The Development of Children

Stephanie Stolarz-Fantino

San Diego State University

SCIENTIFIC AMERICAN BOOKS

Distributed by W. H. Freeman and Company

Contents

To the Student

This Study Guide was written to help you understand and remember the ideas and facts presented in The Development of Children. The guide has 18 chapters corresponding to the 18 chapters of the textbook; each chapter has the following sections, intended to enhance your studying in a different way:

•The introduction will orient you to the ideas presented. You may want to read it before reading the chapter in the text.

•The detailed chapter outline can be read before the textbook chapter, as preparation, or afterwards, as a review; it will also be useful for studying for quizzes and exams. Reading the outline cannot, however, substitute for reading the text; while it contains the basic ideas, it leaves out the many important examples and illustrations that will help you understand and remember these ideas.

•The key terms listed at the end of each textbook chapter are reproduced. There is space for you to write the definition of the terms and a matching exercise that will give you the opportunity to test your understanding by identifying examples that illustrate them.

•The fill-in review exercise recapitulates important points made in the chapter. Uncover the correct answers as you complete each statement.

•Practice questions are multiple choice and cover material that is especially likely to appear on exams.

•Short-answer questions are intended to make you think about important topics introduced in the chapter. Sometimes you will need to utilize ideas presented in different sections of the chapter to answer these questions.

•Putting it all together appears in some, but not all, chapters of the guide. It contains exercises that require you to pull together material from the chapter you are currently studying with information from previous chapters to help you gain a better overall view of development.

•Sources of more information contains suggested readings to supplement those listed at the end of each text chapter.

•An answer key in each chapter lists the correct answers for the key terms matching exercise, the practice questions, and, where appropriate, for the putting it all together section.

The Study Guide concludes with suggestions for observing children. It is hoped that you will find your study of child development to be interesting and enjoyable.

Ideas for Observing Children

As you learn about children's development, you may become interested in observing their behavior. Perhaps you will want to conduct some formal observations or you may be assigned this task by your instructor. These suggestions will help you get started.

There are many opportunities for casual observation of children's behavior in everyday settings. A children's shoe store is a good place to hear the ways preschoolers use language as they argue for one pair of shoes or another. Restaurants provide opportunities to view children's social interactions and observe their fine motor skills. Children can be observed using the equipment at playgrounds, playing in parks, visiting zoos and amusement parks with their parents, and just "hanging around" with their friends at public libraries, in shopping centers, and at beaches or swimming pools. Babies can be observed—sitting in strollers, carried by their parents, and taking their first, unsteady steps—in many of the same settings as they accompany their parents and older siblings. It is also possible to view children in more formal settings—at day-care centers, schools, or in such activities as scouting or Little League. In fact, a good way to get first-hand experience with children is to work as a volunteer in one of these settings. Babysitting also provides excellent opportunities to observe children's behavior in detail.

Observations may focus on particular behaviors—for example, noting instances of aggression among a group of preschoolers—or may consist of records of all the behavior a child performs within a specified period of time. In the first example, you might prepare a chart with the children's names on one axis and the aggressive behaviors under study—hitting, biting, pushing, and so on—on the other. Specific instances of aggression could then be recorded by checking appropriate boxes corresponding to the particular children and behaviors. Other types of behavior would not, of course, be recorded. In the second type of observation, you would target a particular child, a 4-year-old named Jill, for example. First, you would set the scene—for example, "Jill is seated on the floor, cross-legged, in the block area of the classroom. Mark is nearby but is facing in the opposite direction"— then describe everything that occurs in as much detail as possible, keeping track of the time in the left margin in 2- or 5-minute intervals. Motor movements are described in detail, especially when observing babies, and conversations are recorded whenever possible. Naturally, when performing such a detailed observation, it is necessary to take breaks, possibly every 10 minutes.

When you conduct observations, keep in mind the criteria of scientific description discussed in Chapter 1. Your observations should, first of all, be objective. This will be easier to accomplish if you separate your own comments and interpretations ("Jill is angry with Mark") from the facts of the observation ("Jill does not respond to Mark's request") either by placing them in a separate, parallel column or by putting them in parentheses. Observations also need to be reliable. For example, when studying aggression, two observers should be able to agree on whether a particular act was, in fact, an instance of hitting. Validity is important as well; for example, crying when their mothers leave the room may be a valid measure of attachment in 1-year-olds, but it is a less appropriate measure of 6-year-olds' attachment.

Observers also need to remember the ethical guidelines for research with children, also discussed in Chapter 1. In particular, always obtain permission from parents or teachers before conducting a formal observation on a particular child, and be sure not to follow or approach children in any way that might alarm or frighten them. If you use common sense in obtaining subjects, your observations will be enjoyable to carry out and will add greatly to your understanding of children's development.

Entire books can be, and have been, written about techniques for carrying out observations on children. Those listed below will give you additional ideas about how to conduct this kind of psychological research.

Cohen, Dorothy H. and Virginia Stern with Nancy Balaban. *Observing and Recording the Behavior of Young Children*, 3rd Ed. New York: Teachers College Press, 1983.

Irwin, D. Michelle, and M.M. Bushnell. *Observational Strategies for Child Study.* New York: Holt, 1980.

Isaksen, Judith G. *Watching and Wondering: Observing and Recording Child Development.* Palo Alto, Calif.: Mayfield, 1986.

CHAPTER

1

THE STUDY OF HUMAN DEVELOPMENT

For centuries, philosophers have asked, "What is human nature?" Within this question are others, about how individual humans become what they are, and about how the events of their lives help or hinder their development.

Today developmental psychologists bring the techniques of scientific research to bear on these questions. Using interviews, observations, and experiments, they gather information on human behavior and interpret it within the framework of theory.

This research is not of interest solely to philosophers. It helps all of us to make informed decisions in diverse areas; for example: public policy, by asking such questions as "What kinds of day-care arrangements are best for children?"; education, by asking under what conditions children learn best; and child rearing, by asking about what techniques are most likely to help children grow up happy and well-adjusted.

Psychologists do not yet have answers to all our questions. But each year psychological research adds something to our understanding of human nature and to our appreciation of the development of individual human children.

Chapter Outline

I.   A Child of Nature?

Victor, the "Wild Boy of Aveyron," remains something of a mystery nearly two centuries after his discovery. Was he, as believed by many authorities of his time, abandoned by his parents because of innate mental deficiency? Or, as his benefactor Jean-Marc Itard believed, was his development stunted by years of isolation in the forest? These questions, though unanswered, are relevant to the modern-day study of **human**

development, the sequence of changes that begins at conception and continues throughout life.

II. The Legacy of Itard

In his work with Victor, Itard showed that science could be applied to problems of human behavior, and that practical applications can come from such work. The case of the Wild Boy also demonstrated that scientific work has implications for philosophical and political issues. The combination of scientific, philosophical, and public policy goals remains important to today's developmental psychologists.

A. Scientific concern about children grew out of social concerns, as the industrial revolution in Europe and America resulted in large numbers of children working long hours in unhealthy factory conditions. Charles Darwin's theory of evolution also focused interest on children, as scientists drew parallels between evolutionary change and human development. By the late nineteenth century, G. Stanley Hall had formed the Child-Study Association, and child welfare reform was under way.

B. Modern developmental psychologists are dedicated to accumulating knowledge about human behavior at all age levels and applying their knowledge in helpful ways. Their general goal, increasing our understanding of human nature and its development, should be kept in mind while using the textbook.

III. The Central Questions of Developmental Psychology

Developmental psychologists seek answers to two major questions:

• Can we best understand development as continuous change or as discontinuous—a series of transformations?
• Which primarily directs development: the body's genetic program or forces in the environment?
    Psychologists' assumptions about these issues influence both their interpretations of what they observe and their proposals for enhancing development.
 A. Within the question about continuity are several issues:
• Are human beings distinctive? This is a question about **phylogeny,** the evolutionary history of a species. There is disagreement among evolutionary theorists as to whether the process of evolutionary change is continuous or discontinuous. Certainly, humans have much in common with other animals; however, we have unique attributes as well, especially our highly developed systems of language and **culture.**
• Is individual development continuous? This is a question about **ontogeny**—the course of development during an individual person's lifetime—and concerns the notion that children pass through a set of qualitatively different stages on their way to maturity. Some psychologists emphasize these discontinuities, while others stress underlying processes, such as learning, that remain the same throughout life. Psychologists also ask whether people's characteristics remain the same throughout

their lifetimes—for example, can you predict their behavior as adults from their traits as infants?

• Are there **critical periods** in development? Critical periods are times during which particular events must occur in order for development to proceed normally. Critical periods occur in human physiological development and may occur in behavioral development as well.

B. The question about the roles of genes and environment in development is often thought of as a debate about the relative importance of **nature** (a person's inborn capacities and limitations) and **nurture** (the influences on the person of the social environment). This debate, which has its roots in philosophical theories about the nature of mankind, has striking implications for politics and education. The ideas of the English philosopher John Locke, who saw the infant's mind as a blank slate *(tabula rasa)*, and the French philosopher Jean-Jacques Rousseau, who conceived of the child as "natural man," continue to influence our ideas about the nature of children and society's responsibility toward them.

Disagreements about the relative contributions of nature and nurture have resulted in several different theoretical frameworks through which psychologists attempt to explain the processes of development:

• According to the biological-maturation perspective, the basic changes characterizing development are **endogenous** (coming from "inside"), and **maturation** is therefore the major cause of development; from this perspective, the environment plays a secondary role.

• According to the environmental-learning perspective, biological factors provide a foundation, but **learning** is the major cause of developmental change. This theory emphasizes **exogenous** factors (those coming from "outside").

• From the interactional perspective, nature and nurture both play important roles, the specifics of which vary with the type of development being examined. Developmental psychologist Jean Piaget emphasized children's roles as active constructors of their own development.

• The cultural-context perspective is similar to the interactionist perspective; however, it emphasizes the role of children's cultural groups in organizing their experiences, since the same biological or environmental factors may have different consequences for development when they appear in different cultural contexts.

IV. The Discipline of Developmental Psychology

To be able to meaningfully relate their data to their theories, developmental psychologists collect information using various types of research designs.

A. Psychologists judge their findings according to four general criteria:

• **Objectivity.** Observations should not be biased by the investigator's preconceived ideas.

• **Reliability.** The behavior observed should be reliable—consistent and agreed on by independent observers.

• **Validity.** Validity means that the behavior being studied should actually reflect the underlying process the researcher is using it to measure.

• **Replication.** When other investigators perform a replication—that is, when they perform the same study using the same procedures—they should obtain the same results.

It is also important that the subjects being studied are a **representative sample** of the group about which the investigator is drawing conclusions.

B. Some of the ways psychologists obtain information are:

• **Self-reports** which include interviews and responses to questionnaires.

• **Naturalistic observation**, in which people's behavior is studied in real world settings. Observations may be made in a single setting or in many different settings. Baby biographies, diaries recording observations of children, are also examples of naturalistic observation. Naturalistic observation aims at discovering children's ecology, the range of situations they encounter, and the roles they play.

A problem with collecting data through naturalistic observation is that, while some of the factors observed may be correlated with one another, it is not possible to determine which factors are causal. The issue of correlation and causation is discussed in Box 1.2.

• **Experiments**, which are often used to get around the problem of determining causation. In these studies, investigators introduce a change into a child's environment while, if possible, holding all other factors constant; then they measure the effect of this change on the child's behavior. The group of children whose environment is changed are called the **experimental group**. Their behavior is compared with that of the **control group**, who are treated as much as possible like the experimental group except for not undergoing the environmental change. Because some research is potentially harmful to children, researchers must carry out their investigations according to strict standards of ethics, as described in Box 1.3.

• **Clinical methods**, in which interview techniques tailored to the individual subject focus on the particular circumstances that affect that person's development. Clinical methods can reveal a great deal about individual behavior; however, it may be difficult to arrive at general conclusions using this technique.

C. In order to determine how the factors influencing development work over time, psychologists use:

• **Longitudinal designs**, in which the same group of individuals are studied at more than one age. Unfortunately, longitudinal designs frequently confound age changes in behavior with changes due to other influences relating to the subjects' cohorts—the people born at about the same time who share particular experiences unique to those growing up during that era.

• **Cross-sectional designs**, in which groups of people of different ages are each studied at a single time.

Each of these research designs, like each technique for collecting data, has advantages and disadvantages; keeping these in mind, investigators must choose the most practical methods for conducting their particular studies.

D. The information psychologists obtain about children's behavior is only meaningful in the context of a theory—a broad conceptual framework within which facts can be interpreted. As new facts are collected, they point up inconsistencies in current theories; these theories are then replaced by others that provide us with still better explanations.

V. This Book and the Field of Developmental Psychology

While psychologists of all major theoretical orientations regard development from conception to adulthood as encompassing five major periods—the prenatal period, infancy, the preschool period, middle childhood, and adolescence—they have not developed a unifying theory within which their observations can be interpreted. Therefore, the textbook organizes its discussion of developmental change around a series of **bio-social-behavioral shifts**. These shifts are points at which converging changes in children's biology and behavior—which, in turn, cause them to be treated differently by other people—lead to the emergence of distinctively new forms of behavior.

It will be useful, in reading the text, to keep in mind the questions raised in this chapter about the nature of humankind and the developmental process. All the information presented ultimately bears on these questions.

Key Terms I

Following are important terms introduced in Chapter 1. Write the definition for each after the term. Then match the term with the letter of the example that best illustrates it.

_____ Baby biographies _____

_____ Clinical method _____

_____ Cohort _____

_____ Control group _____

_____ Correlation _____

_____ Cross-sectional design _____

_____ Experimental group _____

_____ Experiments _____

_____ Longitudinal design _____

_____ Naturalistic observations _____

_____ Objectivity _____

_____ Reliability _____

_____ Replication _____

_____ Representative sample _____

_____ Self-report _____

_____ Validity _____

a. These diaries of infants' behavior are still used in studying language development.
b. This occurs when changes in one factor are associated with changes in another—for example, the association between age and height in children.
c. A person filling out a questionnaire about his or her behavior would be participating in this method of observation.
d. This occurs when other researchers redo a study and get the same results.
e. Watching children interact on the playground at recess is a form of this.
f. Research designs have this quality if they are not biased by preconceived ideas.
g. A measure has this characteristic when it reflects what it is purported to. (For

example, in order to have it, a written memory test would need to be given to subjects who could read.)

h. A group of subjects in an experiment who undergo a manipulation of their environment.

i. A psychologist who is comparing a group of 8-year-olds, a group of 10-year-olds, and a group of 12-year-olds on a problem-solving task is conducting this type of study.

j. Psychologists try to obtain this in selecting subjects, so that they can generalize their results to a larger population.

k. Subjects in an experiment who do not receive the experimental manipulation, but are otherwise treated the same as those who do.

l. A measure has this when subjects tested on more than one occasion earn nearly the same scores.

m. An example is "American children beginning kindergarten in 1988."

n. In this way of studying development, questions are tailored to the person being interviewed.

o. A psychologist who is studying one group of children's social relationships from kindergarten through sixth grade is conducting this type of study.

p. Teachers who are comparing the effectiveness of a new way to teach spelling with the effectiveness of their previous method are conducting this type of study.

Key Terms II

Following are important terms introduced in Chapter 1. Write the definition for each after the term. Then match the term with the letter of the example that best illustrates it.

_____ Bio-social-behavioral shift _____

_____ Critical periods _____

_____ Culture _____

_____ Ecology _____

_____ Endogenous causes _____

_____ Exogenous causes _____

_____ Human development _____

_____ Learning _____

_____ Maturation _____

_____ Nature _____

_____ Nurture _____

_____ Ontogeny _____

_____ Phylogeny _____

_____ Stage _____

_____ Theory _____

a. An individual's developmental history.
b. A broad conceptual framework within which facts can be interpreted.
c. The process by which new behaviors arise when the organism is modified by experience.
d. The knowledge and beliefs of a group of people are an example of this.
e. The sequence of physical and behavioral changes that occur, among humans, from conception to maturity.
f. Influences on development that come from "inside"—from the child's biological heritage.

g. A species' evolutionary history.
h. Genetically determined patterns of change that occur during development.
i. Influences on development that come from "outside"—from the child's interaction with the environment.
j. This term, derived from the Greek word for "home," refers, in psychology, to the range of situations in which people's behavior occurs.
k. A distinctive period of development marked by discontinuity from the periods occurring before and after.
l. This represents the influence of the environment on the individual.
m. A reorganization of behavior, such as the one that occurs at the end of infancy, which comes about as a result of changes in several different areas of development.
n. Times in a person's life when certain experiences are necessary if normal development is to occur.
o. This refers to the individual's inborn, biologically based capacities.

Fill-In Review

Cover the list of answers next to the statements below. Then uncover each answer after you complete each statement.

1. The study of human _____ involves the changes beginning at conception and continuing throughout life.

   development

2. Scientific concern about children grew both out of social concern and interest in Darwin's theory of _____.

   evolution

3. Modern developmental psychologists accumulate knowledge about human behavior and _____ their knowledge to enhance development.

   apply

4. Two major questions guide developmental psychologists: whether development is best understood as continuous or _____; and whether development is guided mainly by the body's _____ program or by environmental influences.

   discontinuous
   genetic

5. When we ask about ways in which human beings are distinctive, we are asking questions about _____, the evolutionary history of our species.

   phylogeny

6. Questions about continuity relate to _____, an individual person's development.

   ontogeny

7. One question about ontogeny concerns whether individuals pass, on the way to maturity, through qualitatively different _____ of development.

   stages

8. We are not sure whether _____ periods—times during which particular events must happen for normal development to take place—occur in human psychological development.

   critical

9. Questions about the relative importance of genes and environment are often phrased as a debate about the relative influence of nature and _____.

   nurture

maturation

10. According to the biological-maturation explanation, the major cause of development is _____.

environmental-learning

11. The _____ approach emphasizes learning as the main source of developmental change.

interactional

12. The _____ perspective acknowledges the importance of both nature and nurture in development.

cultural

13. The cultural-context perspective emphasizes the importance of the _____ group in organizing children's experience.

objectivity

14. In conducting research, psychologists strive for observations that have _____, or freedom from bias.

reliability

15. When observations are agreed upon by more than one observer, they are said to have _____.

validity

16. Observations have _____ when they actually reflect the process they are used to measure.

replication

17. Obtaining the same result when a study is repeated, or _____, helps an investigator's findings to be accepted by the scientific community.

self-reports

18. Sometimes investigators obtain _____ from subjects by asking them about their own behavior.

observation

19. Sometimes researchers document behavior through naturalistic _____, studying people in one or more settings as they go about their daily lives.

experimental

20. When using _____ methods, investigators introduce some kind of change into the environment and study its effect on behavior.

experimental
control

21. When groups of people are studied, the group whose environment is changed is called the _____ group; their behavior is compared with that of the _____ group.

ethical

22. When conducting research with children, investigators must follow strict _____ standards, in order to avoid harm to the participants.

clinical

23. Research using _____ methods involves interview techniques that are tailored to the individual subject.

longitudinal

24. In _____ studies, researchers examine the effect of time on development by studying the same group of people at more than one age.

cross-sectional

25. In _____ studies, investigators compare single observations of people from different age groups.

theory

26. A _____ provides a conceptual framework within which researchers can interpret the facts they uncover.

27. This textbook organizes its discussion of development around points in children's lives at which changes in biology, behavior, and social expectations converge. New forms of behavior emerge from these bio-social-behavioral

shifts

_____.

Multiple-Choice Practice Questions

Circle the letter of the word or phrase that correctly completes each statement.

1. It was hoped that the case of Victor, the Wild Boy of Aveyron, could help answer questions about
   a. why parents abandoned their children.
   b. what people would be like if they grew up completely apart from others.
   c. how wild animals raised their young.
   d. the causes of mental retardation.

2. John Locke, the seventeenth century English philosopher, believed that most differences between people were
   a. caused by genetic differences.
   b. unimportant.
   c. due to the way they were brought up.
   d. due more to influences in later life than to influences during childhood.

3. Jean-Jacques Rousseau's ideas about _____ remain influential today.
   a. the child's mind as a "blank slate"
   b. original sin
   c. the importance of beginning formal education at an early age
   d. the stagelike character of development

4. The history of a species over thousands or millions of years is called
   a. ontogeny.
   b. continuity.
   c. phylogeny.
   d. development.

5. Knowledge about how to live is passed from one generation of humans to another through
   a. culture.
   b. the genetic code.
   c. mutations.
   d. unknown means.

6. Using the concept of stage to explain development (for example, saying that John has tantrums because he's in the "terrible twos")
   a. helps in understanding children's behavior.
   b. is widely accepted by developmental psychologists.
   c. confirms the usefulness of stage theories.
   d. does not help us understand children's behavior.

7. A possible example of a critical period in human development is the following: In order to develop normally with respect to this behavior, children need to
   a. form a primary attachment during the first year of life.
   b. acquire some form of language before 7 years of age.
   c. learn to walk before 18 months of age.

d. learn to play an instrument before 10 years of age.

8. How can we tell when a child reaches a new stage of development?
   a. quantitative change (for example, the ability to remember more words)
   b. slow, steady improvement (for example, being able to walk more quickly)
   c. simultaneous change in several areas of behavior
   d. the appearance of new behaviors with no obvious input from the environment

9. The _____ perspective views development as being due mainly to factors "inside" the child.
   a. environmental-learning
   b. cultural-context
   c. interactional
   d. biological-maturation

10. The cultural-context approach is similar to the _____ perspective, but also emphasizes the effect on development of the prior experience of the society into which a child is born.
    a. biological-maturational
    b. environmental-learning
    c. interactional
    d. sociobiological

11. Which statement best represents psychologists' current attitudes toward replication of studies?
    a. The findings of a study are more likely to be accepted when, by following the same procedures, other investigators obtain the same results.
    b. To be accepted as true, a study should yield the same results more than once, even when different procedures are used.
    c. A study with conclusive findings is generally accepted as accurate even if other investigators are unable to obtain the same results.
    d. It is a waste of time and money to replicate research that has already been carried out.

12. A person who fills out a consumer questionnaire about what household products he or she uses is participating in which form of data collection?
    a. naturalistic observation
    b. self-report
    c. experiment
    d. clinical

13. In order to be able to generalize their results to other groups, researchers need to conduct their work using
    a. both children and adults as subjects.
    b. as representative a sample as possible.
    c. identical questions for all age groups.
    d. naturalistic observation.

14. When conducting an experiment, researchers usually compare the performance of the experimental group with that of a control group that
    a. is assigned to a different experimental treatment.

b. undergoes no experience at all.

c. consists of people who did not volunteer to be in the experimental group.

d. is treated like the experimental group except for not receiving the experimental treatment.

15. When psychologists compare the performance of 3-year-olds, 5-year-olds, and 7-year-olds on a vocabulary test, they are conducting

a. a kinship study.

b. a clinical study.

c. a cross-sectional study.

d. a longitudinal study.

Short-Answer Questions

Write a brief answer in the space below each question.

1. What might be some reasons why Victor, the Wild Boy of Aveyron, never developed completely normal behavior, despite Itard's educational efforts?

2. What did seventeenth-century English philosopher John Locke consider to be the role of early experience?

3. What is "culture" as psychologists use the term? Why is it important to consider the role of culture in development?

4. Compare the advantages and disadvantages of naturalistic observation and experiments for studying children's behavior.

5. Describe how researchers might use a longitudinal design or a cross-sectional design to gather information on the same aspect of development. What are the advantages and disadvantages of each?

Sources of More Information

Barker, Roger G, and **Herbert F. Wright.** *One Boy's Day: A Specimen Record of Behavior.* New York: Harper & Row, 1951.
This book, which records in detail a day in the life of a 7-year-old boy, illustrates one method of naturalistic observation.

Elkind, David. *Children and Adolescents: Interpretive Essays on Jean Piaget,* 3rd Edition. New York: Oxford University Press, 1981.
Although most of the material has been inspired by Piaget, this book also contains sections comparing the Piagetian and psychometric approaches to development and comparing the work and goals of Piaget and Maria Montessori.

Fraiberg, Selma H. *The Magic Years. Understanding and Handling the Problems of Early Childhood.* New York: Charles Scribner's Sons, 1959.
This book entertainingly describes development during the first five years of life from a psychoanalytic point of view.

Gesell, Arnold, Frances L. Ilg, Louise Bates Ames , and **Janet Learned Rodell.** *Infant and Child in the Culture of Today: The Guidance of Development in Home and Nursery School,* Rev. Ed. New York: Harper & Row, 1974.
This book presents Gesell's maturational approach to infancy and early childhood, with an emphasis on the child's increasing abilities of self-regulation.

Irwin, D. Michelle, and **M. Margaret Bushnell.** *Observational Strategies for Child Study.* New York: Holt, Rinehart and Winston, 1980.
This book serves as an introduction to observing children, and contains both general

guidelines and specific suggestions for using checklists, event sampling, rating scales and other techniques, and instruction on writing up observation reports. Information on theoretical perspectives and history is also included.

Jones, N. Blurton, ed. *Ethological Studies of Child Behavior.* New York: Cambridge University Press, 1972.

This book contains many different ethological studies, including examples of child-child and mother-child interaction.

Patterson, Gerald. *Living With Children: New Methods for Parents and Teachers.* Champaign, Ill.: Research Press, 1976.

In this book, parents and teachers are shown how to change children's behavior for the better by arranging environmental contingencies to encourage desired behaviors and eliminate undesired ones. This book illustrates the environmental-learning approach to development.

Answer Key

Answers to Key Terms I: a, n, m, k, b, i, h, p, o, e, f, l, d, j, c, g

Answers to Key Terms II: m, n, d, j, f, i, e, c, h, o, l, a, g, k, b

Answers to Practice Questions: 1. b, 2. c, 3. d, 4. c, 5. a, 6. d, 7. b, 8. c, 9. d, 10. c, 11. a, 12. b, 13. b, 14. d, 15. c.

2

THE HUMAN HERITAGE: GENES AND ENVIRONMENT

In many ways, all human beings seem very much alike. Yet within that basic similarity, the details of appearance and behavior vary a great deal. In fact, people exhibit an amazing diversity of both talents and troubles.

How do genes and the environment combine to create our unique characteristics as human beings? If we were all raised in identical environments, would we behave completely alike? Nearly all psychologists would say "No." Human development is an interaction between biologically based tendencies and the environmental circumstances in which people live. Nearly all of us are genetically unique, so a hypothetical universal environment would affect each person in a different way. On the other hand, under ordinary circumstances, even genetically identical individuals—monozygotic twins—develop individual interests, abilities, and characters.

Some of the differences among people are shaped systematically by the cultures in which they live. Human beings can adapt to changing conditions through cultural evolution, building upon the expertise of countless generations.

Because biological and cultural evolution have occurred together for so long, it is not easy to distinguish their separate influences on development. But by studying the effects on development of mutations—mistakes in gene replication—and inherited genetic disorders, psychologists can learn more about how genes and environment interact to produce each unique person.

Chapter Outline

I. Sexual Reproduction and Genetic Transmission

The similarities and differences among people result from the interaction of the environments in which they develop and the **genes** they inherit from their parents.

Each person's genes are found on the 46 **chromosomes**—23 inherited from each parent—present in the **zygote**, the single cell from which all the individual's body cells will derive.

A. The zygote creates these new cells through **mitosis**, a process of duplication and division. This is also the way new **somatic cells** are created and replaced throughout a person's lifetime.

B. **Meiosis** is the process by which **germ cells** (sperm and ova) are derived. It results in cells with 23 chromosomes—half the usual number. When a sperm cell fertilizes an ovum, the resulting zygote will have 46 chromosomes.

The mixing of genes during sexual reproduction and the process of **crossing over** (an exchange of genetic material between two chromosomes) during meiosis make each human being, with the exception of monozygotic twins, genetically unique.

Occasionally resulting in 1 of every 250 births, the daughter cells separate during one of the early mitotic divisions to form two genetically alike individuals—**monozygotic**, or identical twins. **Dizygotic**, or fraternal, twins result from the fertilization of two eggs by two sperm; these twins are no more alike genetically than any brothers or sisters.

C. The twenty-third pair of chromosomes in normal females are both X chromosomes; normal males have one **X chromosome** and one **Y chromosome**. While an ovum always contains an X chromosome, a sperm may contain an X or a Y; thus, the sperm cell determines the genetic sex of the resulting child. More boy babies than girl babies are conceived. This may reflect boy babies' greater vulnerability: by 18 years of age there are equal numbers of males and females, and females outnumber males thereafter.

II. The Laws of Genetic Inheritance

Some characteristics are inherited through a simple type of genetic transmission in which one pair of genes determines a trait. The genes controlling the trait (for example, blood type) may have alternative forms, or **alleles** (for example, A, B, and O). People who have inherited the same allele from both parents are **homozygous** for the trait; those who have inherited different alleles are **heterozygous**. How an allelic form of a trait is expressed in a heterozygous person depends on whether the allele is **dominant** (in which case it will be expressed), **recessive** (in which case it will not be expressed), or whether the two alleles have **codominance** (in which case a distinctively different outcome will result). In those instances in which neither allele is dominant, an intermediate outcome will occur (as it may in the case of skin color).

A. An individual's **genotype** represents that person's genetic endowment; the **phenotype**, or the individual's observable characteristics, results from an interaction between that person's inherited traits and the environment. Most phenotypic characteristics (height is an example) are **polygenic traits** resulting from the combined action of many genes as well as a great deal of influence from the environment.

Genes interact with each other in several ways:

•**Modifier genes** influence the expression of other genes; without the action of modifier genes on the allelic forms of the gene for eye color, all people would have either blue or brown eyes.
•Some genes are **complementary** to one another; both must be present for a characteristic to be expressed.
•**Masking genes** prevent or lessen the expression of other genes.

B. **Sex-linked characteristics** are determined by genes found only on the X chromosome; therefore, the phenotypic expression of these traits is seen more often in males, who have only one X chromosome, than in females, whose second X chromosome may contain an allele that will prevent expression. Because of this, certain recessive genetic defects, ranging from red-green color blindness to a form of muscular dystrophy, are far more common among males. Sex-linked abnormalities also vary in frequency among ethnic groups, reflecting differences in the frequencies with which the corresponding alleles occur in different **gene pools**—the total genetic information possessed by a sexually reproducing population.

III. Genes, the Organism, and the Environment

Because genes do not exist in isolation, development occurs only within the context of an organism's environment.

A. Environmental variations may have large effects on an individual's phenotypic characteristics. By varying genotypes within the same environment, or by varying the environment of individuals with the same genotype, researchers are able to learn how genes and environment interact to produce particular characteristics. **Range of reaction** is the term used for the changes in phenotype caused by varying the environment of a particular genotype.

B. We cannot study the range of reaction for human genotypes in the way we can for plants, insects, and animals, but **kinship studies**—comparisons among members of the same biological family—help in estimating which traits have a substantial genetic contribution. If people are increasingly similar with respect to a trait the more closely they are related, this is evidence for an inherited factor. Of course, people who are biologically related also share similar environments; this limits our ability to test for genetic influences using kinship studies.

C. Genotypes, phenotypes, and environment do not interact as unrelated factors in development; complex feedback mechanisms exist. Babies inherit both their genes and their early environment from their parents, and babies' own characteristics influence the types of environments their parents provide. Different babies might experience the same environment in different ways. In any case, while their genotypes remain the same over their lifetimes, the environment in which they develop will change.

D. Some genetically determined traits are not easily influenced by the environment. Biologist C.H. Waddington described these highly **canalized** characteristics as deep valleys in a landscape of development. Shallow valleys represent traits more subject to environmental effects. Children moving through the landscape come upon "decision points"—points of transition at which relatively small environmental influences can lead to large effects on developmental outcome (phenotype).

E. Richard Lewontin has discussed four pitfalls involved in describing gene-environment interactions:

•The genetic code is *not* like a present-day computer program; preset instructions set at conception do not determine the output—development— from that time onward.
•While there are cases (for example, blood type) in which genotype determines phenotype, for most characteristics this is *not* the case.
•We cannot say that genes determine capacity for a particular activity (for example, running) without considering the physical and cultural environments (the jungle, the Himalayas, or a U.S. track meet) in which the capacity is expressed.
•It is not even possible to say for certain that genes determine tendencies unless the behaviors in question are observed to occur consistently over a wide variety of environments.

IV. Mutations and Genetic Abnormalities

Mutations are errors in gene replication that result in a change in the molecular structure of genetic material. The majority of mutations are lethal, resulting in spontaneous abortions early in pregnancy. But about 1 of every 200 babies born has some kind of genetic aberation; because most of these are recessive, they are not often phenotypically expressed. Table 2-2 describes some common genetic diseases and conditions. By studying mutations and genetic abnormalities, researchers can better understand the interaction of genes and environment, and may find ways of preventing defects or lessening their impact.

A. Sickle-cell anemia, a serious blood disorder, is caused by a recessive gene, carried mainly but not exclusively by people of African descent. People who are heterozygous for the gene have the sickle-cell trait but usually do not suffer from the disease; they have been found to be more resistant to malaria than people without the sickle-cell trait. This explains why an otherwise unadaptive trait remains at a relatively high level in the population. Twenty percent of the people in West Africa, where malaria is common, carry the sickle-cell gene, compared to 10% of blacks in the U.S.

B. Down's syndrome is caused by an extra chromosome on the twenty-first pair (*Trisomy* 21) and results in mental retardation as well as a number of distinctive physical characteristics and a susceptibility to leukemia and respiratory problems. The older a woman is when she conceives, the greater her chance of producing a child with this disorder, suggesting that environmental agents may damage the genetic material. Children with Down's syndrome have a wide range of levels of functioning, depending on the severity of the disorder and the environmental interventions they receive.

C. The most common abnormalities of the chromosomes that determine sex are Klinefelter's syndrome, in which a male has an extra X chromosome (XXY), and Turner's syndrome, in which a female has only one X chromosome (XO).

D. Phenylketonuria (PKU) is an inherited metabolic disorder that results in brain damage leading to mental retardation. However, by altering the environment of children with this disorder—specifically, by removing from their diets foods high in the amino acid phenylalanine—the children's brains can develop normally. A blood test given to newborn babies can detect most cases of PKU, so that dietary intervention can begin immediately.

It is now possible to detect some abnormalities before birth. Following **amniocentesis**, a technique in which a needle is inserted into the mother's uterus in order to sample the fluid in the sac surrounding the fetus, amniotic fluid is analyzed for chemical imbalances and fetal cells floating in the fluid are examined for certain genetic disorders. In **chorionic villus sampling,** the fetal cells are harvested from the hairlike projections (villi) on the chorion—the tissue that forms the placenta. The **alpha-fetoprotein test** is a blood test that is used to detect defects in the neural tube.

Parents who have had a child with a genetic defect or who think they may be carriers of a particular disorder can often be helped by genetic counseling. Through test results and family histories, the genetic counselor will try to determine the probability that a couple's future children will be affected. Using this information, the couple can make an informed decision about whether to risk a future pregnancy.

V. Biology and Culture

At the time Darwin wrote *The Origin of Species*, people tended to confuse the processes that produce biological change with those that produce historical change.

A. For example, as explained by the French biologist Jean Baptiste Lamarck, characteristics acquired by parents during their lifetimes could be passed on biologically, it was thought, to their children. Today we know that this process does not account for biological evolutionary change; however, it does illustrate the occurrence of human cultural evolution, in which the skills and knowledge of each generation build on those of the generations before.

B. Evidence from archeology and paleontology tells us that **coevolution** of human biological and cultural characteristics has been occurring for millions of years. The fact of coevolution makes it extremely difficult, when comparing people from different parts of the world, to determine whether the differences between them are due to genetically transmitted characteristics or to differences in the cultures in which they have been raised. Nearly every instance of human development is the result of complex interactions between genes and environment.

Key Terms I

Following are important terms introduced in Chapter 2. Write the definition for each after the term. Then match the term with the letter of the example that best illustrates it.

_____ Allele _____

_____ Canalized characteristics _____

_____ Chromosome _____

_____ Codominance _____

_____ Complementary genes _____

_____ Crossing over _____

_____ Dominant allele _____

_____ Gene pool _____

_____ Genes _____

_____ Heterozygous _____

_____ Homozygous _____

_____ Masking gene _____

_____ Modifier gene _____

_____ Phenotype _____

_____ Recessive allele _____

_____ X chromosome _____

_____ Y chromosome _____

a. There are 46 of these threadlike structures in the nucleus of each cell.
b. This sex-determining chromosome can be inherited only from the father.
c. These molecules, found on chromosomes, contain "blueprints" for development.
d. The cells of normal females contain two of these.
e. This exchange of material between chromosomes helps to increase genetic diversity.
f. These characteristics, such as the tendency to have two eyes and one nose, follow the same developmental path for everyone, despite most environmental variations.
g. An alternative form of a gene; for example, the O form of the gene for blood type.
h. A gene that prevents another gene from completely expressing itself.
i. This kind of gene influences the action of other genes, producing, in one example, hazel eye color.
j. A person's observable characteristics, developing through interaction between genes and environment.

k. Genes that can only produce their effect if other genes are also present.
l. The genetic information available in a whole reproducing population.
m. When a child inherits an allele for type A blood from his mother and an allele for type O blood from his father, we use this term to describe his genotype for blood type.
n. A child inherits an allele for type O blood from each parent; this term describes her genotype for blood type.
o. A less powerful allele—for example, the allele for type O blood—that is not expressed when a more powerful allele is present.
p. A trait is contributed to by two different alleles; for example, type AB blood.
q. An allele whose effects show up phenotypically—in type A blood, for example— even in the presence of another allele (such as the O allele).

Key Terms II

Following are important terms introduced in Chapter 2. Write the definition for each after the term. Then match the term with the letter of the example that best illustrates it.

_____ Alpha-fetoprotein test _____

_____ Amniocentesis _____

_____ Coevolution _____

_____ Chorionic villus sampling _____

_____ Dizygotic twins _____

_____ Genotype _____

_____ Germ cells _____

_____ Kinship studies _____

_____ Meiosis _____

_____ Mitosis _____

_____ Monozygotic twins _____

_____ Mutation _____

_____ Polygenic traits _____

_____ Range of reaction _____

_____ Sex-linked characteristics _____

_____ Somatic cells _____

_____ Zygote _____

a. These come in two varieties: sperm and ova.
b. In this test for genetic defects, a long needle is inserted in the uterus to sample the amniotic fluid.
c. Nearly all the body's cells are produced by this process of duplication and division.
d. All the cells in the body with the exception of the sperm and ova.
e. These result from the fertilization of two ova by two sperm.
f. This prenatal blood test can detect anencephaly or spina bifida.
g. Exposure to radiation can cause this change in the structure of the genetic material.

h. This term refers to a person's genetic endowment.
i. The process through which sperm and ova contain 23 chromosomes, rather than 46.
j. Members of the same family are compared to assess their similarity for a particular trait.
k. Characteristics influenced by the interaction of several genes, as in the case of height and many other human characteristics.
l. This single cell results from the joining of sperm and ovum at conception.
m. Red-green color blindness is an example of this.
n. The fact that this occurs makes it difficult to pinpoint the source of differences between people who have grown up in very different parts of the world.
o. The full range of gene-environment interactions that are compatible with life for a particular genotype.
p. A technique of testing for genetic defects by examining cells from the fetal tissue that forms the placenta.
q. Two individuals with exactly the same genotype.

Fill-in Review

Cover the list of answers next to the statements below. Then uncover each answer after you complete each statement.

1. People's similarities and differences come from an interaction between _____ and environment.

    genes

2. The body's cells contain ____ chromosomes, 23 inherited from each parent.

    46

3. New cells are created by the process of _____.

    mitosis

4. The cells of females contain two ___ chromosomes; those of males contain one X chromosome and one ___ chromosome.

    X
    Y

5. Although a greater number of _____ are conceived and born, by 18 years of age there are equal numbers of males and females.

    males

6. The genes determining a trait can have alternative forms called _____. People who inherit the same allele from both parents are called homozygous for the trait; those who inherit a different allele from each parent are _____.

    alleles

    heterozygous

7. When two alleles are present but only one is expressed, we say that the one whose characteristics are expressed is a _____ allele. The one that is not expressed is a _____ allele.

    dominant
    recessive

8. A person's genetic endowment is represented by his or her genotype; _____ represents the individual's observed characteristics.

    phenotype

9. _____ characteristics are determined by genes found only on the X chromosome. They are phenotypically expressed more often in _____ than in females.

    Sex-linked
    males

reaction

10. By varying the environments of organisms with the same genotype and observing the phenotypic results, researchers can determine the range of _____ for a particular genotype.

Kinship
genetic

11. _____ studies compare people from the same families to assess their similarities. They help to determine what traits might have a substantial _____ contribution.

environments

12. One problem with kinship studies is that closely related people usually have similar _____.

interact

13. Genotype and environment _____ in complex ways to produce phenotypic characteristics.

canalized

14. A characteristic that is relatively unaffected by environmental influences during development is one which is highly _____.

Mutations

15. _____ are changes in genetic material caused by errors in gene replication.

spontaneous

16. The majority of mutations result in _____ abortions early in pregnancy.

trait
malaria

17. People who have the sickle-cell _____ do not develop sickle-cell anemia; in addition, they have increased resistance to _____.

Down's

18. _____ syndrome is a chromosomal disorder that results in mental retardation and characteristic physical abnormalities.

sex

19. Klinefelter's and Turner's syndromes are caused by abnormalities of the _____ chromosomes.

diet

20. Today the inherited metabolic defect PKU need not lead to mental retardation if the _____ of an affected child is controlled.

cultural

21. Inheritance of acquired characteristics is a result of _____ not biological evolution.

coevolution

22. We give the name _____ to the process in which biological and cultural evolution have interacted with one another over the last several million years.

Multiple-Choice Practice Questions

Circle the letter of the word or phrase that correctly completes each statement.

1. The somatic cells of the body each contain
   a. 23 chromosomes.
   b. 23 pairs of chromosomes.
   c. 46 pairs of chromosomes
   d. 50 pairs of chromosomes.

2. A person who is genetically male receives, at conception,
   a. an X chromosome from his mother and a Y chromosome from his father.
   b. a Y chromosome from his mother and an X chromosome from his father.

    c. an X chromosome from each parent.

    d. a Y chromosome from each parent.

3. Sex-linked characteristics are

    a. passed from one generation to the next on the Y chromosome.

    b. phenotypically expressed more often in females than in males.

    c. limited to characteristics that determine a person's physical and psychologi-
       cal sex.

    d. phenotypically expressed more often in males than in females.

4. When two alleles for a trait are present but only one is expressed, we call the one
    that is *not* expressed

    a. dominant.

    b. codominant.

    c. complementary.

    d. recessive.

5. The development of _____ traits is resistant to environmental influence.

    a. learned

    b. canalized

    c. physical

    d. psychological

6. Which is true about gene-environment interactions, according to Richard Le-
    wontin?

    a. For most characteristics, genotype does not entirely determine phenotype.

    b. The genetic code is much like a computer program, and development unfolds
       according to preset instructions.

    c. Genes influence only physical development; they have no impact on the de-
       velopment of most behavior.

    d. For most characteristics, genotype completely determines phenotype.

7. Errors in gene replication, called _____, often have lethal results.

    a. meioses

    b. canalizations

    c. mutations

    d. recessive traits

8. _____ is a genetic disorder caused by an extra chromosome.

    a. Down's syndrome

    b. Sickle-cell anemia

    c. Phenylketonuria

    d. Turner's syndrome

9. A _____ gene prevents another gene from expressing itself completely.

    a. complementary

    b. masking

    c. modified

    d. recessive

10. Which of the following is not a test used to detect birth defects prenatally?
    a. amniocentesis
    b. range of reaction
    c. chorionic villus sampling
    d. alpha-fetoprotein test

11. The total genetic material in a reproducing population is called the
    a. genotype.
    b. phenotype.
    c. range of reaction
    d. gene pool.

12. If a child receives an allele for type A blood from her mother and an allele for type B blood from her father, she is _____ with respect to blood type.
    a. heterozygous
    b. recessive
    c. homozygous
    d. complementary

13. Meiosis is
    a. the process by which the body's cells reproduce.
    b. the process by which the germ cells come to contain fewer chromosomes than the somatic cells.
    c. an error in gene replication.
    d. a polygenic trait.

14. As the word is used by psychologists, _____ refers to the knowledge and beliefs of a group of people.
    a. evolution
    b. culture
    c. language
    d. ontogeny

15. _____ make(s) it difficult to tell whether differences between people are genetically transmitted or environmentally caused.
    a. Coevolution of physical and cultural characteristics
    b. Kinship studies
    c. Mutations
    d. Recessive traits

Short-Answer Questions

1. What is a sex-linked genetic effect, and how is it transmitted from one generation to another? Describe two examples of such an effect.

2. Describe how kinship studies are used to separate genetic and environmental contributions to behavior. What are some problems with such studies?

3. How does feedback complicate the study of gene-environment interactions? Give an example.

4. How does coevolution affect attempts to separate the contributions of nature and nurture to human differences? Describe an example of a human characteristic shaped by coevolution.

Sources of More Information

Asimov, Isaac. *The Genetic Code.* New York: New American Library of World Literature, 1962.
This book traces the research that led to the discovery of DNA.

Darwin, Charles. *The Origin of Species.* New York: New American Library of World Literature, 1958.
Charles Darwin's classic account of the origin of man.

Genes: Our Individual Programming System. Bostonia, Sept./Oct. 1984: 26-33.
This article reviews findings about how genes, hormones, and environment affect biological sex characteristics and gender identity.

Jensen, Arthur R. *The Heritability of Intelligence.* Saturday Evening Post, Summer 1972.*
The author marshalls evidence for genetic influences on intelligence and demonstrates how heritability is determined.

Kimura, Doreen. *Male Brain, Female Brain: The Hidden Difference.* Psychology Today, Nov. 1985: 50-52.
This article examines the relationship between genetic sex, physiological functioning, and some forms of behavior.

Norwood, Christopher. *At Highest Risk. Protecting Children from Environmental Injury.* New York: Penguin Books, 1980.
In this book the risks of radiation, environmental contaminants, and drugs to children and fetuses are described.

Stockton, William. *Altered Destinies. Lives Changed by Genetic Flaws.* New York: Doubleday, 1979.
A medical reporter follows the lives and experiences of families affected by genetically based disorders.

Vishup, Amy. *Perfect People?* New York Magazine, July 27, 1987: 26-34.
This article discusses genetic testing techniques and the moral dilemmas that accompany their increasingly widespread use.

Whimbey, Arthur. *Something Better than Binet?* Saturday Review, June 1, 1974.*
The author argues that, while genetic factors affect the development of intelligence, the extent of their influence depends upon the environment in which children are raised.
* The Jensen and Whimbey articles are also available in **Rubinstein, Joseph** and **Brent D. Slife,** *Taking Sides: Clashing Views on Controversial Psychological Issues.* Guilford, Conn.: Dushkin Publishing Co., 1980.

Answer Key

Answers to Key Terms I: g, f, a, p, k, e, q, l, c, m, n, h, i, j, o, d, b

Answers to Key Terms II: f, b, n, p, e, h, a, j, i, c, q, g, k, o, m, d, l

Answers to Practice Questions: 1. b, 2. a, 3. d, 4. d, 5. b, 6. a, 7. c, 8. a, 9. b, 10. b, 11. d, 12. a, 13. b, 14. b, 15. a.

CHAPTER

3

PRENATAL DEVELOPMENT

During the 9 months between conception and birth, rapid development transforms the human organism from a single cell to a baby capable of life outside the mother's body. Development proceeds through the processes of differentiation and integration: differentiation of one type of cell into many, and integration of bodily systems into a smoothly functioning whole.

At no time during the course of prenatal development is the developing organism completely buffered from the outside world. On the one hand, while still in the womb, the fetus registers signals from its sense organs, particularly those of balance and hearing. It may even learn to recognize familiar experiences. On the other hand, outside influences such as malnutrition, chemicals, and disease organisms may set obstacles to normal development. Even stresses on the family are experienced by the fetus through substances produced by the mother's body and passed into its bloodstream along with nutrients and oxygen.

While many psychologists agree that an understanding of prenatal development is essential to understanding later developmental processes, they do not always agree on why. Nevertheless, our increasing knowledge about the first nine months of development may someday allow each newborn to face the world with the best possible start.

Chapter Outline

Many developmental theorists consider an understanding of development during the 9 months from conception to birth to be essential for explaining the processes of development that occur throughout postnatal life.

I. The Periods of Prenatal Development

As a zygote develops from one-celled organism to newborn baby, it passes through three periods of development: the germinal period, the period of the embryo, and the period of the fetus. Each period is characterized by distinctive patterns of growth and interaction with the environment.

A. The **germinal period** begins at conception and lasts until, 8 to 10 days later, the organism is implanted in the uterine wall. During its journey through the fallopian tube, the zygote—contained within the **zona pellucida**, an envelope only a few molecules thick—divides, through the process of mitosis. These initial mitotic divisions are called **cleavage**; after the first few cleavages occur, a cluster of identical cells—the **morula**—takes shape. By the time it reaches the uterus, the organism is a **blastocyst** consisting of about 100 cells. Interaction with the environment results in differentiation of the blastocyst into the **inner cell mass**, that will become the organism itself, and the **trophoblast**, which will become the membranes that will supply it with nourishment. **Implantation** occurs when the trophoblast puts out branches which burrow into the uterine wall and contact maternal blood vessels.

A major question in embryology is: How do new forms arise from a single type of cell? The **preformationist hypothesis** argues that all forms are already present in the first cells; the **epigenetic hypothesis**, which is now generally favored, suggests that new forms come about as the result of interactions between previous forms and the environment.

B. The period of the embryo begins at implantation and continues until, at about the end of the eighth week of gestation, the bones begin to **ossify**. During this period, the basic organs take shape.
•From the trophoblast come the membranes that will protect and nourish the developing embryo: the **amnion**, holder of the fluid surrounding the embryo; and the **chorion**, which becomes the fetal portion of the **placenta**, which is made from both maternal and embryonic tissue. The placenta is linked to the embryo by the **umbilical cord**. It delivers nutrients and oxygen to the embryo and carries away waste products.
•The inner cell mass differentiates into three cell layers: the outermost, or **ectoderm**, from which the skin and nervous system, among other things, develop; the **mesoderm**, which becomes the bones, muscles, and circulatory system; and the innermost, or **endoderm**, which develops into the digestive system and lungs.
•Beginning during the prenatal period and continuing through adolescence, development occurs in **cephalocaudal** (from the head down) and **proximodistal** (from the midline outward) **patterns**. The pattern of development for all but the sexual organs is the same for all human embryos. As discussed in Box 3.1, sexual differentiation for genetically male (XY) embryos begins in the seventh week of gestation with the formation of the testes, while the formation of ovaries in genetically female (XX) embryos will not begin until several weeks later. The rest of the process of sexual differentiation is controlled by hormones: in the presence of the male hormone testosterone, the external genitalia will be male; in the absence of testosterone, female genitalia will develop.
•By about 4 weeks after conception, the embryo's heart begins to beat; by 8 weeks, it can open its mouth, turn its head, and flex its body in response to a stimulus.

C. During the period of the fetus, which lasts from the eighth or ninth week of gestation until birth, the organ systems integrate their activities and the central nervous system undergoes a great deal of development. The fetus greatly increases in length and in strength.

The fetus also becomes more active, engaging in more varied and smoother movements that, by the end of the fourth month, can be felt by the mother. The fetus's activity decreases temporarily at 17 or 18 weeks, inhibited by higher brain regions that are taking greater control. From the sixth month on, activity once again increases. Experiments with fetuses of other species suggest that fetal movement may be necessary for normal development to take place; for example, chick embryos paralyzed with drugs fail to demonstrate the elimination of excess **neurons**—nerve cells—that ordinarily accompanies neuromuscular development, and their joints become fused as a result. The exact role of fetal movement in human prenatal development is, however, not known.

II. The Developing Organism in the Prenatal Environment

Even though it is protected and nourished by the mother's body, the fetus interacts with both the uterine environment and the outside world.

A. An understanding of the fetus's sensory capacities helps to determine how its development is affected by the environment.
• About 4 months after conception, the fetus begins to develop a sense of balance and can sense changes in its mother's posture. Floating in the fluid-filled amniotic sac is beneficial for fetal development; in fact, premature babies placed on waterbeds grow more quickly than those placed in ordinary cribs.
• Toward the end of pregnancy, fetuses are able to respond to light and may actually see light through the stretched wall of the mother's abdomen.
• Fetuses hear, and respond to, loud noises in the outside environment, though these sounds are muffled by background noise in the uterus.

B. While there is no evidence that fetuses learn likes or fears while still in the womb, after birth they do seem to recognize some familiar sounds, such as their mothers' heartbeats, to which they were repeatedly exposed prenatally.

C. Fetuses are indirectly affected, biochemically, by events affecting their mothers.
• Psychological stress during pregnancy puts women at risk for miscarriage and premature or difficult labor. Their babies may be irritable and have eating and sleeping difficulties. Having a supportive mate can reduce a woman's stress during pregnancy. As discussed in Box 3.2, fathers-to-be also must adjust to the changes that a pregnancy brings. Their involvement sometimes even includes sharing their wives' physical discomforts.
• Adequate maternal nutrition during pregnancy is necessary for normal fetal development. Extreme malnutrition early in pregnancy can lead to spontaneous abortions,

malformations, or stillbirths; for those born alive, it can result in low birth weight. Less extreme nutritional deprivation is also harmful, in particular because it usually accompanies low income, poor health care, and lack of educational opportunity; together, these factors may interfere with babies' cognitive development. Studies suggest that food supplementation for low-income pregnant women helps reduce the health costs of undernutrition. And special educational help as well as health care and nutritional supplementation can improve the cognitive and social development of children who have been undernourished prenatally.

D. **Teratogens** are environmental agents—for example, drugs, radiation, infections, and chemical pollutants—that can kill the developing embryo or fetus or cause serious abnormalities.

•*Drugs*, both prescription and nonprescription, can cross the placenta to affect the developing child. Some, like thalidomide, cause major deformities; no drug should be taken during pregnancy without medical advice.

•*Smoking* increases the rate of stillbirths and is associated with low birth weight.

•*Alcohol* consumption during pregnancy, particularly during the first 3 months, can lead to the set of abnormalities known as fetal alcohol syndrome. Even moderate drinking is thought to put the fetus at some risk.

•*Narcotics* addiction (for example, to heroin or methadone) on the part of mothers results in the birth of addicted infants who are also at risk for prematurity, low birth weight, respiratory illness, and impaired motor control.

•*Infections* can be passed to an embryo or fetus across the placental barrier or during the birth process. Rubella (German measles) and AIDS (Acquired Immune Deficiency Syndrome) are two examples. Rubella causes major developmental defects; transmission of the AIDS virus causes the baby to be infected with the disease.

•*Rh incompatibility* can result in a mother forming antibodies that destroy the red blood cells of the fetus. Rh disease can be treated by blood transfusions; however, most cases are now prevented by an anti-Rh serum that prevents Rh-negative mothers from forming antibodies to their Rh-positive children's blood.

•*Radiation* exposure can lead to spontaneous abortions, malformations, and mental retardation, and can also cause genetic damage to future generations.

•*Pollution* by chemicals which can become concentrated in the body can cause birth defects in unborn children. Additional research is needed to determine the effects of many of the chemicals to which we are routinely exposed.

Principles of teratogenic effects:

•The impact of teratogens on the developing organism depends on when exposure occurs. Exposure during the first 2 weeks may destroy the organism; after that time, exposure will affect whatever system is in the process of developing.

•Each teratogen causes a particular pattern of abnormal development.

•The genotypes of the mother and the developing organism help determine how strong the effect of a teratogen will be.

•Factors such as the mother's age and health can intensify or decrease the risk from exposure to a teratogen.

•The greater the concentration of a teratogen to which the organism is exposed, the greater the risk.

•Levels of a teratogen that can harm the developing organism may produce little or no effect on the mother.

III. Prenatal Development Reconsidered

In examining prenatal development, some general principles become clear: sequence and timing of development are important; development consists of both differentiation and integration; development occurs unevenly and appears stagelike; and regressions in development occur during periods of reorganization. These principles, according to many psychologists, can help us to understand the processes involved in postnatal development as well.

Key Terms I

Following are important terms introduced in Chapter 3. Write the definition for each after the term. Then match the term with the letter of the example that best illustrates it.

_____ Amnion _____

_____ Blastocyst _____

_____ Chorion _____

_____ Ectoderm _____

_____ Endoderm _____

_____ Inner cell mass _____

_____ Mesoderm _____

_____ Morula _____

_____ Placenta _____

_____ Trophoblast _____

_____ Umbilical cord _____

_____ Zona pellucida _____

a. A membrane that develops into the fetal component of the placenta.
b. The layer of cells from which the lungs and digestive system develop.
c. This organ, made from tissues of both the mother and the embryo, helps the embryo obtain nourishment and dispose of wastes.
d. This structure links the embryo to the placenta.
e. The layer of cells from which the bones and muscles are formed.
f. A thin but tough membrane that contains the fluid surrounding the embryo.
g. This extremely thin "envelope" forms the boundary that separates the zygote from the outside world.
h. The skin and the central nervous system develop from this layer of cells.
i. A cluster of identical cells that forms during the first few days after conception.
j. The name for the organism very early in development when, for the first time, two different types of cells can be distinguished.
k. A layer of cells within the blastocyst that develops into the protective membranes which will surround the developing organism.
l. A knot of cells within the blastocyst that develops into the organism itself.

Key Terms II

Following are important terms introduced in Chapter 3. Write the definition for each after the term. Then match the term with the letter of the example that best illustrates it.

_____ Cephalocaudal pattern _____

_____ Cleavage _____

_____ Epigenetic hypothesis _____

_____ Germinal period _____

_____ Implantation _____

_____ Neurons _____

_____ Ossify _____

_____ Period of the embryo _____

_____ Period of the fetus _____

_____ Preformationist hypothesis _____

_____ Proximodistal pattern _____

_____ Teratogens _____

a. The period of prenatal development, lasting about 6 weeks, during which the body's basic organs take shape.
b. A word that, applied to bones, means "to harden."
c. The blastocyst attaches itself to the wall of the uterus.
d. The period of prenatal development that begins at conception and ends when implantation occurs.
e. This is illustrated by the fact that the embryo's arms begin to form earlier than its legs.
f. These come from the environment and harm the developing fetus by causing deviations in development.
g. The idea that the adult forms of the body are each already present in some way within the fertilized ovum.
h. The period of prenatal development during which the organ systems develop sufficiently to allow the fetus to be able to survive outside the mother's body.
i. Examples are that the upper arm develops before the forearm and the forearm before the hand.
j. About 24 hours after conception, the zygote divides into two daughter cells that, in turn, each divide into two daughter cells.
k. This is another word for "nerve cells."
l. The idea that new forms arise during development through the interaction of existing forms with the environment.

Fill-in Review

Cover the list of answers next to the statements below. Then uncover each answer after you complete each statement.

implantation   1. The germinal period begins at the time of conception and lasts until _____, 8 to 10 days later.

blastocyst   2. The single-celled zygote divides again and again; eventually, the organism becomes a _____ with two distinctly different kinds of cells.

trophoblast   3. Some cells of the blastocyst form the inner cell mass; the others form the _____, which nourishes and protects the developing organism.

conception   4. The preformationist hypothesis assumes that all the different types of cells and physical features that characterize adults are already present at the time of _____.

5. According to the _____ hypothesis, these forms emerge later, through interaction with the environment.

   epigenetic

6. Today we know that both hypotheses have some truth. However, what is present at conception is not the adult forms themselves, but coded instructions contained in the _____.

   genes

7. After implantation, the period of the _____ begins, and continues for about 6 weeks.

   embryo

8. The embryo is surrounded by fluid that is contained by the _____, a thin but tough membrane.

   amnion

9. Another membrane, the chorion, becomes a component of the _____, which contains both maternal and embryonic tissue.

   placenta

10. Different layers of the inner cell mass form the various organ systems of the body: the digestive system and lungs are formed from the inner layer, or _____; the middle layer, or _____, becomes the bones, muscles, and circulatory system; and the outer layer, or _____, gives rise to, among other things, the skin, nails, and central nervous system.

    endoderm
    mesoderm
    ectoderm

11. Embryonic development occurs in patterns that are cephalocaudal—from the ___ down—and _____—from the inside out.

    top; proximodistal

12. Sexual differentiation begins at 7 weeks gestation for male embryos, several weeks _____ than for females.

    earlier

13. An XY pattern of sex chromosomes results in a person who is genetically _____; an _____ pattern results in a person who is genetically female.

    male; XX

14. Most of sexual differentiation is determined by the presence or absence of male _____, especially testosterone.

    hormones

15. The period of the _____ begins once the basic organ systems have been formed.

    fetus

16. Although it has been capable of activity for some time, it is not until about the end of the fourth month that the mother can feel the fetus _____.

    move

17. Fetal activity may temporarily _____ at 17 or 18 weeks, due to inhibition by higher brain centers.

    decrease

18. Fetuses are able to _____ to light, sound, and changes in their mothers' posture.

    respond

19. There is some evidence that newborns may recognize certain sounds, such as the mother's heartbeat, that became familiar to them _____.

    prenatally

20. The changes associated with pregnancy can cause a mother-to-be to experience psychological _____, which can adversely affect the fetus.

    stress

21. The fetus may also suffer if the mother is _____, either because of economic deprivation or poor eating habits.

    undernourished

22. Drugs, radiation, or pollutants—which are all _____—can kill the embryo or fetus or cause it to develop abnormalities.

    teratogens

when 23. The effects of teratogen exposure depend on _____ during gestation exposure occurs.

24. Levels of teratogen exposure that can harm the embryo or fetus do not necessarily
mother affect the _____.

developing 25. In general, whatever system is in the process of _____ when exposure occurs is the one that will be affected.

Multiple-Choice Practice Questions

Circle the letter of the word or phrase that correctly completes each statement.

1. During the prenatal period, the one-celled _____ develops into a fully formed baby.
   a. ovum
   b. blastocyst
   c. zygote
   d. embryo

2. The germinal period of development begins at conception and ends when
   a. the organism divides into two cells.
   b. the organism is implanted in the uterine wall.
   c. the major organ systems are formed.
   d. the heart begins to beat.

3. According to the _____ explanation for development, new forms occur during development through differing interactions of existing forms with the environment.
   a. epigenetic
   b. embryonic
   c. preformationist
   d. constructivist

4. The fluid-filled _____ protects and supports the developing embryo.
   a. chorion
   b. placenta
   c. amnion
   d. zona pellucida

5. The bones and muscles of the developing organism are formed from which layer of the inner cell mass?
   a. endoderm
   b. mesoderm
   c. ectoderm
   d. trophoblast

6. During prenatal development, the embryo's arms
   a. are formed earlier than the legs.

b. are formed at the same time as the legs.

c. are formed later than the legs.

d. are formed later than the hands.

7. In the absence of testosterone during prenatal development, the external genitalia will be _____ in appearance.

a. male

b. undifferentiated

c. both male and female

d. female

8. During the _____ period of prenatal development, the organism engages in smoother and more varied movement.

a. conceptual

b. embryonic

c. fetal

d. germinal

9. When chick embryos are given a drug that prevents them from moving, what happens if the drug is removed after 2 days?

a. The embryos begin to move again, but their muscles are somewhat behind normal in development.

b. The embryos begin to move again and are at the normal stage of muscle development for their gestational ages.

c. The embryos are unable to move because their joints have grown rigid and immobile.

d. The embryos die unless the drug is continued.

10. Studies of fetal hearing indicate that

a. fetuses are capable of hearing, but the uterine environment is very quiet, so there is little to hear.

b. fetuses "hear" only by feeling vibrations on their body surfaces, not with their ears.

c. fetuses hear most sounds in the immediate vicinity of their mothers, including most conversations.

d. fetuses hear only very distinct sounds from the world outside, as the background noise level in the uterus is fairly high.

11. Women who are under stress during pregnancy

a. secrete hormones that affect their fetuses' behavior.

b. give birth to larger babies than women who experience peaceful pregnancies.

c. give birth to babies who are placid and regular in their bodily functions.

d. experience no special problems or advantages in their pregnancies.

12. It is recommended that pregnant women consume well-balanced diets of at least

a. 1200 calories per day.

b. 1800 calories per day.

c. 2400 calories per day.

d. 3000 calories per day.

13. In an experiment on the consequences of undernutrition, Philip Zeskind and Craig Ramey found that children who had been prenatally undernourished
    a. were not distinguishable from those who had not been prenatally undernourished.
    b. were lower in birth weight than those who had not been undernourished but suffered no later effects on cognitive or social development.
    c. caught up to nonmalnourished children in cognitive and social skills when they were given food supplementation and health care.
    d. developed cognitive and social skills at normal rates when they received health care, food supplementation, and enriched educational experiences.

14. Which of the following causes birth defects?
    a. alcohol
    b. radiation
    c. environmental pollutants
    d. all of these

15. Exposure to a teratogen during prenatal development
    a. invariably leads to fetal death.
    b. affects whatever system is developing at the time of exposure.
    c. affects all fetuses with comparable exposure in the same way.
    d. does not affect the fetus at exposure levels that are safe for the mother.

Short-Answer Questions

1. What are the major features of the three periods of prenatal development? How would exposure to a teratogen affect development during each of these periods?

2. In the context of the epigenetic hypothesis, what is the environment? Give an example.

3. Is there evidence that fetuses are capable of learning? If so, what is an example of this?

4. Why is it difficult to determine the effect on development of nutritional deprivation alone?

5. In what ways do experiences originating outside the mother affect the developing fetus?

Putting It All Together

As discussed in Chapter 1, developmental psychologists interpret the facts they collect in terms of two major questions about development: Is development continuous or do discrete changes take place?

Which is more important in development—the genetic program or environmental forces?

Using what you know about prenatal development, find an example of each of the following during the prenatal period

•stages of development

•continuous change

•critical periods

•genetic influence

•effects of the environment

Sources of More Information

Boston Children's Medical Center. *Pregnancy, Birth, and the Newborn Baby.*
New York: Dell, 1972.
A guide to pregnancy, childbirth, and the newborn, including a discussion of the cultural context of childbearing.

Bremner, J. Gavin. *Infancy.* New York: Basil Blackwell, 1988.
The first chapter of this textbook covers physical growth and motor development both before and after birth.

Cherry, Sheldon H. *Understanding Pregnancy and Childbirth.* New York: Bobbs-Merrill, 1983.
An authoritative discussion of pregnancy and birth, including conception, prenatal development, prepared childbirth, and medical problems of pregnancy.

Nilsson, Lennart. *A Child Is Born.* New York: Dell, 1977.

Poole, William. *The First Nine Months of School.* Hippocrates July/Aug. 1987: 68-73.
This article gives the reader a lighthearted, though scientifically accurate, look at fetal learning.

Wallis, Claudia. *The New Origins of Life.* Time, Sept. 10 1984: 46-50; 52-53.
A guide to new techniques designed to combat infertility.

Answer Key

Answers to Key Terms I: f, j, a ,h, b, l, e, i, c, k, d, g

Answers to Key Terms II: e, j, l, d, c, k, b, a, h, g, i, f

Answers to Practice Questions 1. c, 2. b, 3. a, 4. c, 5. b, 6. a, 7. d , 8. c, 9. c, 10. d, 11. a, 12. c, 13. d, 14. d, 15. b

CHAPTER

4

BIRTH: STARTING LIFE ON THE OUTSIDE

The birth of a human infant is a dramatic transition, both physically and behaviorally. It also marks the beginning of children's first social relationships, starting with their first face-to-face encounters with their parents. And finally, at birth, the beliefs and customs of the cultural group into which children are born begin to shape their development in more direct ways. The influence of culture can be seen in how preparations for birth are carried out—whether in a hut or a hospital—in the rituals surrounding the process, and in the expectations with which the infant is greeted by parents and other members of the community.

Newborn infants are well-equipped to meet the challenges of postnatal life. Most of their senses are fairly well developed, and an array of reflexive behaviors allows them not only to breathe on their own and take in food, but also to attract responsive adults who will attend to their needs.

Newborns are individuals, and variations in temperament—mood, regularity of eating and sleeping, and ways of responding to new experiences—help determine how infants' development will be affected by their particular environments. Psychologists have long wondered whether infants' characteristics predict later behavior. Apparently, there are limits to predictability. But both temperament and the expectations of parents are important sources of continuity across the years, contributing to what stability can be observed in behavior as individuals develop from infancy to adulthood.

Chapter Outline

I.   Giving Birth

A. Labor, the process that forces the fetus out of the mother's body, occurs approximately 266 days after conception, and is divided into three stages:
•During the *first stage of labor*, contractions of the uterus dilate, or open, the cervix—

the opening of the uterus into the vagina.

•The *second stage of labor* begins when the baby's head enters the vagina and continues until the baby's head, then body, emerge from the mother's vagina.

•During the *third stage of labor*, the placenta and membranes are expelled.

B. The experience of giving birth depends, in part, on the traditions surrounding it in the culture in which the mother lives. These customs vary widely from culture to culture.

C. In the United States today, most women give birth in hospitals. The change to hospital-based birth has helped to lower infant mortality to less than 11 out of 1000 births and maternal mortality to 1 out of 10,000 births; however, medical intervention is not without controversy.

•Drugs used to relieve the pain of childbirth may affect babies' breathing and sucking responses and other postnatal behavior. In large doses, they may have long-term effects.

As discussed in Box 4.1, **prepared childbirth** techniques are, for some women, an alternative to the use of medication during labor and delivery.

•Medical interventions—for example, *induction of labor* or *caesarean section*—are thought to occur more frequently than is necessary. As cited in Box 4.2, the stresses of labor and delivery may actually help babies adapt to postnatal life; caesarean-born infants are more likely to have breathing difficulties than those born vaginally.

II. The Baby's Condition

Newborn babies weigh, on average, 7 to 7 1/2 pounds (5 1/2 to 10 pounds is the normal range) and are, on average, 20 inches in length.

A. The neonate's physical and behavioral condition can be assessed using rating scales:

•The **Apgar Scale** measures babies' heart rate, respiratory effort, muscle tone, reflex responsivity, and color at 1 and 5 minutes after birth.

•The **Brazelton Neonatal Assessment Scale** tests reflexes, muscle tone, motor capacities, responsiveness to objects and people, and infants' ability to control their own behavior and attention. Scales like Brazelton's do well in pointing out babies who need medical intervention, but are less useful in predicting later development from neonatal behavior.

B. Some babies are at risk for developmental problems, often because they are born prematurely and/or underweight.

•**Premature**, or preterm, babies are born before 37 weeks of gestation. Prematurity affects 5 to 7 percent of U.S. births. Premature babies may have immature digestive and immune systems, and may suffer from respiratory distress syndrome. The causes of prematurity are not well understood; however, mothers who are poor, very young, in poor health, who smoke, or are carrying more than one fetus are more likely to give birth prematurely.

Low birth weight means birth weight of 2500 grams (5 1/2 pounds) or less, regardless of **gestational age**, or age from conception. **Fetal growth retardation**—especially low weight for gestational age—is associated with multiple births, maternal malnutrition, smoking, infection, or certain abnormalities.

Very small babies are more likely to die during the first year or have permanent impairments. Preterm babies are developmentally delayed during infancy, by about the number of weeks of gestation they missed. Those who grow up under favorable environmental conditions have the best chance to catch up developmentally with their peers.

III. Newborn Behavior

Psychologists now know that infants are born able to perceive and react to the world in ways that help them to survive.

A. Newborns' sensory systems are all functioning, but some capacities are more mature than others. Psychologists study infants' sensory capacities by observing their reactions to stimuli—for example, does a child turn his or her head in the direction of a sound? Another common method relies on infants' tendency to pay less and less attention to a repeatedly presented stimulus (**habituation**); if the stimulus is changed in a way that makes it seem new to the infant, he or she will once again pay attention (**dishabituation**).

•Newborn hearing, while not as acute as that of older children and adults, is sensitive to the same range of frequencies. Newborns turn their heads toward the sources of sounds, startle when they hear loud noises, and can even distinguish—and prefer—the human voice compared to other sounds. As discussed in Box 4.3, newborns are also able to perceive distinctions between the basic speech sounds called **phonemes**—even ones not present in the language they hear around them.

•Infants' vision is not fully developed at birth. They are quite nearsighted with an acuity that has been estimated as between 20/300 and 20/800. However, they can see fairly clearly objects about as far away as their mothers' faces when they are nursing.

•Newborns also demonstrate both endogenous looking, which originates in the neural activity of the brain, and exogenous looking, which is stimulated by the external environment.

•Babies prefer to look at patterned figures rather than unpatterned ones. At 1 month of age, they focus on areas of high contrast and ignore internal details. By 2 or 3 months, they scan figures more thoroughly and concentrate more on internal contours.

•Newborns have been found to prefer schematic faces to jumbled face patterns, though this probably does not occur until the third month of life. Still, when faces are seen under natural conditions, moving, 45-hour-old infants prefer their mothers' faces to those of other women.

•Newborns are sensitive to a variety of odors and can distinguish them from one another. Their sense of taste is acute, and they prefer sweet substances.

•Newborns are sensitive to touch, to changes in temperature, and to sudden changes in position.

B. Infants are born with a number of ways to respond to or act on the world.

•They are equipped with an array of **reflexes**—involuntary and specific responses to specific types of stimulation.

•They appear to express **emotions**—for example, surprise, interest, pleasure, and anger, although it is difficult to know whether infants' emotional expressions have the same meanings as those of adults.

•Many psychologists believe that the elements of **temperament**—reflecting dominant mood and the tendency to react to the world in certain ways—are present at birth.

Alexander Thomas, Stella Chess, and their colleagues found that babies could be classified as *easy* (playful, adaptable, and regular in biological functions), *difficult* (irritable, negative toward new experiences, and irregular), and *slow to warm up* (low in activity level and needing some time to adapt to new situations). There appear to be genetic influences on infant temperament; however, as with other psychological phenomena, stability of temperament over time depends, in part, upon the environment in which the child develops.

IV. Beginning the Parent-Child Relationship

A. As has been discovered through **ethology**—the study of animal behavior in an evolutionary context—the appearance of **babyness** influences animals' responses to their offspring. There is evidence that for humans, also, the large heads, protruding cheeks, and large, low-set eyes of infants are appealing. Research shows that, beginning at about the age of puberty, children switch from preferring to look at pictures of adults to preferring pictures of babies.

B. Animal mothers will often reject babies who are removed from them immediately after birth, unless they have first had the opportunity to interact with them. According to Marshall Klaus, John Kennell, and their colleagues, human mothers given extra contact with their infants after birth are later more responsive to them. These findings have not been consistently replicated, however; in any case, we know that strong parent-infant attachments are formed even without extended, early contact.

C. When a baby is born, parents must begin to adapt to their actual child, not the child they may have imagined. From the time of birth, parents' reactions to their infants reflect their, and their societies', beliefs and expectations. Boys may be described as "big," girls as "cute," regardless of their actual appearance. From the beginning, parents treat their infants in ways consistent with the community's ideas and knowledge about people and their future roles. The parent-infant relationship will serve as the foundation for children's future development.

Key Terms

Following are important terms introduced in Chapter 4. Write the definition for each after the term. Then match the term with the letter of the example that best illustrates it.

_D_ Apgar Scale _____

_E_ Babyness _____

_K_ Brazelton Neonatal Assessment Scale _____

_O_ Dishabituation _____

_H_ Emotion _____

_F_ Ethology _____

_L_ Fetal growth retardation _J_ _____

_C_ Gestational age _____

_M_ Habituation _____

_J_ Low birth weight ___|_____

_N_ Phonemes _____

_____ Premature _____

_____ Prepared childbirth _____

_____ Reflexes _____

_____ Temperament _____

a. Birth that occurs before the 37th week of gestation.
b. The Lamaze method is an example.
c. From conception to birth, this normally measures 37 to 43 weeks.
d. An assessment of the baby's physical condition at 1 and 5 minutes after birth.
e. Protruding cheeks and a large, high forehead are indicators of this.
f. Study of the evolutionary basis of behavior.
g. One study of this attribute classified children as "easy," "difficult," or "slow to warm up."
h. Some examples of this—including anger, pleasure, and surprise—appear to be present at birth.
i. These well-integrated but involuntary responses comprise much of the newborn's behavior.
j. When this occurs, babies are born particularly small for their gestational ages.
k. This evaluates newborns' neurological condition by testing their behavior.
l. A factor that increases an infant's risk for developmental problems, whether or not it is accompanied by prematurity.
m. A newborn who stops paying attention to the repetitive sound of the washing machine has this response pattern.
n. These are responsible for the difference in sound between "bear" and "pear."
o. A baby who has stopped paying attention to the sound of the radio and perks up when the station is changed has this response pattern.

Fill-in Review

Cover the list of answers next to the statements below. Then uncover each answer after you complete each statement.

labor   1. _____, the process that forces the fetus out of the mother's body, begins at about 266 days after conception.

2. During the first stage of labor, contractions of the uterus cause the _____ to dilate. *cervix*

3. During the _____ stage of labor, the mother feels the urge to bear down and push the baby out. *second*

4. Under ordinary circumstances, the baby's _____ is the first part to emerge from the mother's body. *head*

5. The _____ and membranes are delivered during the third stage of labor. *placenta*

6. Although this was not always the case, most babies in the U.S. are born in _____. *hospitals*

7. During many deliveries, obstetric medications are used: for example, _____ to reduce feeling; analgesics to reduce perception of _____; or sedatives to relax the mother. *anesthetics* *pain*

8. It is now known that drugs administered during childbirth can cross the _____ and affect the fetus. *placenta*

9. _____ childbirth methods, such as Lamaze, provide alternatives to medication for controlling the pain of labor and delivery. *Prepared*

10. The stresses of the birth process stimulate fetuses to produce adrenaline and other _____, which help their breathing and circulation adjust to postnatal conditions. *hormones*

11. Average American babies weigh between 7 and 7 1/2 pounds at birth, but _____ several ounces during the first few days of postnatal life. *lose*

12. Babies' length, 20 inches on average, is mainly determined by the size of the _____. *uterus*

13. The _____ scale assesses a baby's physical condition at 1 and 5 minutes after birth. *Apgar*

14. The Brazelton Neonatal Assessment Scale evaluates a baby's _____ condition after delivery. *neurological*

15. Babies born at fewer than 37 weeks of gestation are considered _____. *premature or preterm*

16. Preterm infants often suffer from respiratory _____ syndrome. *distress*

17. Infants are classified as having a ____ birth weight if they weigh 2500 or fewer grams at birth. *low*

18. Preterm infants reach early developmental milestones, such as sitting up and crawling, somewhat _____ than infants born at normal gestational age. *later*

19. Whether preterm babies "catch up" with their full-term peers depends in part on what _____ conditions they are exposed to after birth. *environmental*

20. Sometimes, prolonged separation in the hospital results in disturbed relationships between preterm infants and their _____. *parents*

21. Researchers sometimes study newborns' sensory capacities using _____, the tendency for infants to stop paying attention to a repeated stimulus. *habituation*

speech   22. Newborn infants prefer _____ sounds to nonspeech sounds, and, by several
language   days after birth, may prefer the sounds of the _____ they hear spoken around
them.

nearsighted   23. Infants are quite _____ at birth, but their visual acuity reaches adult levels
crawl   by the time they are old enough to _____.

24. Although it is not clear what aspects they are responding to, newborns like to look
faces   at human _____.

sweets   25. Newborns have a well-developed sense of taste and prefer _____ tastes to sour
ones.

reflexes   26. Infants are born with many _____—for example, blinking and grasping—
which represent specific responses to specific kinds of stimulation.

emotions   27. Even very young infants appear to feel _____, such as pleasure, anger, and
surprise.

28. Infant humans and many infant animals have physical characteristics, such as
babyness   large eyes and round cheeks, that signify _____ and evoke caregiving behaviors in adults of their species.

expectations   29. Parents' _____ about their infants, shaped by culturally organized beliefs, are an important source of continuity in development.

Multiple-Choice Practice Questions

Circle the letter of the word or phrase that correctly completes each statement.

1. The baby actually emerges from the mother's body during
    a. the first stage of labor.
    b. the second stage of labor.
    c. the third stage of labor.
    d. the fourth stage of labor.

2. The main problem with obstetric medications is that
    a. they are not effective in relieving the pain of labor.
    b. while they do not affect the fetus, they may adversely affect the mother.
    c. they enter the bloodstream of the fetus and may cause adverse effects.
    d. in order to use them, it is necessary to give birth in a hospital.

3. The "stress" hormones that babies produce during labor are now thought to
    a. help their circulation and respiration adjust to life outside the womb.
    b. be the basis for psychological birth trauma.
    c. prevent them from making a smooth adjustment to postnatal life.
    d. have no effect on them.

4. The _____ evaluates the baby's condition at 1 and 5 minutes after birth.
   a. Apgar Scale
   b. PKU test
   c. Brazelton Neonatal Assessment Scale
   d. Bayley Mental and Motor Scales

5. The most critical problem for preterm newborns is
   a. lack of a subcutaneous fat layer.
   b. a weak sucking reflex.
   c. respiratory distress syndrome.
   d. an immature digestive system.

6. Women who _____ are more likely than others to give birth prematurely.
   a. are of middle-class socioeconomic status
   b. are carrying more than one fetus
   c. are in their twenties
   d. have no known risk factors

7. Premature babies who _____ are especially likely to have long-term developmental problems.
   a. have small head size and slow head growth
   b. have respiratory distress syndrome
   c. are of normal birth weight for gestational age
   d. gain weight quickly

8. On which would a newborn best be able to focus?
   a. his mother's face while he nurses
   b. a mobile hanging on the far end of his crib
   c. a person standing across the room
   d. all of the above, equally well

9. A baby has stopped paying attention to a repeated tone. Then, when a higher frequency tone is played, he begins to respond again. This is called
   a. classical conditioning.
   b. sensory adaptation.
   c. dishabituation.
   d. operant conditioning.

10. Newborns distinguish syllables such as /pa/ and /ba/ on the basis of
    a. auditory frequency.
    b. voice-onset-time (VOT).
    c. rhythm.
    d. none of the above—they cannot make this distinction.

11. Which is an example of endogenous looking?
    a. scanning with short eye movements in a completely dark room
    b. scanning that occurs after the lights are turned on in a previously dark room
    c. looking longer at a patterned stimulus than at an unpatterned stimulus
    d. all of the above

12. When 1-month-olds are shown simple geometric figures,
    a. they look away.
    b. they focus on areas of high contrast.
    c. they systematically scan the entire outline of the figure.
    d. they look first at the outside of the figure, then scan the interior.

13. Some theorists believe that the _____ was important during earlier evolu-
    tionary stages, but has no current function.
    a. eyeblink reflex
    b. sucking reflex
    c. Babinski reflex
    d. Moro reflex

14. Some researchers infer from newborns' facial expressions, sounds, and move-
    ments that they experience
    a. love for their parents.
    b. thoughts.
    c. emotions.
    d. memories from before birth.

15. Infants who are regular in biological functions, playful, and adaptable have been
    labeled "easy" with respect to
    a. temperament.
    b. personality.
    c. motor development.
    d. emotion.

16. Which is *not* a sign of babyness, as Konrad Lorenz describes it?
    a. small head in proportion to body
    b. round cheeks
    c. large eyes
    d. high forehead

17. Parents tend to describe their newborns as
    a. "easy" if they are girls, and "difficult" if boys.
    b. "big" if they are boys, and "cute" if girls.
    c. "big" and "beautiful" regardless of sex.
    d. "resembling their mothers," regardless of sex.

Short-Answer Questions

1. Why is it difficult to predict which premature babies will have long-term developmental problems? What factors are associated with such problems?

2. In what ways do researchers determine that infants are experiencing emotions? Can we know for certain that infant and adult emotions are similar? Why or why not?

3. What do psychologists mean by "temperament"? What evidence is there that it has a heritable component?

4. Why did Marshall Klaus and John Kennell believe that mother-infant bonding would be enhanced by early prolonged contact between them? To what extent has their claim been supported by research?

5. What are some positive and negative aspects of parents' expectations about their newborns on the basis of the infants' sex?

Sources of More Information

Boston Children's Medical Center. *Pregnancy, Birth, and the Newborn Baby.* New York: Dell, 1972.
A guide to pregnancy, childbirth, and the newborn, including a discussion of the cultural context of childbirth.

Cherry, Sheldon H. *Understanding Pregnancy and Childbirth.* New York: Bobbs-Merrill, 1983.
An authoritative discussion of pregnancy and birth, including conception, prenatal development, prepared childbirth, and medical problems of pregnancy.

Fincher, Jack. *Before Their Time.* Science 82 July/Aug. 1982.
This is a look inside the newborn intensive-care nursery, where physicians, nurses, technicians, and parents handle the problems of extreme prematurity.

Haith, Marshall. *Rules That Babies Look By.* Hillsdale, NJ: Erlbaum, 1980.
The characteristics of visual behavior in early infancy are described by an expert in the field.

Klaus, Marshall and John H. Kennell. *Maternal-Infant Bonding.* St. Louis: The C. V. Mosby Co., 1976.
The physician-authors hypothesize a sensitive period for the formation of early parent-infant attachment. This is a controversial but thought-provoking book.

Lamaze, Fernand. *Painless Childbirth: The Lamaze Method.* New York: Pocket Books, 1983.
The psychoprophylactic method is explained by the physician who brought it from the Soviet Union to France.

Pryor, Karen. *Nursing Your Baby.* New York: Pocket Books, 1984.
In this book, nursing is discussed from the point of view of the prospective mother; it should, nevertheless, be interesting to students of infant development.

Schaffer, Rudolph. *Mothering.* Cambridge: Harvard University Press, 1977.
The author describes the organization of infants' behavior in the context of their mothers' stimulation of and reaction to them.

Answer Key

Answers to Key Terms: d, e, k, o, h, f, j, c, m, l, n, a, b, i, g

Answers to Practice Questions: 1. b, 2. c, 3. a, 4. a, 5. c, 6. b, 7. a, 8. a, 9. c, 10. b, 11. a, 12. b, 13. d, 14. c, 15. a, 16. a, 17. b.

CHAPTER

5

DEVELOPMENTAL CHANGE IN EARLY INFANCY

During the first 2 1/2 postnatal months, infants are mainly adjusting to life outside their mothers' bodies, and parents are adjusting their lives to accommodate their new offspring. Some changes seem to be the result of maturation of infants' nervous systems. Several reflexes present at birth—stepping and involuntary grasping, for example—disappear during the first weeks or months. But learning also plays a role, and other reflexes are modified by use, becoming part of more complex behaviors, as when rooting, sucking, swallowing, and breathing become integrated with one another (and with maternal behaviors as well) in nursing.

Cultural variations in the ways parents organize their infants' experiences exert some influence on development. For example, infants from cultures—such as that of the U.S.—in which they are expected to sleep all night without waking to feed will, in fact, learn to sleep through the night sooner than infants from cultures in which this is not an important expectation.

The various broad approaches to the study of development—biological-maturation, environmental-learning, interactional, and cultural-context—each emphasize different factors in explaining the changes of the first months of infancy. But at the end of about 2 1/2 months, it is possible to see how changes at all levels—biological, behavioral, and social—move infants to a new level of development, in a bio-social-behavioral shift.

Chapter Outline

I. Becoming Coordinated

Coordination of babies' inborn abilities with their parents' caretaking skills allows babies' basic needs to be met. In addition, when babies and parents coordinate their schedules—for example, for eating and sleeping—babies fit smoothly into their families' lives.

A. An important area for coordination is sleep. Peter Wolff, studying newborns' activity patterns, found that they display seven different states of alertness, in four of which they are asleep or nearly asleep. Electroencephalographic research indicates that different brainwave patterns accompany these levels of arousal.

•For the first 2 to 3 months of life, babies begin their sleep periods with active or REM (rapid eye movement) sleep, and later enter quiet or NREM sleep. After a few months, this pattern is reversed.

•Newborns sleep about two-thirds of the time, but their sleep comes in many short periods. As they grow older, sleep periods become longer and begin to coincide with adult day/night schedules.

•Both cultural expectations and brain maturation affect how quickly babies adopt adultlike sleep cycles. American expectations for babies to sleep through the night may be at the limit of what they can adjust to.

B. Adults and babies must also coordinate feeding schedules. If fed on demand, newborns prefer to eat about every 3 hours, but adjust, by 7 to 8 months, to eating about four times per day.

C. Crying alerts parents to babies' discomfort. Birth, pain, and hunger cries can be distinguished both by electronic analysis of sound patterns and by adult listeners, as can those of "at risk" and normal babies. Still, parents may not always be able to interpret their babies' cries. Adults react to infant cries with increased heart rate and blood pressure, and even, among nursing mothers, with milk flow.

•Hunger and gastrointestinal pain are two major causes of crying, but all infants have periods in the first few months during which they cry for no identifiable reason.

•Changing their diapers often quiets babies, but it may be the handling involved in diapering that has this effect. Holding babies to the shoulder, rocking, patting, cuddling, swaddling, and giving them pacifiers to suck—all effective techniques—provide babies with rhythmic stimulation while reducing the sensations from their own movements. Crying gradually decreases during the first few months of life.

II. Mechanisms of Developmental Change

A. During early infancy, existing behaviors become more efficient and new behaviors develop. Nursing provides a good example. At birth, rooting, sucking, swallowing, and breathing are not yet smoothly coordinated; but by 6 weeks, the components of nursing occur in an efficient, integrated sequence. Since each of the four broad developmental frameworks introduced in Chapter 1 emphasizes different factors in explaining its development, nursing is a behavior that can be used to compare these approaches.

B. The biological-maturation perspective emphasizes the way changes in physical structure and physiological processes bring about development, and assigns only a small role to the environment. According to this approach, postnatal development is a continuation of embryological processes, and changes in behavior, such as the development of nursing, are accounted for by changes in infants' nervous systems.

Infants' reflexes illustrate some of these changes.

•Infants' simplest behaviors are spinal reflexes, involving **sensory receptors**, motor neurons, a **synapses** (the gaps between neurons) in the spinal cord. The hand withdrawal reflex (in response to pain) is an example.

•More complex reflexes such as sucking involve additional neurons both in the spinal cord and in the **brain stem**. The brain stem also controls newborns' vital functions, such as sleeping and breathing, and is involved in their emotional responses.

•When sensory inputs are directed to the **cerebral cortex**, memories of past events are integrated with current information, and information from several sources can be combined. The cortex, which allows "higher psychological processes" to take place, undergoes many changes after birth:

1. The cortex becomes larger and more complex.

2. **Myelination**, the formation of **myelin**, a fatty sheath along nerve cells, allows the cells to transmit information more quickly. As myelination better connects the cortex to underlying parts of the nervous system, infants' abilities expand. Structural developments in the **primary motor area**, the first to develop after birth, allow infants first to raise their heads voluntarily, to control their arms, trunks, and legs, and, finally, to walk.

3. Changes in the **primary sensory areas** (including those responsible for touch, vision and hearing) take place mainly during the first 3 months after birth.

•Babies born with intact brain stems but without cerebral cortexes can suck, yawn, stretch, cry, and track visual stimuli, but do not develop the well-coordinated behaviors, such as nursing, seen in normal babies the same age.

•After birth, the increasingly active cerebral cortex begins to suppress certain reflexes. The **Moro reflex** occurs in response to a sudden noise or to the sensation of being dropped. It resembles the clinging of infant apes and disappears by about the fifth month; the **stepping reflex** by 2 months. Some researchers feel that the stepping reflex, inhibited by cortical activity, reappears later as voluntary walking (at about 1 year of age) under cortical control; others believe that the stepping reflex is not directly related to voluntary walking. As the visual and motor systems develop in the months after birth, visually initiated reaching (or **prereaching**), based on independent and reflexive reaching and grasping movements, is replaced by the coordinated movements of visually guided reaching.

As discussed in Box 5.2, interaction with the environment affects development of the nervous system. Austin Riesen demonstrated that chimpanzees needed visual stimulation for normal development of their retinas and visual cortexes, and Hirsch and Spinelli demonstrated the effect of visual stimulation in kittens. Mark Rosenzweig and his colleagues found that rats allowed to actively explore enriched environments developed larger brains and learned faster than those housed in standard laboratory conditions. Thus, not only does the brain affect behavior, but behavior affects development of the brain.

C. The environmental-learning perspective emphasizes the role of learning in the coordination of innate reflexes with environmental events. One type of learning, habituation, was discussed in Chapter 4. Other types of learning are **classical conditioning**, operant conditioning, and imitation.

•Through classical conditioning, infants learn what events in the environment tend to occur together. They are then able to anticipate events rather than simply react to them. Classical conditioning was first described by physiologist Ivan Pavlov during his experiments on digestion in dogs. In his studies, a tone served as a **conditional stimulus** (CS), which was paired with food in the dog's mouth—an **unconditional stimulus** (UCS). This UCS invariably caused salivation—an **unconditional response** (UCR). After many pairings, presentation of the CS alone caused the dog to salivate—a **conditional response** (CR) had been learned.

It appears that babies can learn expectancies through classical conditioning within hours of birth. Elliot Blass and his colleagues demonstrated that infants could learn to pucker their mouths (CR) in response to being stroked on the forehead (CS), when the stroking had been paired with a sugar-water solution (UCS).

For reasons not yet clear, **aversive conditioning**, or anticipation of unpleasant events, does not appear until several months after birth.

•While classical conditioning explains how behaviors come to be elicited by new circumstances, instrumental or **operant conditioning** provides a means for adding new forms of behavior to infants' repertoires. **Reinforcement** occurs when actions that produce rewarding consequences are repeated; those which fail to produce rewards are not. Einar Siqueland demonstrated that newborns could learn to either turn their heads (experimental group) or keep their heads still (control group) in order to obtain the opportunity to suck on a pacifier (a reinforcing stimulus).

•There is controversy about whether imitation is possible for newborn infants. Andrew Meltzoff and Keith Moore found that newborns appeared to imitate adults' facial expressions, such as opening their mouths wide or sticking out their tongues, and Tiffany Field and her colleagues used habituation to demonstrate that newborns do pay attention to adults' expressions. However, researchers have not always been able to produce newborn imitation. Imitation may be part of newborns' repertoire of reflexive behaviors; it is probably not an important way of learning about the world for several months after birth.

While the environmental-learning perspective has contributed many practical means for overcoming behavior problems, such as shyness, school difficulties, and bedwetting, it does not do well in accounting for developmental change and individual differences.

D. The interactional perspective, as exemplified by the theory of Jean Piaget, emphasizes the interaction of infants' environments with their biological capacities, and views developmental change as originating in children's own ongoing activity.

•**Schemas** are the basic psychological units in Piaget's theory; children's inborn reflexes are also their first schemas. These schemas are strengthened and transformed through the processes of **assimilation** and **accommodation**.

Experience is assimilated to infants' schemas much the same as food is assimilated by their digestive systems. Infants may assimilate breast, bottle, pacifier, and fingers to their inborn sucking schemas.

At the same time, it is necessary for infants to modify their schemas to fit the variety of objects to which they are applied. This process is called accommodation. Somewhat different sucking techniques are necessary to get milk from breast and bottle. Infants who are fed both ways must accommodate to each.

•**Equilibration** is a balancing of assimilation and accommodation, bringing children to a new level of development. Soon, however, biological changes or environmental demands will create new imbalances that will in turn push children's development even further.

•Piaget identified six substages within infancy, which he referred to as the **sensorimotor stage**. Substages 1 and 2 are described in this chapter.

In substage 1 (birth to about 1 month), infants mainly exercise their first schemas, the inborn reflexes. The most important aspect of this "functional exercise" is that the reflexes themselves produce further stimulation, which then stimulates further reflex activity.

Substage 2 (from about 1 to about 4 months) is characterized by **primary circular reactions**: infants now repeat, for their own sake, primary actions that are centered on their own bodies , such as sucking their fingers, waving their hands, or kicking their feet. These actions are also called circular because they lead back to themselves, serving only to prolong interesting events.

• Although Piaget did not actually study the social context of early development, it is clear that changes in the mother's behavior are essential to an infant's development. In nursing, for example, the mother's behavior (holding the infant properly or joggling the infant during pauses in sucking) combines with the baby's efforts to maximize the amount of milk received.

E. The cultural-context perspective emphasizes cultural variations in the way that adults arrange their interactions with their children. For example, children may be breastfed by their mothers, fed by a wet nurse, or given infant formula in a bottle. More important for development than these variations in feeding practices, though, are the larger cultural patterns of which they are a part. The ways in which infants are treated in a particular culture depend on what that culture views babies to be. American mothers, who have a high opinion of newborns' capacities, react to them as though each of their behaviors were highly meaningful. The Kaluli of Papua New Guinea (as studied by Eleanor Ochs and Bambi Schieffelin), view infants as quite helpless and speak *for* their infants to other members of the social group, rather than speaking *to* their infants.

III. Integrating the Separate Threads of Development

Children's behaviors do not develop in isolation, but as part of a complex system. Because it is not possible to study all aspects of this system at once, Robert Emde and his colleagues developed a strategy for tracing development in biological, behavioral, and social domains as they relate to one another. Periodically, changes in these domains converge, resulting in a qualitative reorganization that represents a new level of development, a bio-social-behavioral shift.

A. The first bio-social-behavioral shift occurs, in full-term babies, at about 2 1/2 months after birth. Changes in smiling illustrate the importance of this shift for infants' interactions with the world.

B. Robert Emde, T.J. Gaensbauer, and R.J. Harmon observed that infants' earliest smiles were controlled by events occurring in the brain stem. These have been called REM smiles because they are associated with drowsiness and REM sleep. In the first few months, these endogenous smiles are replaced by exogenous smiles, which are reactions to environmental stimuli. Between 1 month and 2 1/2 months of age, infants may smile in response to nearly any outside stimulus.

At 2 1/2 to 3 months of age, as part of the first bio-social-behavioral shift, infants' smiles become truly social—they smile in response to others' smiles and, in turn, elicit others' smiles. At this point, parents report a new quality of emotional contact with their infants.

Feedback from the social world—in the form of others smiling back—is important in the development of social smiling. Blind infants, unable to make these visual connections, may not shift to social smiling at 2 1/2 months. According to Selma Fraiberg, parents of blind infants often use touch to stimulate their babies' smiles; in this way, they establish the kind of social interaction seen in sighted babies and their parents.

C. During the first 10 to 12 weeks of postnatal life, infants grow larger and stronger, their nervous systems develop, and they perform reflexive behaviors more efficiently. These developments take place through support from and interaction with their caretakers. At about 2 1/2 months after birth, converging developments in the biological, behavioral, and social domains allow new behaviors and a new social relationship between infants and their caretakers.

Key Terms I

Following are important terms introduced in Chapter 5. Write the definition for each after the term. Then match the term with the letter of the example that best illustrates it.

_____ Accommodation _____

_____ Assimilation _____

_____ Equilibration _____

_____ Learning _____

_____ Moro reflex _____

_____ Myelination _____

_____ Prereaching _____

_____ Primary circular reaction _____

_____ Primary motor area _____

_____ Primary sensory areas _____

_____ Schema _____

_____ Sensorimotor stage _____

_____ Stepping reflex _____

a. The time of life during which developments in behavior primarily involve co-ordination between motor behaviors and sensory circumstances.
b. A baby learns to suck differently to get milk from a bottle than to nurse from his mother's breast.
c. A newborn, when startled, flings out her arms and legs, then brings them back toward her body, as if clinging to something.
d. A baby sees his hand pass across his field of vision, finds this interesting, then repeats the movement over and over again.
e. This balance between assimilation and accommodation brings the child into a new stage of development.
f. Habituation, classical conditioning, and operant conditioning are examples.

g. Development in this part of the cortex allows changes such as that from prereaching to voluntary reaching.

h. A baby uses her sucking schema to explore a pacifier.

i. When held upright on her parents' bed, a week-old girl repeatedly touches the surface with first one foot, then the other.

j. As this process occurs, the cerebral cortex becomes more directly connected to the lower-lying areas of the nervous system.

k. According to Piaget, the infant's early reflexes (for example, sucking) are primitive examples of this unit of psychological functioning.

l. A newborn girl stretches out her hand toward her mother's bright necklace.

m. The area responsible for the sense of touch is the first of these to become active.

Key Terms II

Following are important terms introduced in Chapter 5. Write the definition for each after the term. Then match the term with the letter of the example that best illustrates it.

_____ Aversive conditioning _____

_____ Brain stem _____

_____ Cerebral cortex _____

_____ Classical conditioning _____

_____ Conditional response _____

_____ Conditional stimulus _____

_____ Myelin _____

_____ Operant conditioning _____

_____ Reinforcement _____

_____ Sensory receptor _____

_____ Synapse _____

_____ Unconditional response _____

_____ Unconditional stimulus _____

a. An infant learns to suck a pacifier in order to activate a mobile above her crib.
b. The light-sensitive rods and cones in the eye are examples.
c. The part of the nervous system that controls vital functions such as breathing and inborn reflexes.
d. This substance coats nerve fibers, allowing nerve impulses to travel more efficiently.
e. Through this process, infants learn to anticipate events rather than simply reacting to them.
f. A stimulus that automatically elicits some response (as a puff of air in the eye elicits blinking).
g. Infants do not demonstrate this type of learning before several months of age.
h. In simple reflexes, the small gaps between sensory and motor neurons.
i. In Pavlov's study, a tone, which signaled that food was about to be presented.
j. An infant smiles at his father and receives a smile in return, making him more likely to direct smiles at his father in the future.
k. This part of the nervous system allows infants to integrate new sensory information with memories of previous experiences.
l. A response that automatically occurs to a particular stimulus (as when a baby turns his head in the direction of a touch on the cheek).
m. A baby makes sucking movements with his mouth when he sees his nursing bottle approaching.

Fill-in Review

Cover the list of answers next to the statements below. Then uncover each answer after you complete each statement.

short 1. Newborns sleep for a large number of fairly _____ periods.

expectations 2. Both brain maturation and cultural _____ affect the age at which babies adopt an adultlike sleep cycle.

three 3. If fed on demand, newborns prefer to eat about every _____ hours.

4. Both adult listeners and electronic analysis can distinguish among infants' birth cries, pain cries, and _____ cries.
hunger

Nursing 5. _____ is not a reflex, but involves coordination of the sucking, swallowing, and breathing reflexes.

biological-maturation 6. The _____ perspective explains developmental change in infancy as a continuation of embryological processes.

reflexes 7. An infant's simplest _____ involve a sensory neuron, a motor neuron, and a synapse in the spinal cord.

brain stem 8. The _____ _____ controls newborns' sleeping and breathing, and is involved in their emotional responses.

cerebral cortex 9. The _____ _____ is involved in "higher psychological processes" including language and memory.

myelination 10. In the months after birth, _____ of neurons more closely connects the cortex to the brain stem and spinal cord.

11. While the primary motor area is not fully developed until sometime in the second
sensory year, the primary _____ area is relatively mature by 3 months after birth.

12. Some reflexes present at birth—for example, the Moro and stepping reflexes—
inhibition disappear in the next few months, possibly due to _____ by the cortex.

environmental-learning 13. The _____ perspective emphasizes the importance of learning in explaining developmental change.

conditional 14. In classical conditioning, a _____ stimulus (for example, a bell), when paired with an unconditional stimulus (for example, food), comes to elicit a con-
response ditional _____ (for example, salivation).

aversive 15. Infants do not display _____ conditioning (involving anticipation of unpleasant events) until several months after birth.

operant 16. In _____ conditioning, behavior increases in frequency when followed
reinforcement by _____ (rewards or escape from unrewarding circumstances).

imitation 17. There is controversy about whether the form of learning called _____ occurs in newborn infants.

18. The _____ framework, exemplified by Piaget's theory, emphasizes the role of children's own activity in developmental change.

    interactional

19. In Piaget's theory, the basic psychological units are _____; for example,
sucking, grasping, and looking.

    schemas

20. In the process of _____, schemas are applied to new experiences;
through _____, the schemas are modified to fit the demands of the environment.

    assimilation
    accommodation

21. _____, the balancing of assimilation and accommodation, brings children to new stages of development.

    Equilibration

22. Piaget referred to the first 2 years as the _____ stage of development.
He divided this period into _____ substages.

    sensorimotor
    six

23. In substage 1 (birth to about 1 month), infants exercise their first schemas, the inborn _____.

    reflexes

24. During substage 2 (1 to 4 months), infants engage in primary _____ reactions, such as sucking their fingers and kicking their feet.

    circular

25. The _____ perspective emphasizes the ways in which develop-
ment is affected by cultural differences in adults' interactions with their children.

    cultural-context

26. When developments in the biological, behavioral, and social domains converge,
the result is the qualitative reorganization of development known as a
_____ shift. The first such shift takes place at about _____ months
of age.

    bio-social-behavioral;2 1/2 to 3

27. _____ smiling (smiling in response to others' smiles and eliciting the smiles
of others) occurs as part of the first bio-social-behavioral shift.

    Social

Multiple-Choice Practice Questions

Circle the letter of the word or phrase that correctly completes each statement.

1. Newborn babies sleep
   a. in one 14-hour period each day.
   b. in several long stretches each day.
   c. in many short periods each day.
   d. many hours at night and rarely during the day.

2. Babies' cries usually cause adults to
   a. react with increased heart rate and blood pressure.
   b. avoid contact with the babies.
   c. react with decreases in heart rate.
   d. react with signs of depression.

3. Research on the effect on crying of changing babies' diapers showed that
   a. wet diapers are the most important source of discomfort for babies.

b. putting wet diapers back on crying babies made them cry more than before.

c. changing diapers had no effect on babies' crying.

d. the handling involved in changing diapers seems to have an effect in soothing babies.

4. Nursing

a. is present at birth in the same form as seen in older infants.

b. develops greater efficiency and coordination during the first weeks of life.

c. is composed of several reflexes that are and remain separate from one another.

d. takes longer in older infants than in newborns.

5. Theorists with the _____ perspective view development during infancy as a continuation of embryological processes.

a. environmental-learning

b. interactional

c. cultural-context

d. biological-maturation

6. The _____ controls vital functions such as breathing and sleeping.

a. cerebral cortex

b. cerebellum

c. brain stem

d. midbrain

7. Myelination is

a. a process of brain growth through the formation of new neurons.

b. the formation of a fatty sheath around nerve fibers.

c. a structural part of brain development that is nearly complete at birth.

d. the formation of reflex arcs in the spinal cord.

8. The _____ reflex involves flinging out the arms, then hugging them back to the center of the body.

a. grasping

b. reaching

c. swimming

d. Moro

9. Experiments with animals indicate that

a. visual experience with patterns is necessary for the normal development of connections between eye and brain.

b. the visual system requires no experience for its development, so long as it is not completely deprived of stimulation by light.

c. even raising animals in the dark has no effect on the development of their visual systems.

d. there are no "critical periods" in development of the visual system.

10. Through _____, babies learn to anticipate events that often occur together.

a. operant conditioning

b. imitation

c. classical conditioning

d. habituation

11. When an infant turns her head, she is given a taste of sugarwater. After a series of trials, she turns her head consistently. This is an example of
    a. habituation.
    b. classical conditioning
    c. imitation.
    d. operant conditioning.

12. Piaget's theory of intellectual development views _____ as the originators of developmental change.
    a. children themselves
    b. children's environments
    c. children's genes
    d. children's parents

13. Which might be a primary circular reaction?
    a. An infant opens his mouth for milk when he sees his mother approach.
    b. An infant repeatedly brings her hand to her mouth and briefly sucks her fingers.
    c. A baby learns to ignore the sound of the highway outside his window.
    d. A newborn copies his mother when she opens her eyes wide in a surprised expression.

14. American mothers generally behave as though everything their infants do is
    a. random.
    b. evidence of helplessness.
    c. meaningful.
    d. evidence of superior intelligence.

15. Which is associated with the first postnatal bio-social-behavioral shift?
    a. social smiling
    b. complete development of the cerebral cortex
    c. walking
    d. the first meaningful spoken words

Short-Answer Questions

1. How do both mother and infant contribute to the development of efficient nursing?

2. How do infants form expectancies through classical conditioning? Describe a situation in which this might actually occur.

3. Describe an instance in which cultural variations influence infants' development.

4. Show how biological, behavioral, and social factors interact in infants' development of social smiling.

Putting It All Together

Find examples from prenatal development and early infancy to show what happens when higher centers in the nervous system begin to take charge of particular motor functions.

Sources of More Information

Bower, T.G.R. *Development in Infancy.* San Francisco: W.H. Freeman and Co., 1982.
This discussion of perceptual and cognitive development during infancy gives readers a look at how a clever researcher tries to determine what babies really know.

Brazelton, T. Berry. *What Every Baby Knows.* New York: Ballantine Books, 1987.
This account of early development follows five families during the first two years of

their children's lives, showing how they solve problems and adapt to the changes brought about by their children's births.

Ginsburg, Herbert P. and Sylvia Opper. *Piaget's Theory of Intellectual Development*, Third Edition. Englewood Cliffs, N.J.: Prentice-Hall, 1988.
This is a readable, up-to-date presentation of Piaget's work and theory, aimed at undergraduate-level students.

Metzger, Mary and Cynthia Whittaker. *The Childproofing Checklist. A Parent's Guide to Accident Prevention From Birth to Age Five.* New York: Doubleday, 1988.
This book deals with one of the major adjustments that must be made by families with new babies—making the home safe for infants and young children.

Montagu, Ashley. *Touching. The Human Significance of the Skin*, Third Edition. New York: Harper & Row, 1986.
The author describes the importance of tactile interaction for human development.

Towle, Alexandra (Ed.). *Mother.* New York: Simon & Schuster, 1988.
This book contains many views of motherhood, expressed through the words and images of famous writers and poets.

Answer Key

Answers to Key Terms I: b, h, e, f, c, j, l, d, g, m, k, a, i

Answers to Key Terms II: g, c, k, e, m, i, d, a, j, b, h, l, f
Answers to Practice Questions: 1. c, 2. a, 3. d, 4. b, 5. d, 6. c, 7. b, 8. d, 9. a, 10.c, 11. d, 12. a, 13. b, 14. c, 15. a.

CHAPTER

6

THE ACHIEVEMENTS OF THE FIRST YEAR

At no time after birth does development occur so quickly as in the first year. During their first 12 months, infants move from relative helplessness to independent locomotion. Gradually, they gain control over their bodies. By 1 year of age, they can reach for and grasp objects smoothly and accurately and let them go voluntarily; they can even, using thumb and forefinger, pick up objects the size of beads or raisins.

Infants' growing cognitive abilities parallel the development of their motor skills. Toward the end of the first year, they demonstrate newly developed powers of memory and are able to coordinate actions to reach a goal. Linguistically, they are also making progress; their strings of babbling begin to resemble adult speech.

Changes are occurring in infants' social lives as well. By 7 or 8 months of age, they begin to be wary of strangers and to resist being separated from their caretakers. In fact, they depend on their caretakers' reactions to show them how to react in unfamiliar situations.

These many changes in different domains result in a bio-social-behavioral shift between about 7 and 9 months of age. At this time, infants are prepared for more active exploration of their physical and social worlds.

Chapter Outline

I. Biological Changes

Changes in babies' motor and cognitive abilities between 2 1/2 months and 1 year depend on changes in the physical structures of their bodies and brains.

A. Most babies grow about 10 inches and triple their weight during the first year—their fastest growth spurt until adolescence. Their bodies grow differentially; by 12 months, their heads account for a smaller and their legs a greater proportion of overall length. This lowers their center of gravity and makes walking easier.

B. Infants' bones start to ossify, or harden, beginning with those of the hands and wrists. Their muscles become longer and thicker, another development that prepares them to walk.

C. Babies' nervous systems—especially the cortexes of their brains—become larger and more complex. Growth and myelination lead, between 7 and 9 months, to increased functioning of the frontal lobes and changes in electrical activity. The hippocampus, which is involved in memory, and the cerebellum, related to motor coordination, undergo similar development.

II. Motor Development

Dramatic improvements in babies' ability to move around and to manipulate objects occur during the first year.

A. At first, babies reach for objects in front; later, they can reach for objects to the side. This is a proximodistal pattern.
   By about 2 1/2 months, babies perform visually guided reaching. By 9 months, they can pick up objects using a pincerlike movement of thumb and forefinger; their movements appear almost reflexive, but are now under voluntary control.

B. Babies can raise their heads before they can sit, and sit before they can stand, a cephalocaudal pattern of development. Crawling develops when the actions of arms and legs are not only mastered but coordinated with one another. This occurs at about 8 months of age; it will be followed by walking several months later.

C. Giving babies practice in specific motor skills—walking, for example—causes them to learn these skills at earlier ages. However, at least for skills involved in basic motor development, untrained children quickly catch up.

III. Cognitive Changes

As they become more mobile, infants also become better able to understand the basic properties of objects and spatial relations. They also learn to recognize and respond to categories, and to compare present with past experiences. These achievements help their thinking to become more systematic and their problem-solving more planned.

A. In substages 1 and 2 of Jean Piaget's period of sensorimotor development (described in Chapter 5), infants first practiced their inborn reflexes (substage 1), then developed ways of making enjoyable activities continue (substage 2). Between 4 and 12 months, they will complete substages 3 and 4.

•In substage 3 (4 to 8 months), babies perform **secondary circular reactions**, in which they repeat actions that cause interesting results in the outside environment; for example, kicking at a mobile in order to see the dangling objects move.
•In substage 4 (8 to 12 months), they become able to combine secondary circular reactions, performing one as a means to perform another. For example, a baby may sweep a cushion out of the way (one action schema) in order to reach for and grasp a stuffed toy (a second action schema).

B. Piaget believed that newborns had no sense of **object permanence** but gradually develop it during the sensorimotor period. Until babies actively began to search for hidden objects, he thought, it was not possible to know that they believed in the objects' continued existence when out of sight. This notion has generated a considerable amount of scientific work.

C. Piaget traced six levels of understanding of the object concept, which parallel the six substages of the sensorimotor period.
•In stages 1 and 2 (birth to 4 months), when an object disappears, babies stare at the place where they last saw it, then turn their attention elsewhere.
•During stage 3 (4 to 8 months), they react more strongly to an object's disappearance. Also they will reach for a covered object if it is only partially hidden.
•During stage 4 (8 to 12 months), babies search for an object that has been completely hidden under a cover, showing that they believe in the object's continued existence. However, if an object that was first hidden in one location is then hidden in a second location—in full view of the babies—they continue to search for it in the first location, where they had previously found it. This is called the **A-not-B error**.

Babies seem to pass through the same stages in understanding the permanence of people. However, while they may lose interest in objects that disappear, babies are distressed at the disappearance of their caretakers. Both familiar people and objects are treated as permanent somewhat earlier than unfamiliar ones.

It is possible, by using clever experimental techniques, to show that infants of less than 8 months of age actually know more about hidden objects than they appeared to in Piaget's observations. For example, Renee Baillargeon and her colleagues demonstrated that 3 1/2-month-olds continued to believe in the existence of a hidden object by showing that the infants were surprised when the object seemed to have disappeared. Why, then, do they fail to actively search? When T.G.R. Bower and Jennifer Wishart used a transparent cover to "hide" an object, stage 3 babies were able to retrieve it, showing that their motor coordination was good enough to uncover hidden objects. Adele Diamond varied the time before babies could search for an object and found that memory limitations were a factor in their performance. Linda Acredolo showed that—as hypothesized by Piaget—in predicting the location of a person, young infants (6 months old in her study) paid little attention to outside location cues, relying instead on their own previous movements to orient themselves. By the time they were 16 months old, all these infants were using external landmarks to direct their responses.

Piaget's views on the importance of children's own activity in cognitive development have led to many studies. Richard Held and Alan Hein, working with kittens, discovered that experience with locomotion is necessary for developing an understanding of spatial relations. Joseph Campos and his colleagues demonstrated that babies who had experience with moving around in baby walkers developed fear of heights (as measured on a visual cliff) at an earlier age and also were better at locating hidden objects than children of the same age without walker experience.

D. For many years, it was assumed that, at birth, babies respond to the sight, sound, and other sense impressions of objects as though these impressions were completely separate. Recent studies, however, indicate that babies are either born with the ability to integrate their sense impressions or learn this ability quite early in infancy. For example, Elizabeth Spelke found that, when infants were shown two different films but heard only one soundtrack, they spent more time looking at the film that matched the sounds they heard.

E. Between 2 1/2 and 12 months, babies begin to notice categories. Categories occur when we treat two objects as equivalent (for example, both apples) even though they differ in some ways (as a tall, red Delicious apple looks and tastes different from a round, green Pippin). Between 6 and 9 months, there is a transition in infants' **categorizing** abilities. For example, 9-month-olds spend more time than 6-month-olds examining a test stimulus whose parts are arranged so that they seem to form a new kind of object. And 9- and 12-month-olds, but not six-month-olds, tend to touch like objects in a display before touching objects from another category.

F. Infants also improve in their ability to remember what they learn. Carolyn Rovee-Collier and her colleagues found that, when they were taught to move a mobile by kicking it, 3-month-olds remembered their training for about a week; however, if "reminded" by being shown the mobile the day before testing, they remembered even after a month. Interestingly, babies tested on a different mobile the day after training would not kick to make it move, while those tested 4 days after training would. It seems that babies, like adults, come to forget the specific details of an event while remembering its generalized properties.

G. Between 7 and 9 months, infants show that they are able to recall things which are not present, and begin to act wary or afraid of unfamiliar things. Rudolph Schaffer found that, while 4-month-olds immediately reached for an unfamiliar object, 6-month-olds hesitated a short time, and 9-month-olds hesitated longer or turned away from the object. Nathan Fox, Jerome Kagan, and Sally Weiskopf suggest that infants become wary when confronted with objects and events which do not fit into any familiar category.

These changes in cognitive abilities are linked to changes in babies' emotional relationship with their caretakers and in their ability to communicate.

IV. A New Relationship to the Social World

A. Babies categorize people, as well as objects, into the familiar and the strange, and act wary or afraid of those who are strange. This wariness, which typically develops between 6 and 9 months of age, has been studied extensively using a laboratory procedure, developed by Mary Ainsworth and her colleagues, called the **strange situation**. In the strange situation, observers measure babies' reactions to a room containing toys when their mothers are present, when their mothers leave, and when they are approached by a strange adult. The observers note the babies' reactions to their mothers' leaving and their reactions to the stranger's attempts to comfort them as they wait for them to return. Results show that, compared to when they were younger, 6- to 9-month-old babies do not find strange adults very comforting in their mothers' absence.

What accounts for this change? Babies are fairly limited in the ways in which they can function in the world; therefore, they depend on adults to help them perform many actions that they will later be able to perform by themselves. Cultural-context theorist Lev Vygotsky called this a **zone of proximal development**. The adults perform only those parts of the action that the child cannot yet perform; thus, their actions are finely tuned to those of the child. Only familiar adults can be counted on to perform according to babies' expectations and babies may therefore feel uncertain about how to interact with unfamiliar adults.

B. At the same time that infants begin to react with wariness to unfamiliar people, their emotional relationships with their caretakers take on a new quality, which psychologists call **attachment**. Attachment is an enduring emotional tie to a specific person or people. Attachment develops between the ages of 7 and 9 months; and infants' first attachment is usually to their mothers. According to Eleanor Maccoby, the signs of attachment are:
•Seeking to be near the other person.
•Showing distress if separated.
•Being happy when reunited.
•Orienting (for example, watching, or listening for) toward the other person.
Attachment appears to be a universal characteristic of babies.

C. Babies who can move about by themselves need to be able to keep in touch with their caretakers from a distance. **Social referencing** is one such form of communication, in which babies' reactions to unusual situations are affected by their mothers' facial expressions—the expressions tell them "how to feel." New forms of vocal communication allow mothers and babies to remain coordinated even when out of sight of one another.
•From the first few months of life, babies make cooing and gurgling noises, and will even engage in conversationlike turn taking.
•**Babbling** (involving consonant-vowel combinations) begins, around 4 months of age, as a form of vocal play. Babies from all cultures babble in the same way until, at about 9 months, they begin to drop sounds that do not belong to the language they hear around them.
•In **jargoning**, which begins around the end of the first year, babies imitate the stress intonations of the language they are learning while putting together long strings of syllables. Deaf babies, whose early cooing and babbling follow the same patterns as those of hearing children, now begin to "babble" with their hands.
•Sometime before the end of the first year, babies begin to use certain sounds repeatedly in the same situations, as though they mean something.

V. A New Bio-Social-Behavioral Shift

Changes in physical and cognitive development and in social relationships create a new bio-social-behavioral shift between 7 and 9 months of age. From this higher level of development, infants are prepared to actively explore the world around them.

Key Terms

Following are important terms introduced in Chapter 6. Write the definition for each after the term. Then match the term with the letter of the example that best illustrates it.

_____A-not-B error _____

_____Attachment _____

_____Babbling _____

_____Categorizing _____

_____Jargoning _____

_____Object permanence _____

_____Secondary circular reactions _____

_____ Social referencing _____

_____Strange situation _____

_____Zone of proximal development _____

a. An 11-month-old boy sounds as if he is explaining something to his family; however, no one can understand a bit of what he says.

b. When a nurse enters the examination room and greets a 9-month-old girl, the infant glances at her mother's face, then smiles at the newcomer.

c. Tim cries when his mother leaves the room, but gives her a big hug when she returns.

d. Although she has just watched her dad hide his shiny watch under the sofa cushion, Jennifer searches for it behind the throw pillow, where she found it the last time.

e. A baby plays with language sounds: "ba-ba-ba-ba."

f. John's mother gets the applesauce on the spoon, then lets John guide it to his mouth.

g. An infant takes part in an experimental study in which his mother leaves him alone in an unfamiliar room, and a strange adult tries to comfort him until she returns.

h. Becky, confronted with an array of toys, touches all the toy cars, one after another.

i. A 7-month-old boy has learned to pull the ring his parents have dangled over his crib, causing a music box to play. He pulls it over and over again.

j. A 10-month-old girl immediately whisks her mother's handkerchief off the rattle after her mother has covered it.

Fill-In Review

Cover the list of answers next to the statements below. Then uncover each answer after you complete each statement.

faster 1. Babies grow _____during their first year than at any other time until adolescence.

ossify 2. Infants' bones _____, beginning with those of the hands and wrists.

memory; motor 3. Two parts of the brain to develop during the first year are the hippocampus, which aids in _____, and the cerebellum, which controls _____coordination.

center *feet* 4. Infants' motor development proceeds from the _____ of their bodies outward, and from their heads to their ____.

voluntary 5. "Preprogrammed" reaching looks almost reflexive, but is really under _____ control.

practice 6. Infants can learn some motor skills at earlier ages if given the opportunity to _____ them.

secondary *outside* 7. Substage 3 of the sensorimotor period is called _____ circular reactions; during this time, infants learn to repeat actions with interesting results in the _____ world.

8. Piaget believed that, at birth, infants have no sense of the _____ of objects, behaving as if they no longer existed when out of sight.

   permanence

9. During substage 4, infants learn to _____ secondary circular reactions in order to achieve a goal.

   coordinate

10. It is not until stage 3 (4 to 8 months), Piaget thought, that infants react to an object's disappearance; at that time, they will search for a covered object so long as it is not completely _____.

    hidden

11. Stage _____ children (8 to 12 months) will uncover a completely hidden object, but also make the _____ error when an object has been hidden in another place.

    4
    A-not-B

12. Infants appear to understand the permanence of _____ people and objects earlier than unfamiliar ones.

    familiar

13. Babies have more trouble searching for hidden objects when they have to wait to begin the search. This shows that part of their problem is limited _____.

    memory

14. Another problem in finding hidden objects is that many younger infants rely on their own _____, rather than on external cues, to orient themselves.

    position

15. Studies with both kittens and human infants have demonstrated that experience with _____ leads to better understanding of spatial relations.

    locomotion

16. Between 6 and 9 months of age, infants begin to treat objects that are similar in important ways (though dissimilar in others) as though they belong to the same _____.

    category

17. Once objects and people can be categorized, infants begin to react with wariness to those that are not _____.

    familiar

18. Between 6 and 9 months of age, infants form an enduring emotional tie, called _____, to their primary caretakers.

    attachment

19. Mary Ainsworth and her co-workers have studied infants' attachments to their caretakers by placing them in the _____.

    strange situation

20. At around 4 months of age, babies begin _____, vocalizing in consonant/vowel combinations.

    babbling

21. Later in the first year, they engage in _____, reproducing the sound patterns and intonation of the language they are learning.

    jargoning

22. Deaf babies engage in cooing and babbling, showing that these begin as _____ actions.

    reflex

23. Deaf babies eventually stop vocal babbling and begin to "babble" using _____ movements.

    hand

Multiple-Choice Practice Questions

Circle the letter of the word or phrase that correctly completes each statement.

1. What, if any, changes occur in infants' body proportions during the first year of life?
   a. The head becomes a larger proportion of total body length.
   b. The head becomes a smaller proportion of total body length.
   c. The head and body maintain the same relative proportions.
   d. The head and body each maintain the same overall size.

2. The _____, a part of the brain involved in memory, undergoes development between 3 and 12 months after birth.
   a. cerebellum
   b. brain stem
   c. primary motor area
   d. hippocampus

3. Babies gain control earliest over which of the following?
   a. head
   b. legs
   c. trunk
   d. all at about the same time

4. In the long run, which of the following skills should benefit most from extensive early practice?
   a. sitting
   b. walking
   c. dancing
   d. crawling

5. According to Piaget, during the last few months of the first year infants are learning to
   a. modify their basic reflexes.
   b. make interesting experiences, centered on their own bodies, last.
   c. make interesting events in the outside world last.
   d. coordinate actions to reach a goal.

6. Infants in _____ of developing object permanence tend to search for hidden objects in places they have found them before, even when they have seen them being moved to another place.
   a. stage 1
   b. stage 2
   c. stage 3
   d. stage 4

7. "Person permanence"
   a. seems to follow basically the same rules as object permanence.
   b. only develops for familiar people.
   c. is present beginning at birth.

    d. only develops for unfamiliar people.

8. Research has shown that 7 1/2-month-old babies can avoid the A-not-B error
    a. when they are given extensive practice in finding hidden objects.
    b. when they are kept from searching for several seconds to prevent impulsive choices.
    c. when they are allowed to begin searching immediately after the object is hidden.
    d. under no known circumstances.

9. Studies measuring infants' understanding of categories have shown that
    a. by 6 months of age, infants are already mentally categorizing objects.
    b. 9- and 12-month-olds seem to think of objects as belonging to categories, but 6-month-olds do not.
    c. infants show no evidence of attending to objects' categories before 12 months of age.
    d. infants pay no attention to objects' categories until late in the second year.

10. Between the ages of 7 and 9 months, infants begin to act _____ people and things that are unfamiliar.
    a. afraid of
    b. attracted to
    c. indifferent to
    d. attached to

11. With respect to parent-infant interaction, a zone of proximal development refers to
    a. the parent directly training the child to learn new skills.
    b. the parent allowing the child to learn new skills entirely on his or her own.
    c. the child following the parent around wherever the parent may go.
    d. the parent helping the child do things he or she cannot yet accomplish alone.

12. Which is *not* a sign of attachment to the mother during the first year of life?
    a. The child cries when his mother leaves the room.
    b. The child is perfectly happy to be left by his mother.
    c. The child follows his mother around the house.
    d. The child is happy when his mother returns after a separation.

13. Mary Ainsworth and her colleagues have studied attachment using
    a. a zone of proximal development.
    b. the strange situation.
    c. videotapes of male and female faces and voices.
    d. the visual cliff.

14. Infants' earliest babbling sounds
    a. may contain the sounds of any language.
    b. contain only the sounds of the language they hear around them.
    c. are performed with the hands, rather than vocally, by deaf babies.
    d. do not occur without reinforcement from parents.

15. The development of _____ seems to improve infants' abilities to re-member the location of hidden objects.
    a. babbling
    b. social referencing
    c. stranger wariness
    d. locomotion

Short-Answer Questions

1. How are improvements in memory and in locomotion related to infants' ability to search for hidden objects?

2. In what ways might the growth of memory and the ability to classify contribute to infants becoming wary of strange objects and people?

3. Show how the biological changes in body and brain that occur during the first year prepare infants for independent locomotion.

4. What evidence is there that infants may believe in the continued existence of hidden objects even though they fail to search for them?

Putting It All Together

Look back to Chapter 3, on prenatal development. What are some examples of development proceeding in cephalocaudal and proximodistal directions?

Now list some examples of cephalocaudal and proximodistal principles in motor development during infancy.

Sources of More Information

Brazelton, T. Berry. *Infants and Mothers. Differences in Development* (Rev. Ed.). New York: Dell, 1986.
The author follows the progress of an active baby, a quiet baby, and an average baby through the first 12 months of life.

Caplan, Frank (Ed.). *The First Twelve Months of Life. Your Baby's Growth Month by Month.* New York: Grosset & Dunlap, 1973.
This is a month-by-month look at the physical, cognitive, and social changes taking place during an infant's first year.

McCall, Robert B. *Infants.* Cambridge, Mass.: Harvard University Press, 1979.

This book about infants covers physical growth and the development of personality, cognition, and attachment.

Walden, Tedra A. and **Tamra A. Ogan.** "The Development of Social Referencing." *Child Development*, 1988, *59*, 1230-1240.
This study examines the course of development of social referencing in infants from 6 to 22 months of age.

Zucker, Kenneth J. "The infant's Construction of His Parents in the First Six Months of life. In Tiffany Field and Nathan Fox (Eds.), *Social Perception in Infants*. Norwood, NJ: Ablex, 1985.
This chapter traces the development during the first 6 months of infants' ability to recognize their parents.

Answer Key

Answers to Key Terms: d, c, e, h, a, j, i, b, g, f

Answers to Practice Questions: 1. b, 2. d, 3. a, 4. c, 5. d, 6. d, 7. a, 8. c, 9. b, 10. a 11. d, 12. b, 13. b, 14. a, 15. d

CHAPTER

7

THE END OF INFANCY

Between 12 and 30 months of age, children develop in important ways—physically, cognitively, and in their social relations. During this time, they develop increasing control over their bodies, as reflected in "gross motor" skills such as walking and running, "fine motor" skills such as scribbling with crayons, and in the ability to feed, dress, and toilet themselves.

New developments in thought allow children to reflect on what has happened in the past and to set themselves goals for the immediate future. Being able to call objects and events to mind helps them avoid some of the trial and error on which younger infants depend when solving problems.

While older infants are still dependent on their caretakers for support when coping with unfamiliar situations, they are learning to predict and understand their caretakers' periodic absences and returns. Development in the ability to communicate with language helps infants make their needs better known.

The changes of late infancy—physical, cognitive, and social—allow children a greater degree of independence and self-direction. Their behavior begins to reveal a sense of "selfhood" at this time. These developmental changes complement one another—changes in one area helping development in another. At about 2 years of age, developments in physical growth and coordination, thinking and language skills, and greater self-directedness will result in a new bio-social-behavioral shift and a transition to a new level of development.

Chapter Outline

I. Biological Maturation

During the second and third years of life, children raised in the United States continue to grow substantially, adding, on the average, 32 inches and 24 pounds.

A. Important changes are also taking place in children's brains. Individual cells grow new and longer dendrites, forming connections to other cells. Fibers that connect parts of the brain stem with areas of the cerebral cortex become covered with a coat of myelin, allowing them to transmit messages more efficiently. And brain areas that had, until now, been maturing at different rates finally reach similar levels of development.

B. These developments in the nervous system give children much greater control over physical movement. Although most babies develop the neural capacity for walking at about 12 months of age, most cannot walk up and down stairs until they are 17 months old. Between 12 and 30 months, they will develop greater coordination of fine hand movements, allowing them to learn to string beads, throw balls, and feed and dress themselves. Voluntary control over elimination is not possible until at least 15 months, and many children are not dry during the day until 3 years of age. Walking, toileting, and other voluntary behaviors give children a measure of independence from their caretakers.

II. A New Mode of Thought

Children's increased ability to control their actions is accompanied by new mental skills that allow them to think about themselves and about the world around them as well. By 12 months, toddlers have demonstrated early means-end problem-solving, performing one action in order to be able to perform another, desired action.

A. Piaget described two additional substages that occur during later infancy and that mark the end of the sensorimotor period:
• In substage 5 (**tertiary circular reactions**)—12 to 18 months—children explore the world in more complex ways by varying the actions they use to reach their goals. They do not yet make use of mental trial and error, so these actions must still be performed physically.
• In substage 6 (**representation**) 18- to 24-month-old children literally "re-present" the world to themselves mentally. This allows them to plan solutions to problems before carrying them out. They are now able to imitate past events, make use of language, and engage in pretend play.

B. Children master the remaining stages of what Piaget called object permanence during the second year of life.
• Beginning at about a year of age (stage 5), they will search for a toy in a place it has not previously been, so long as they see it being hidden there.
• Between 18 and 24 months, they achieve stage 6; now they can find the toy in a new place even if they have not seen it hidden there.

C. Developments in sensorimotor intelligence and in the ability to reason about the location of hidden objects are accompanied by changes in children's problem-solving behavior. They now become less dependent on trial and error and are better able to plan their solutions before carrying them out.

D. Play gives children a chance to practice new motor, thinking, and social skills. Twelve-month-olds begin to use familiar objects in ways similar to adult usage. Between 18 and 24 months, children begin to engage in **symbolic play**, in which one object may stand for another; for example, a rock for a baby. Symbolic play continues to develop during the third year of life. Theorists have suggested several purposes that children's play might serve.

•Peter Smith has described four kinds of play—locomotor, object, social, and fantasy—which, he feels, provide practice in activities that are important in children's development.

•Piaget considered play an opportunity for children to interact with the world—to assimilate it to their goals—with little need to adjust, or accommodate, to external reality.

•Lev Vygotsky's view was that play serves as a mental support system which allows children to perform developmentally more advanced actions than they can perform on their own.

E. While playing, children bend reality to their own ideas. In imitation, on the other hand, they closely adjust their behavior to what they see in the outside world. During the second year, children become able to imitate actions they have seen at an earlier time. This is called **deferred imitation**, and it is a sign that children can mentally represent events which happened in the past. Deferred imitation and symbolic play appear at about the same time in development and are thought to be closely related. Each serves as a zone of proximal development, helping children carry out, with others' help, actions they cannot yet perform alone.

F. One way to study children's mental representations is to see how—or whether—they classify objects. A study by Susan Sugarman explored classification in 12- to 30-month-old toddlers. While 1-year-olds noticed similarities between objects, they did not yet place similar objects together. Eighteen-month-olds, on the other hand, created a "work space" and filled it with objects of a particular category—for example, all the boats in a collection of toys. Twenty-four-month-old toddlers divided the objects into two groups, and 30-month-olds divided their collections into subcategories—for example, red boats and blue boats.

G. Children's vocabularies grow quickly during the second and third years of life. By 14 to 18 months, they can name a few common objects and identify some objects or animals from pictures. By the time they are 2 years old, children can speak in two-word combinations and can follow fairly complicated directions. Cognitive ability parallels language development. For example, when children are putting two words together in speech, they can categorize objects along two dimensions.

III. The Development of Child-Caretaker Relations

As babies begin to move around on their own, they need to be able to learn about the world while, at the same time, avoiding its hazards. The development of attachment, an emotional bond between children and their caretakers, helps provide a balance between security and opportunities to explore.

A. Sometime between 7 and 9 months of age—at about the same time they begin to search for hidden objects—infants begin to resist being separated from their caretakers. This behavior has been observed in many different cultures; psychologists see it as a sign that infants are attached to those who care for them.

B. Psychologists have suggested several different explanations for why attachment occurs.
•Freud's theory emphasizes the importance of **biological drives** (for example, hunger) and proposes that infants become attached to those who help them satisfy these drives. Children first become attached, during what Freud called the oral stage, to those who satisfy their hunger; during the second year of life, while in the anal stage, they will strive for independence and self-control. Freud believed that children's relationships with their mothers were models for their adult relationships.
•Erik Erikson emphasizes society's influence on development. He believes that, at each of eight stages of development, from birth through old age, people meet and resolve a particular conflict or crisis. Erikson's theory stresses that attachment is related to children's development of trust in their caretakers during the earliest stage and to the development of autonomy—control of their bodies and actions—during stage 2.
•In John Bowlby's evolutionary explanation, attachment serves to regulate the distance between infants and their caretakers. In unfamiliar situations, the caretaker serves as a **secure base** from which the infant can explore, occasionally returning for reassurance.

Studies using **animal models** suggest that bodily contact is important in fostering attachment. Infant monkeys became attached to terry-cloth-covered "surrogates" in preference to wire-bodied ones even when only the wire "mothers" provided them with food. But, attachment—and the sense of security it brings—will not, by itself, ensure healthy social development; monkeys who became attached to nonliving surrogates did not learn how to behave with other monkeys. Two-way interaction with a responsive caretaker teaches the infant how to relate to others of its kind.

C. Mary Ainsworth and her colleagues studied attachment in the "strange situation," in which children were left alone in an unfamiliar room, approached by a strange adult, then reunited with their mothers.

Several different behavior patterns emerged. *Securely attached* infants were upset when their mothers left, but were quickly reassured when they returned. *Anxious/avoidant* infants appeared indifferent to their mothers and ignored them when they returned. *Anxious/resistant* infants became upset when their mothers left, but struggled to resist comfort from them when they returned.

Some, though not all, studies show that infants of responsive mothers are more likely to behave in a securely attached manner in the "strange situation"; in contrast, it is more certain that infants of abusive or neglectful mothers are more likely to be rated avoidant or resistant.

Children's own characteristics can affect attachment. For example, communication handicaps can interfere with parent-infant attachment. Children's own temperaments may also affect their attachment behavior.

Cultural differences in child-rearing practices result in differences in babies' behavior in the "strange situation." For example, Japanese children and communally raised Israeli infants are more often rated anxious/resistant, and a study of German children showed more anxious/avoidant infants than are usually found in American samples. The possible significance of these differences is not known, but they suggest that cultural factors are an important influence on child-caretaker relationships.

Children's attachment patterns are likely to remain stable, at least in the short term, but only so long as their life circumstances also remain the same.

IV. A New Sense of Self

Two-year-olds' capabilities in thinking, motor skills, language, and the ability to do things on their own combine to give them a greater awareness of themselves as people.

A. Children become more sensitive to adult standards of "rightness"; they notice when toys are broken or clothing is soiled. They may even feel responsible for living up to adult standards—for example, by being able to imitate adults' behavior. They seem to set themselves goals—perhaps, making a tower of *all* the blocks—and to check their progress in achieving them.

B. Between 18 and 24 months, children begin to describe their own actions in their speech.

C. Eighteen- to 24-month-old children also begin to identify their own images in the mirror.

The biological, behavioral, and social changes occurring at the end of the second and the beginning of the third year mark the end of the period we call infancy.

Key Terms

Following are important terms introduced in Chapter 7. Write the definition for each after the term. Then match the term with the letter of the example that best illustrates it.

_____ Animal model _____

_____ Biological drives _____

_____ Deferred imitation _____

_____ Representation _____

_____ Secure base _____

_____ Symbolic play _____

_____ Tertiary circular reactions _____

a. A girl watches her mother apply lipstick. The next day, she tries to apply her mother's lipstick to her own lips.
b. A boy places pebbles in a bowl, stirs them around, and serves "soup" to his teddy bear.
c. Hunger and thirst are examples of these.
d. A child, sitting in a high chair, repeatedly drops peas onto the floor. Sometimes holding his arm straight out, sometimes to the side, he varies the position from which each pea is dropped.
e. A child is able to think about things that are not present to her senses.
f. Harry Harlow's work on attachment in infant monkeys is an example.
g. A 1-year-old plays by himself in the living room, but comes into the kitchen periodically to make contact with his mother.

Fill-in Review

Cover the list of answers next to the statements below. Then uncover each answer after you complete each statement.

walking

1. At about 12 months of age, babies have the neural connections necessary for independent _____.

elimination

2. Children are usually unable to voluntarily control _____ until about 15 months of age.

3. In substage 5 of Piaget's period of sensorimotor development, infants begin to vary the action sequences they use to attain goals. These sequences are called _____ circular reactions.

tertiary

4. The sensorimotor period comes to an end during substage 6, when infants become able to use _____ to act on objects mentally, rather than solely through physical manipulation.

representation

5. Babies in stage _____ of the object concept will search for an object in a new location, provided they have actually seen the object being moved. Stage _____ infants do not need to see the change in order to search in a new location.

5
6

6. At about 12 months of age, babies begin to use objects similarly to the ways they are used by _____.

adults

7. Between 18 and 24 months, children begin to use one thing to stand for another as they engage in _____ play.

symbolic

8. Peter Smith described four kinds of play that provide practice for later activities. Three of these—locomotor, object, and social play—occur among the young of many species; however, _____ play appears to occur exclusively among human beings.

fantasy

9. Lev Vygotsky described play as providing a mental support system that allows children to perform developmentally more _____ actions before they can do so independently.

advanced

10. During the second year, children begin to engage in _____ imitation, copying events that have occurred in the past.

deferred

11. While infants less than 1 year of age can recognize that an array of objects has a categorical structure, they do not begin to generate _____ until sometime in the second year.

categories

12. One clear indicator of representational thought is the use of _____ to stand for objects and events.

words

13. At about 18 months of age, children can combine two symbolic actions in their play; they can also combine two _____ to make a sentence, and categorize objects along _____ dimensions.

words
two

14. According to Freud's explanation of attachment, babies become attached to those who satisfy their need for _____.

nourishment

15. According to Erik Erikson, infants become attached to those whom they can _____ to minister to their needs. Toddlers (1 1/2 to 3) are better able to tolerate separation as they develop a sense of_____ in their relations with the environment.

trust
autonomy

16. John Bowlby emphasized that, in unfamiliar situations, the mother provides a secure base from which the child can _____.

explore

17. Harry Harlow's studies with baby monkeys who were raised with wire or cloth surrogates provided evidence against the _____ theory of attachment.

drive-reduction

securely; anxious

18. Mary Ainsworth found three basic patterns of infant response to the "strange situation": _____ attached, _____/avoidant, and anxious/resistant.

responsive

19. Mary Ainsworth and Sylvia Bell found that the infants of mothers who were rated as highly _____ when the infants were 1 to 3 months of age were found to be more securely attached several months later.

responsiveness

20. While parental responsiveness is important in forming attachments between children and parents, _____ on the part of the child is also important.

temperament

21. A source of variation in children's response to the "strange situation" is _____; for example, timidity or irritability.

attachment

22. Cultural factors provide an additional source of variation in patterns of _____.

less

23. In families under stress, there is often a change from more to _____ securely attached from one testing session to the next.

standards; goals

24. At about 1 1/2 years of age, children seem to develop a recognition of adult _____ for what is proper and improper. They also begin to set _____ for their own behavior and work to achieve them, alone or with adult help.

words

25. Between 1 1/2 and 2 years of age, children begin, for the first time, to use _____ to describe their own actions.

mirror

26. Starting at about 18 months, children show themselves able to use a _____ for self-recognition.

Multiple-Choice Practice Questions

Circle the letter of the word or phrase that correctly completes each statement.

1. Brain development during the second year of life is characterized by
   a. an increase in myelination.
   b. growth in the length and complexity of neurons.
   c. balance between systems that before had been maturing at different rates.
   d. all of the above

2. Children younger than _____ are usually not able to voluntarily control their bladder and bowel functions.
   a. 5 months
   b. 15 months
   c. 3 months
   d. 3 years

3. In sub-stage 5, tertiary circular reactions, children begin to
   a. repeat interesting action sequences without variation.
   b. carry out actions in thought rather than physically.
   c. vary the action sequences they use to reach a goal.
   d. imitate objects and events that are not present.

4. At the end of infancy, children are able to _____ the world to themselves.
    a. assimilate
    b. accommodate
    c. represent
    d. explain

5. Which is an example of symbolic play?
    a. using a banana as a telephone
    b. making cookies out of playdough
    c. serving a doll a cup of sand coffee
    d. all of the above

6. According to Peter Smith, humans are the only species who definitely engage in _____ play.
    a. locomotor
    b. fantasy
    c. object
    d. social

7. Because play with other children creates a zone of proximal development, it allows children to perform
    a. only those actions they can already perform independently.
    b. actions that their parents ordinarily do not allow.
    c. actions developmentally more advanced than those they can perform independently.
    d. less advanced actions than they can perform independently.

8. The appearance of _____ imitation in the middle of the second year is one of the signals of the beginning of representational thought.
    a. deferred
    b. immediate
    c. reflexive
    d. assimilative

9. Children learn to _____ the categorical structure of a group of objects before they are able to _____ categories by themselves.
    a. make use of; recognize
    b. accommodate; assimilate
    c. rearrange; recognize
    d. recognize; generate

10. John Bowlby's explanation of attachment emphasizes the role of attachment in
    a. satisfying biological drives.
    b. building trust between infant and caretaker.
    c. balancing safety and exploration.
    d. promoting object permanence.

11. While children's first few words tend to be _____, they soon begin using words to _____

    a. symbols of objects or events; directly imitate adult speech
    b. direct imitations of adult speech; represent objects and events
    c. pure assimilations; accommodate new ideas
    d. completely meaningless; imitate adult language forms

12. Harry Harlow found that his surrogate-raised infant monkeys
    a. became attached to the wire surrogate, whichever surrogate fed them.
    b. always became attached to the surrogate, wire or cloth, that fed them.
    c. always became attached to the cloth surrogate, whichever surrogate fed them.
    d. did not become attached to either kind of surrogate.

13. In Mary Ainsworth's "strange situation," _____ children calm down
quickly and resume playing when their mothers return after a brief separation.
    a. securely attached
    b. anxious/avoidant
    c. anxious/resistant
    d. all of the above

14. Cross-cultural studies on patterns of attachment indicate that
    a. similar distributions of attachment patterns occur in all societies studied.
    b. different cultures produce varying patterns of attachment as measured in the
"strange situation."
    c. good parenting practices produce the same distribution of patterns of attach-
ment in any culture.
    d. attachment as we know it only exists in societies with "nuclear" families.

15. Children show signs of recognizing their mirror images
    a. starting shortly after birth.
    b. at about the time they say their first words.
    c. at about the time they develop representational thought.
    d. at about the time they begin preschool.

Short-Answer Questions

1. In what ways do imitation and play each serve as a zone of proximal development?
What is an example of behavior in which imitation and play occur together?

2. Psychologists believe that, starting at about 18 months of age, children begin to set goals for themselves and to become more aware of adult standards. What are some indications of this change? What changes in children's language and problem-solving capabilities occur at about the same time?

3. What are some of the ways we can tell that children have begun to mentally represent things to themselves?

4. Why do psychologists say that there are different kinds of attachment relationships between parents and babies? Why might nature allow for a certain amount of variability in the characteristics of attachment?

Putting It All Together

In this section, you will need to put together information from Chapters 5, 6, and 7 to get a more complete picture of development throughout infancy.

I. Reviewing Piaget's stages of sensorimotor development

Here are some behaviors that Piaget observed his own children performing during the sensorimotor period. Match each behavior with the substage in which you would expect it to occur.

Substages
1. Reflexes
2. Primary circular reactions
3. Secondary circular reactions

4. Coordination of secondary circular reactions
5. Tertiary circular reactions
6. Representation

____Laurent strikes at a pillow to lower it, then grasps a box of matches.

____Laurent repeatedly brings his hand to his mouth in order to suck his fingers.

____Lucienne sees her father hide a chain inside a slightly open matchbox. She looks at the opening, opens and shuts her mouth several times, and finally reaches in a finger to open the box and grasp the chain.

____Laurent becomes quicker at finding the nipple when it touches him anywhere on his face.

____Laurent lifts toys and lets them fall, varying his arm position each time.

____Lucienne, lying in her bassinet, sees a doll hanging above her and kicks it. The doll sways, and Lucienne attempts to kick it again and again.

Try to think of another example of infant behavior that would illustrate each substage.

II. The Object Concept—A Review

Match each description of behavior with the appropriate substage.

Substage	Approximate ages	Behavior
1 & 2	Birth - 4 months	_____
3	4 - 8 months	_____
4	8 - 12 months	_____
5	12 - 18 months	_____
6	18 - 24 months	_____

a. The child does not search actively for hidden objects. "Out of sight, out of mind."
b. The A-not-B error appears.
c. The child will search for an object hidden in a new place if he sees the object being moved there.
d. The child will search for a partially hidden object.
e. The child will search for a hidden object in a new place, even if he has not seen the object moved there.
f. The child is not disturbed if the same object appears in two places at once.
g. The child will search for his mother at the door where he has seen her go out on a previous occasion.
h. For the first time, the child will search actively for a completely covered object.
i. The child will stare at the place where an object was last visible.
j. The child is handicapped in her ability to search by limited memory capacity.

Sources of More Information

Ames, Louise B. and **Frances L. Ilg.** *Your Two-Year Old: Terrible or Tender.* New York: Delacorte Press, 1976.
The authors describe typical 2-year-old behavior in the tradition of Gesell's maturational approach.

Caplan, Frank and **Theresa Caplan.** *The Second Twelve Months of Life.* New York: Bantam Books, 1980.
This book describes the development of mental, motor, and language skills, month by month, during the second year.

Erikson, Erik. *The Life Cycle Completed: A Review.* New York: W. W. Norton and Co., 1982.
This is a compact discussion of Erikson's psychosocial theory of development.

Kaplan, Louise J. *Oneness and Separateness: From Infant to Individual.* New York: Simon & Schuster, 1978.
A discussion of Margaret S. Mahler's theories of development, this book chronicles infants' "second birth," in which, during late infancy, they develop individual identities.

Sheridan, Mary D. *Spontaneous Play in Early Childhood.* Great Britain: NFER Publishing Co. (U.S. distributor: Humanities Press, Inc.), 1977.
This book presents information about play from birth through 6 years of age, and suggests ways of promoting and enhancing play experiences. Suggestions for handicapped children are included.

Smith, Helen Wheeler. *Survival Handbook for Preschool Mothers.* Chicago, Ill.: Follett Publishing Co., 1976.
While aimed primarily at mothers, this book contains suggestions that should be helpful to anyone who works with young children. Suggestions for age-appropriate activities, books, and discipline techniques are included.

Answer Key

Answers to Key Terms: f, c, a, e, g, b, d

Answers to Practice Questions: 1. d, 2. b, 3. c, 4. c, 5. d, 6. b, 7. c, 8. a, 9. d, 10. c, 11. b, 12. c, 13. a, 14. b, 15. c

Answers to Putting It All Together I: 4, 2, 6, 1, 5, 3

Answers to Putting It All Together II: 1&2: a, i; 3: d, f, j; 4: b, g, h; 5: c; 6: e.

8

EARLY EXPERIENCE AND LATER LIFE

For thousands of years, philosophers have expressed the belief that children's earliest experiences have the greatest impact on their development—that "As the twig is bent, so grows the tree." Modern psychologists, for the most part, agree. But do early experiences invariably set the course of development? Chapter 8 explores this issue and the related question of what kinds of early experiences help or hinder normal development.

It seems clear that one of children's needs is a certain amount of stimulation from and interaction with other people. Babies raised in poorly staffed orphanages with little human contact have been found to be both mentally and socially retarded. The longer they live under these conditions, the less complete their recovery when moved to more favorable environments. On the other hand, children in well-staffed orphanages have fared much better, even when cared for by as many as 24 nurses during their first 2 years! Children who have been totally isolated become severely retarded; still, under certain circumstances, recovery is apparently possible even for them.

Children who live in environments in which a number of stress-producing factors combine are at risk for later psychiatric problems. However, some children are remarkably resilient because of counterbalancing circumstances such as good schools or supportive extended families. Psychologists cannot predict developmental outcome with certainty. There are enough discontinuities in development to make it difficult to know for sure how the circumstances of babies' lives help to shape the adults they will someday be.

Chapter Outline

Some theorists believe that the experiences children have in infancy determine their later development. This idea is called the **primacy** of infant experience.

I. Optimal Conditions for Infant Development

Optimal rearing conditions are generally thought to involve mothers' responsiveness to their babies' signals. However, mothers of different cultures have different strategies for raising children with the characteristics that are valued in their societies.

A. Parents often worry that overresponsiveness to their children's signals will "spoil" the children. However, as observed by Silvia Bell and Mary Ainsworth, mothers who respond slowly to their infants' cries have infants who cry more frequently than those who respond promptly.

B. Parents also worry that unresponsiveness to their infants will result in **learned helplessness**—that the infants will learn that their actions have no effect on the world and will be discouraged from acting in the future. John S. Watson demonstrated that infants who had learned to control the movement of mobiles at home learned more quickly to control similar mobiles in the laboratory than infants who had previously observed the mobiles but were unable to control them. Neal Finkelstein and Craig Ramey showed that infants as young as 8 months of age generalize what they learn in one situation—in this case, pushing a panel to get an interesting result—to learning new behaviors—vocally activating a stimulus panel, for example. While infants are learning how actions are connected to outcomes, they also seem to be learning about their personal effectiveness in controlling their environment.

II. Effects of Separation

Children are separated from their parents for various reasons, ranging from temporary separations due to parental employment to long-term separations caused by war or natural disasters. Psychologists study the effects of these separations in an effort to learn how to counteract any negative effects that may result.

A. A common form of temporary separation occurs when infants are placed in out-of-home day care while their parents work. The effects on development of out-of-home care during infants' first year is still hotly debated. On one side, Jay Belsky cites findings that show less secure attachment on the part of children with extensive day care experience during the first year. On the other side, Lindsay Chase-Landsdale and Margaret Owen have found no differences in attachment between children cared for at home and children cared for in various day care arrangements. What everyone agrees on is that the quality of care infants receive is important.

Children are sometimes separated from their parents for hospitalization. A study by Michael Rutter showed that, while a single hospitalization before age 5 had no long-term effect on children's emotional development, repeated hospitalization was associated with psychological problems. Because hospitalized children were somewhat more likely to come from disadvantaged families, the exact contribution of hospitalization to their problems of separation is not known.

Children were evacuated from English cities during World War II bombing and were sent to live in the countryside. While the children found the separation distressing, their experiences did not cause them to develop mental illnesses or markedly abnormal behavior.

B. Children living in orphanages experience a much more severe form of separation. A well-known study by Wayne Dennis and his colleagues showed that normal infants placed in the unstimulating environment of a Lebanese orphanage shortly after birth were, by the end of their first year, developing at only half the normal rate. Those of the children who were adopted before age 6 eventually reached normal or near-normal levels of development, depending on how young they were when adopted. At age 6, the girls who remained institutionalized were sent to live in another impersonal, unstimulating situation; by the time they reached their teens, they were severely retarded. The boys, sent to a more stimulating environment, made substantial intellectual recovery.

C. Children raised in better-equipped, more stimulating nurseries in England were studied by Barbara Tizard and her co-workers. Because they were cared for by large numbers of nurses, these children had no opportunity to form close attachments to their adult caretakers. Those who were adopted between 2 and 8 years of age formed attachments with their adoptive parents no matter how old they were when adopted. Those returning to their biological families fared less well, perhaps because their parents gave them less attention; still, they did better than the children who remained institutionalized.

D. Occasionally, cases are discovered in which children have been separated, not only from their parents, but from all human company. Victor, the Wild Boy of Aveyron, is one example. In another case, twin boys, isolated in a closet until 6 years of age with only one another's company, eventually recovered normal intelligence. Genie, a girl who was severely isolated for 11 years, recovered somewhat but never developed normal language. We do not know exactly how long or how severe deprivation must be in order to cause lasting damage.

III. Vulnerability and Resilience

Michael Rutter and his colleagues discovered that children's behavior problems were strongly associated with four factors: family discord; criminal or psychiatric deviance on the part of a parent; social disadvantage; and a poor school environment. The combination of two or more of these factors affecting a child resulted in a greatly increased risk for developing a psychiatric disorder. Still, some children subject to these risk factors manage to develop normally; psychologists are searching for the source of their resilience.

A. Study of a large group of low-income children on the island of Kauai highlights family factors as buffers contributing to children's resilience in the face of threats to their development. In particular, children from cohesive families who received ample attention from their caretakers and had a network of relatives and friends to provide support were less likely to suffer developmental problems.

B. Characteristics of the community in which children live are related to their likelihood of developing problems. Children from poor, inner-city areas are more at risk than those from poor, rural communities; children from affluent communities are less at risk. Social support networks provided by social service agencies reduce the impact of negative community characteristics. Good experiences at school also seem to counteract stressful home circumstances.

C. Children's temperaments are also, to some extent, associated with the tendency to develop problems. Infants whose temperaments are classified as "difficult" are more likely to have psychological problems as adults. On the other hand, the Kauai study revealed that children who were well-adjusted while growing up had been described by their mothers as "very active" and "socially responsive" in infancy.

D. These influences on development work, not in isolation, but in combination with one another. **Transactional models** trace these interactions over time as they influence developmental outcomes. For example, Michael Rutter and his colleagues found that, in their sample, the poor parenting practices of women raised in institutions in infancy were not a straightforward result of their early experience, but resulted from a chain of events which could be broken at various points by more favorable life circumstances.

IV. Recovery From Deprivation

How might children best be helped to recover from early deprivation? Harry Harlow's research with monkeys tells us something about this.

A. Harlow demonstrated that, when infant monkeys were deprived of normal social contact and raised by inanimate mother surrogates, the duration and timing of deprivation affected the monkeys' long-term behavior. Monkeys isolated for their first 3 months developed normal social behavior when placed with a group of other monkeys. Monkeys isolated for their second 6 months after 6 months of normal interaction became aggressive and fearful when returned to the group, but recovered and later were able to mate normally. In contrast, those monkeys isolated for their first 6 months only partially recovered and later were unable to mate. Isolation for the first year of life produced monkeys who showed no recovery without "therapy."

B. Was 6 to 12 months after birth a critical period for normal social development? Harlow and his colleagues tried several methods, all ineffective, for easing isolated monkeys' transition to group interaction. However, when previously isolated female monkeys had infants, they began to recover (assuming the infants survived their abusive behavior). The longer they interacted with their infants, the more normal their behavior became. The researchers found that, by giving them 2- to 3-month-old monkeys to interact with, they could reverse the abnormal social behavior of 12-month isolates before they gave birth to infants of their own.

C. Both Harlow's monkey studies and research with human children suggest that interaction with younger children may be more therapeutic than interaction with peers in reversing the effects of social isolation. Wyndol Furman, Donald Rahe, and Willard Hartup found that socially isolated 2 1/2- to 5-year-olds who played, over a 6-week period, with 1- to 1 1/2-year-olds more than doubled their social intractions with peers, while those who played with peers showed much less improvement. This suggests that socially isolated children can be helped substantially by the proper arrangement of the environment.

V. The Primacy of Infancy Reconsidered

There is no doubt that the experiences of infancy have an effect on later development. But this effect is lessened by certain changes in children's environments. Further, as children develop new capacities during the course of infancy, they experience their environments in different ways. Therefore, instead of speaking of the primacy of infant experience, many psychologists instead focus on continuities and discontinuities between infancy and later periods of development as they relate to specific areas of interest.

A. Studies of long-term effects of different patterns of attachment have reported mixed results. For example, Leah Matas, Richard Arend, and Alan Sroufe found that children rated "securely attached" earlier in infancy were more successful in working with their mothers on a problem-solving task than children rated as anxious/ avoidant or anxious/resistant. But John Bates, Christine Maslin, and Karen Frankel reported no relationship between attachment behavior at 12 months and behavior problems at 3 years. Inge Bretherton hypothesizes that early attachments affect later development through their effect on an "internal working model" of the way to behave toward other people. Later behavior will not be entirely predictable, however, because effects of the environment may either strengthen or modify the internal working model.

B. Studies of the predictive reliability of measures of infant psychological functioning have produced conflicting evidence. For example, standardized developmental tests given during infancy do not predict children's later IQ scores. This makes cognitive development seem discontinuous between infancy and later childhood. However, studies have shown that some continuity is revealed when similar behaviors are measured at each age. For example, babies who are inhibited in unfamiliar circumstances are likely to be fearful when they first enter nursery school.

C. Freud noted that when we trace development backward—from outcome to origins—the steps seem to have led, one to another, in an inevitable sequence. He also pointed out, however, that when we trace development forward, the sequence no longer appears inevitable. We see alternatives that might have occurred. It is just as well that development is not perfectly predictable; otherwise, parents would have no opportunities to influence and enhance the development of their children.

Key Terms

Following are important terms introduced in Chapter 8. Write the definition for each after the term. Then match each term with the letter of the example that best illustrates it.

_____ Learned helplessness _____

_____ Primacy _____

_____ Transactional model _____

a. The idea that, for example, children's earliest attachments have the greatest effect on their later love relationships.
b. Children who learn that their actions have no effect on the environment are slower to learn actions which do have effects.
c. The characteristics of individual children interact with changes in the caregiving environment; these interactions can be traced through time.

Fill-in Review

Cover the list of answers next to the statements below. Then uncover each answer after you complete each statement.

1. The idea that children's earliest experiences have the greatest effect on their development is called _____.   *primacy*

2. Parents sometimes worry that, if they are too responsive to their infants' signals, their babies will become _____.   *spoiled*

3. According to one study, babies whose mothers respond promptly to their cries tend to cry _____ often than those whose mothers respond slowly.   *less*

4. Babies whose signals are ignored may develop "learned _____."   *helplessness*

5. By observing that their actions have effects, infants learn that they can, to some extent, _____ their environments.   *control or influence*

6. Babies resist being separated from their parents, but _____ separations seem to have no negative consequences.   *short*

7. Some studies show that extensive day care experience before 1 year of age has negative effects on the quality of children's _____ to their parents; other studies show no effect.   *attachment*

quality   8. The _____ of out-of-home care infants receive is important in determining its effect on them.

stimulation   9. Studies of children raised in institutions indicate that children cannot develop properly unless they receive sufficient _____ from the environment.

attached   10. It appears that even children 8 years of age who have never formed a primary attachment can still become _____ to adoptive parents.

isolation   11. Even children who have lived under conditions of _____ from other humans may show substantial recovery.

resilient   12. Children from supportive families are more likely to be _____ in the face of risk factors that threaten their development.

difficult   13. Infants classified as temperamentally _____ are more likely to have later psychological problems.

Transactional   14. _____ models of development trace, over time, the interactions of factors that influence development.

younger   15. Harry Harlow discovered that a good therapy for formerly isolated monkeys was placing them with monkeys who were much _____.

securely   16. A study by Leah Matas, Richard Arend, and Alan Sroufe found that children rated as _____ attached were later more successful at working with their mothers on a problem-solving task.

attachments   17. Some psychologists have proposed that children's early _____ serve as models for their later relationships with others.

infancy   18. Developmental tests given during _____ are not very predictive of children's later IQ's.

similar   19. More continuity in development is revealed when the tests given at each age measure _____ behaviors.

backwards   20. As Freud pointed out, developmental outcomes always look more inevitable when we trace their steps _____.

Multiple-Choice Practice Questions

Circle the letter of the word or phrase that correctly completes each statement.

1. Infants whose mothers respond quickly to their cries
   a. are usually spoiled.
   b. cry more than those whose mothers respond slowly.
   c. feel helpless to influence the environment.
   d. cry less than infants of slowly responding mothers.

2. Infants who had learned to control mobiles at home, when confronted with similar mobiles in the laboratory
   a. were afraid of them.
   b. quickly learned to control them.
   c. were not able to learn to control them.
   d. behaved similarly to infants who had seen mobiles before without learning to control them.

3. Some studies have shown that infants with extensive day care experience during the first year of life
   a. are less intelligent than children cared for at home.
   b. are more securely attached to their mothers than children cared for at home.
   c. are less securely attached to their mothers than children cared for at home.
   d. are more cooperative than children cared for at home.

4. Children reared in unstimulating Lebanese orphanages
   a. became severely retarded unless removed before about 6 years of age.
   b. were not affected intellectually, but failed to develop secure attachments.
   c. developed slowly during infancy but recovered later, even if they remained in the same environment.
   d. were not distinguishable in their development from children raised in families.

5. Children who come from cohesive, supportive families are more likely to be _____ in the face of risk factors for developmental problems.
   a. vulnerable
   b. indifferent
   c. logical
   d. resilient

6. In a _____ model, the interaction between children's characteristics and their environments is traced over time.
   a. stage
   b. environmental-learning
   c. transactional
   d. biological-maturation

7. For Harry Harlow's formerly isolated monkeys, the best therapy leading to normal social behavior was
   a. interacting with humans.
   b. interacting with other formerly isolated monkeys.
   c. interacting with younger monkeys.
   d. interacting with a mate.

8. The primacy of infant experience refers to the notion that the experiences of infancy are
   a. the earliest experiences people remember.
   b. more important for development than later experiences.
   c. the only experiences with any importance for development.
   d. qualitatively different from later experiences.

9. Research shows that infants' attachment classifications are
    a. inconsistent in predicting their later behavior.
    b. good predictors of their later behavior.
    c. useless in predicting their later behavior.
    d. nearly perfect predictors of their later behavior.

10. A major objection to using infant tests to draw conclusions about continuity in development is that
    a. the degree of continuity is likely to appear exaggerated.
    b. continuity in development is, by definition, impossible.
    c. the infant tests do not measure the same psychological processes as the later measures.
    d. infants' psychological characteristics cannot be measured.

Short-Answer Questions

1. Discuss how optimal mothering strategies may differ between cultures whose life circumstances are very different. Give examples of this.

2. What do studies of orphanage-raised children tell us about the importance of early experience?

3. What characteristics of children and their environments put them at risk for later psychiatric problems? What factors make children resilient in unfavorable environments?

4. What do animal studies of recovery from isolation tell us about how effective recovery programs for isolated children might be designed?

Putting it All Together

I. The question of the importance of early experience is related to questions about continuities and discontinuities in development, introduced in Chapter 1.

Look back to the material on critical periods in Chapter 1. How does the material on early experience presented in Chapter 8 support or refute the idea that human development is affected by critical periods?

What were philosopher John Locke's views on the importance of early experience?

II. Sometimes, experiences during infancy interact with experiences during the prenatal period. Chapter 3 includes material on the later effects of prenatal undernutrition. Under what circumstances does mitigation of these effects occur? Under what circumstances not? What similarities exist between the developmental insults of prenatal undernutrition and postnatal social isolation?

Sources of More Information

Dennis, Wayne. *Children of the Creche.* New York: Appleton-Century-Crofts, 1973.
A description of the author's well-known study of children raised in a Lebanese orphanage.

Harlow, H., M. Harlow, and **S. Suomi.** "From Thought to Therapy: Lessons From a Primate Laboratory." *American Scientist,* 1971, 59(5), 538-549.
A discussion of the work of Harlow and his colleagues with infant monkeys including their work on rehabilitation.

Leiderman, P., S. Tulkin, and **A. Rosenfeld.** *Culture and Infancy: Variations in the Human Experience.* New York: Academic Press, 1977.
This volume contains several cross-cultural studies of infancy that illustrate how infant care practices prepare children to become culturally socialized members of their particular societies.

Scarr, Sandra. *Mother Care Other Care.* New York: Basic Books, 1984.
Aimed primarily at parents, this book integrates discussion of child development with suggestions for making and implementing informed childcare decisions. It also concisely reviews the relevant literature on the effects of early care experiences on children's later development.

Thompson, Angela M. "Adam—A Severely-deprived Columbian Orphan: A Case Report." *Journal of Child Psychology and Psychiatry,* 1986, 27, 689-695.
A demonstration of a child's progress after intervention to counteract severe deprivation resulting from poverty.

Wachs, T., and **G. Gruen.** *Early Experience and Human Development.* New York: Plenum, 1982.
The authors explore the ways that biological and environmental influences interact to influence development.

Werner, Emmy E. "Children of the Garden Island." *Scientific American,* April 1989, 106-111.
Emmy Werner reports on the "resilient" children, now adults, whom she has been following since their births.

Answer Key

Answers to Key Terms: b, a, c

Answers to Practice Questions: 1. d, 2. b, 3. c, 4. a, 5. d, 6. c, 7. c, 8. b, 9. a, 10. c

CHAPTER

9

LANGUAGE ACQUISITION

One of the most amazing accomplishments of children's preschool years is the rapid acquisition of language. With language, children can make their needs known more clearly and can state their opinions; they also become able to learn more easily from the experiences of others, including those of people who lived generations earlier.

Despite its importance for human beings, language development has yet to be thoroughly explained by psychologists and linguists. No single theory is able to account for all the known facts; however, learning, structural-innatist, and interactionist theories can each explain certain aspects of language acquisition.

As Elizabeth Bates has expressed it, language acquisition can be thought of as learning "to do things with words." In order to be able to do things with words, children must learn to produce the sounds and master the grammatical rules of the language they are learning; they must also learn to select words and constructions that will best express what they want to say.

What experiences must children have in order to learn a language? Certainly they must be exposed to the language itself. Adults provide children with informal language instruction in the course of socializing them as members of the family and community. And while adults in some cultures engage in more deliberate teaching, this is apparently not necessary for children to learn to communicate in this uniquely human way.

Chapter Outline

I. The Puzzle of Language Development

While a great deal is known about language, much about its acquisition remains a mystery.

A. It is still not known how children learn which objects or relations words refer to.

B. Children do not learn **syntax**, the rules of language, solely by imitating adult speech, and **recursion**, the ability to embed sentences within one another, does not appear to be consciously taught. How, then, do these properties of language appear in children's speech?

II. Explanations of Language Acquisition

Theories about language acquisition correspond roughly to the explanations of human development proposed by the various theoretical approaches discussed in Chapter 1.

A. According to the learning-theory explanation, language is learned in the same way as other forms of behavior.
•Children can learn to understand language—that is, to associate words with particular referents—through classical conditioning.
•Children's repertoires of vocalizations can be shaped into the words of the language they are learning through operant conditioning.
•Imitation obviously plays a role in learning language, especially in adding new words to the vocabulary. Explaining how more complex grammatical constructions are learned requires an additional explanatory principle such as **abstract modeling**— proposed by Albert Bandura—in which it is assumed that, as children imitate specific utterances, they abstract the underlying linguistic principles from them.

B. A structural-innatist explanation is proposed by linguist Noam Chomsky, who has suggested that the ability to acquire language is a uniquely human trait and is different from other kinds of learning. According to this view, each child is born with a **language acquisition device (LAD)** which recognizes the underlying rules of whichever language the child hears and triggers his or her innate ability to learn that language.

C. There are two basic kinds of interactionist explanations for language acquisition.
•According to the cognitive interactionist explanation, language develops from the basic structures of sensorimotor thought. Mastery of the rules of language is a by-product of using language to get things done.
•A cultural-context interactionist explanation emphasizes the role of adults in shaping children's language acquisition. According to Jerome Bruner, a **language acquisition support system (LASS)**, inherent in the way adults structure their language input to children, complements Chomsky's LAD.

D. A comparison of the theoretical approaches reveals strengths and weaknesses in each. The strength of Chomsky's structural theory is its formal description of the workings of syntax. Learning theory and the interactionist explanations have made more substantial progress in determining the experiences necessary for language acquisition and the role of other people in the process. At this time, no one theory is adequate to explain all of the known facts about language acquisition.

III. Four Subsystems of Language

A. Beginning at birth, infants are sensitive to the sounds of human language; within a few months, they begin to produce speech sounds themselves.

•Toward the end of the first year, infants begin to restrict their utterances to the sounds and sequences that characterize the language they hear spoken around them. At first, children compensate for difficulties in pronunciation through substitution and simplification; mastering the sound system of their language may take several years.

•Phonemes are the categories of sounds that are meaningful in a language. These differ somewhat from one language to another. **Morphemes** are the meaning-bearing parts of words. They may be whole words, prefixes, suffixes, or other grammatical markers.

B. The first real words appear late in the first year and acquire meaning through a joint effort between children and their adult listeners.

•As children notice that adults react to the sounds they make, their speech comes to anticipate, guide, and stimulate action. Now, children can operate on the world indirectly through language—that is, in a mediated manner.

•Most of children's early words are **general nominals**. They label classes of things, such as "ball" or "juice." **Specific nominals** such as "Mommy" label particular things and are the next most common word category in early speech; the rest of children's first words are action words ("bye-bye"), modifiers ("mine!"), and personal-social words ("no!"). Early words are closely linked to actions; objects on which children can perform actions are those most likely to be named.

•Words can be thought of as cultural objects that mediate activity. Their meanings are not fixed; therefore, as children's activities change over time, so do the meanings they attach to the words they use. **Overextension** occurs when children apply a word too broadly; for example, by calling all animals "doggie." **Underextension** refers to too-narrow application of a word, for example, using the word "animal" only for mammals. Children must also learn to use words at an appropriate level of abstraction. Their first words tend to refer to objects at an intermediate level of abstraction.

•As children accumulate experience with objects and events they have learned to label, the organization of their **lexicons**—the store of words in their vocabularies—changes and words acquire conceptual meanings that are not tied to particular experiences.

•Some investigators believe that each of a child's first words expresses a whole idea—a **holophrase**. Others believe that children's one-word utterances are part of a complex that includes nonverbal actions as well.

C. Toward the end of infancy, syntax appears in children's speech as they begin to form multiword utterances.

•Two-word utterances are more explicit and therefore easier to interpret than one-word utterances. Word order aids in this interpretability. Still, early multiword utterances are telegraphic; it is often necessary to know the context in order to choose between possible interpretations.

•The length of young children's sentences, measured in terms of "mean length of utterance" (MLU), increases rapidly during the period from 1 1/2 to 4 years of age. Children come to make greater use of **grammatical morphemes**, which create meaning by showing the relations between sentence elements. The sequence in which these appear in the speech of English-learning children is roughly constant. By the time they are 6 years old, children will have mastered most of the grammatical rules that govern adult speech although, as demonstrated by Carol Chomsky, they may continue to have difficulties with subtle syntactic constructions.

D. While learning words and the rules for putting them together, children also master the **pragmatic uses of language**—how to use speech in ways appropriate to their actions in different contexts.
•Even 2-year-olds are able to use and understand speech forms as conversational acts intended to accomplish particular results.
•Children's early language is not fully communicative because it often does not take account of the listener's point of view. This improves between 2 1/2 and 7 or 8 years of age. Interestingly, Marilyn Shatz and Rochel Gelman found that 4-year-olds simplified their speech when speaking to 2-year-olds.

IV. Language and Thought

Each major theoretical approach to development has a different view of the relationship between language and thought.

A. According to the environmental-learning perspective, language serves as a symbolic system that can be substituted, in thought, for external events. Acquiring language, in this view, greatly enhances a child's cognitive development.

B. According to Piaget's interactionist perspective, representational thought develops from the sensorimotor schemas of infancy. Children's language abilities reflect their cognitive abilities rather than determining them. Piaget emphasized the egocentric nature of preschoolers' speech; for example, **collective monologues**—conversations in which no actual communication takes place—appear to mirror egocentrism in their thinking.

C. Structural-innatist theorist Noam Chomsky has explained language acquisition as the activity of a mental module. In this view, there are no similarities between language acquisition and the development of sensorimotor intelligence.

D. In a cultural-context view of the relationship between language and thought, Soviet psychologist Lev Vygotsky regarded early language as primarily a social and communicative activity. Egocentric speech, he believed, later split off from social speech and became internalized as the earliest form of linguistically mediated thought. In this view, thought and language develop separately until children are about 2 years of age; then they begin to intermingle, with the result that thinking becomes verbal and language becomes intellectual.

V. Essential Ingredients of Language Acquisition

By examining special cases of language development, psychologists and linguists can gain some understanding of what is required for the acquisition of human language.

A. Psychologists agree that language acquisition has a significant inherited component. To what extent is this ability unique to humans? Chimps raised in human families do not learn speech, but they can be taught to use a manual/visual communication system similar to sign language. The continuity between the language capabilities of lower primates and humans is limited, however; the utterances of human children soon surpass chimps' most sophisticated attempts to use human language.

B. What kinds of environmental input are necessary for normal language development?
•Interaction with other people appears crucial for normal language acquisition. Children do not learn language from exposure to television alone, nor will deaf children in hearing homes spontaneously learn language through lip-reading; however, deaf children do learn to communicate through "home sign," a pantomime they develop themselves. Children raised in linguistically impoverished environments develop the rudiments of human language, but their language is not fully developed— lacking, for example, such subtle features as grammatical morphemes.
•Children learn a great deal about language through the ways that the language they hear varies with the actions they perceive. For example, Elsa Bartlett and Susan Carey found that preschool children learned the name of an unfamiliar color after one experience in which their teacher introduced the color name into classroom conversation.
•What role does deliberate instruction by adults play in language acquisition? Adults simplify their speech when talking to children; they also expand children's utterances. However, explicit tutoring does not seem to affect children's language development, and in some cultures no tutoring is provided. Integrating children into a culturally organized world, of which language is a part, is more important than explicit teaching, at least until they are old enough to need instruction in specialized skills, such as literacy, that will prepare them for adult life.

Key Terms

Following are important terms introduced in Chapter 9. Write the definition for each after the term. Then match each term with the letter of the example that best illustrates it.

_____ Abstract modeling _____

_____ Collective monologues _____

_____ General nominals_____

_____ Grammatical morphemes _____

_____ Holophrase _____

_____ Language acquisition device (LAD) _____

_____ Language acquisition support system (LASS) _____

_____ Lexicon _____

_____ Morphemes _____

_____ Overextension _____

_____ Pragmatic use of language _____

_____ Recursion _____

_____ Specific nominals _____

_____ Syntax _____

_____ Underextension _____

a. The belief that a baby's one-word utterances each carry the meaning of a whole sentence.
b. Seven of these are contained in the sentence "The boys are playing ball."
c. "Mommy" and "Daddy" belong to this word category.
d. An 18-month-old does this when he applies the word "doggie" to all four-legged animals.
e. The sentence "The boy who petted the dog was bitten" illustrates this property of language.
f. Most of the words in children's early vocabularies belong to this category.
g. Piaget gave this name to speech by preschoolers in which remarks are made in the presence of others but with no apparent intent to communicate.
h. A hypothetical structure, similar to an organ, that underlies children's ability to acquire language, according to linguist Noam Chomsky.
i. A child is doing this when she uses the word "dog" only for pictures of dogs but not for live dogs.
j. Albert Bandura hypothesizes this activity as an explanation for children's ability to apply grammatical rules in sentences they have never heard anyone else say.
k. Some examples are *ing*, *the*, and *ed*.
l. The rules that determine the ordering of words in sentences and the ordering of parts within words.
m. The words in an individual's vocabulary.
n. An example is saying "Who left the window open?" when you mean "Please shut the window."
o. Jerome Bruner uses this term to refer to the way adults structure their language input to children.

Fill-in Review

Cover the list of answers next to the statements below. Then uncover each answer after you complete each statement.

refer

1. Psychologists and linguists still do not know how children figure out that words _____ to objects and relations.

syntax

2. The _____ of a language governs the ordering of words in sentences and the ordering of parts within words.

learning-theory

3. According to the _____ explanation of language development, children learn language through imitation and through classical and operant conditioning.

4. Noam Chomsky's structural-innatist explanation of language development hypothesizes a _____ programmed to recognize the universal rules that underlie language.   *language acquisition device*

5. The cognitive hypothesis is an interactional approach which assumes that language grows out of the the basic structures of _____ thought.   *sensorimotor*

6. A language acquisition _____ is a feature of the cultural-context version of the interactional explanation of language development.   *support system*

7. _____ are the categories of sound that are meaningful in a language.   *phonemes*

8. The word "implanted" is made up of three meaning-bearing parts called

    _____.   *morphemes*

9. Language allows children to act on the world and to be influenced by others in an indirect or _____ manner.   *mediated*

10. Most of children's earliest words are in the category of _____ nominals, such as "dog," "milk," or "ball."   *general*

11. Children's early speech often contains _____; for example, calling a skunk "kitty."   *overextensions*

12. In general, children's early words tend to refer to objects at an _____ level of abstraction.   *intermediate*

13. The term _____ refers to the idea that children's single-word utterances express the meaning of whole sentences.   *holophrase*

14. Because of the _____ nature of children's two-word utterances, they must be interpreted in context.   *telegraphic*

15. All children master _____ morphemes, such as *ed* to indicate past tense or '*s* to indicate possession, in much the same order.   *grammatical*

16. When children master the _____ uses of language they learn to select words and word orderings that are appropriate to their actions in particular contexts.   *pragmatic*

17. Piaget observed that preschool children sometimes engage in _____ monologues, in which they talk to one another but do not really respond to what their conversational partners are saying.   *collective*

18. Noam Chomsky has described human language-using capacity as a "mental

    _____."   *module*

19. Lev Vygotsky asserted that the relationship between language and _____ undergoes a fundamental change at about 2 years of age.   *thought*

20. Chimpanzees are capable of learning the rudiments of a gestural _____.   *language*

21. Deaf children raised by hearing, non-signing parents often spontaneously develop a kind of "____ sign" as a means of communication.   *home*

22. In order to acquire language beyond a rudimentary level, children must experience covariation between _____ and action.   *language*

simplify 23. When adults talk to young children, they _____ their speech to make it easier for the children to understand.

expand 24. Adults often _____ children's utterances into a grammatically correct adult version.

Practice Questions

Circle the letter of the word or phrase that correctly completes each statement.

1. The aspect of language that deals with the ordering of words in sentences and the ordering of parts within words is called
   a. pragmatics.
   b. phonetics.
   c. semantics.
   d. syntax.

2. The learning-theory approach to understanding language development does best at explaining
   a. how children learn to produce language.
   b. how children learn the meanings of words.
   c. the relationship between thought and language.
   d. how children learn the rules of syntax. ✗

3. Which theorist has hypothesized a language acquisition device (LAD) that is programmed to recognize universal linguistic rules?
   a. Jean Piaget
   b. Lev Vygotsky
   c. Elizabeth Bates
   d. Noam Chomsky

4. The sounds that carry meaning in a particular language are called
   a. morphemes.
   b. graphemes.
   c. phonemes.
   d. semantics.

5. Which utterance contains five morphemes?
   a. "Doggie!"
   b. "John is eating an apple."
   c. "She jumps rope fast."
   d. "Bobby, have some gum."

6. Children's early words are mainly
   a. specific nominals.
   b. grammatical morphemes.

c. general nominals.

d. verbs.

7. Which is an example of an overextension?

   a. Using the word "bird" for both a parakeet and a baby chick.

   b. Calling a cow "doggie."

   c. Using the word "eeow" to refer to all cats.

   d. Saying "fis" instead of "fish."

8. The term "holophrase" refers to

   a. the idea that children's one-word utterances may carry the meaning of entire sentences.

   b. adults' expansions of children's one-word utterances.

   c. children's belief that all words refer to "things."

   d. one-word exclamations used by children and adults.

9. Grammatical morphemes

   a. are the same in all languages.

   b. appear in all children's speech in about the same order.

   c. are the rules for ordering words in sentences.

   d. do not appear in children's speech until the end of the preschool period.

10. Marilyn Shatz and Rochel Gelman found that, when talking to 2-year-olds, 4-year-olds

   a. simplify their speech to make it easier for the 2-year-olds to understand.

   b. use a larger vocabulary in order to teach new words to the 2-year-olds.

   c. speak just as they would to other 4-year-olds but louder.

   d. speed up their speech to make it more difficult for the 2-year-olds to understand.

11. According to _____, language is a verbal reflection of children's nonlinguistic understanding.

   a. the structural-innatist

   b. Piaget's interactionist

   c. the environmental-learning

   d. the cultural-context

12. Lev Vygotsky believed that children's egocentric speech

   a. is a reflection of their egocentric thought.

   b. serves no communicative function.

   c. helps them to regulate their behavior.

   d. occurs more frequently in the presence of "listeners" who cannot understand (because, for example, they are deaf).

13. Chimpanzees in captivity

   a. communicate with sounds but not with gestures.

   b. have successfully learned the rudiments of human vocal language.

   c. have learned to communicate in simple ways using nonvocal languages.

   d. have demonstrated language development comparable to that of 3-year-old children.

14. Which of the following is sufficient for children to acquire language?
    a. Hearing language on the radio.
    b. Hearing language on television.
    c. Being in an environment where others are communicating with one another, even if not directly with the child.
    d. Participating in activities of which language is a part.

15. The speech of American adults to young children
    a. is adjusted according to the level of complexity of the children's speech.
    b. is more repetitive, but otherwise similar to their speech to adults.
    c. is slower, but is otherwise similar to their speech to adults.
    d. is not significantly different from their speech to adults.

Short-Answer Questions

1. Why is it difficult for psychologists and linguists to explain how children acquire language?

2. Discuss the factors that influence how adults interpret the utterances of 1- and 2-year-old children.

3. In what ways does language appear to be a reflection of thinking? In what ways does it seem unique?

4. To what experiences must children be exposed in order to acquire language? What happens if these requirements are not met?

Putting It All Together

I. Match each milestone in language development with the age at which it occurs. You may need to refer back to material in Chapters 4, 6, and 7.

_____Children can perceive the categorical sound distinctions used in all the world's languages.

_____Children's language typically contains overextensions.

_____Children simplify their speech when talking to younger children.

_____Children begin to practice consonant-vowel sound combinations.

_____Children's vocalizations take on the intonation and stress patterns that characterize the language they are learning.

a. At birth
b. At about 4 months of age
c. Toward the end of the first year
d. At 2 years of age
e. By 4 years of age

II. Match up the facts about language development with the theories that are strongest at explaining them. Refer back to previous chapters when necessary.

_____ Babies can distinguish categorical differences between phonemes.
_____ Children's earliest "words" usually do not have clear meanings and must be interpreted by adults.
_____ Children acquire much of their early vocabularies by repeating the names they hear others give to objects.
_____ Deaf babies begin to babble at about the same time as hearing babies.
_____ Some of children's early sensorimotor accomplishments—for example, delayed imitation—appear to be necessary preconditions for learning language.
_____ Children engage in less egocentric speech when playing with children who cannot hear.
_____ Compared with nonhuman primates, children pick up human language quite easily.
_____ Children who are able to put together two-word utterances usually are also able to combine two symbolic actions in play.

a. Biological-maturation theories
b. Environmental-learning theories
c. Interactionist theories
d. Cultural-context theories

Sources of More Information

Berk, Laura E. Why Children Talk to Themselves. *Young Children*, July 1985, 46-54.
This article discusses Piaget's and Vygotsky's ideas about the nature of children's private speech and attempts to resolve the conflict between these views.

de Villiers, Peter A., and **Jill G. de Villiers.** *Early Language.* Cambridge: Harvard University Press, 1979.
This is an informative and entertaining discussion of children's early language development by two experts in the field.

Lenneberg, Eric H. On Explaining Language. *Science*, 1969, 164 (3880), 635-43.
A discussion of the biological underpinnings of language development which demonstrates that varying approaches to the study of language acquisition need not be antagonistic.

Pepperberg, Irene M. The Importance of Social Interaction and Observation in the Acquisition of Communicative Competence: Possible Parallels Between Avian and Human Learning. In Thomas Zentall and G. Galef Bennet, Jr. (Eds.), *Social Learning: A Comparative Approach.* Hillsdale, N.J.: Erlbaum, 1988.
The subject of this study is an African Grey parrot named Alex, but the topic is how language might be acquired by interacting with others and by watching others interact with one another.

Piaget, Jean. *The Language and Thought of the Child*, trans. M. Gabain. London: Routledge and Kegan Paul, 1926.
In this volume, Piaget presents his work on children's language, including egocentric speech.

Answer Key

Answers to Key Terms: j, g, f, k, a, h, o, m, b, d, n, e, c, l, i.

Answers to Practice Questions: 1. d, 2. b, 3. d, 4. c, 5. c, 6. c, 7. b, 8. a, 9. b, 10. a, 11. b, 12. c, 13. c, 14. d, 15. a.

Answers to Putting it All Together I: a, d, e, b, c.

Answers to Putting it All Together II: a, d, b, a, c, d, a, c.

10

PARADOXES OF THE
PRESCHOOL MIND

Because of their lack of knowledge about the world, preschoolers expend great effort to understand some of the situations they experience each day. Their lack of experience also results in uneven thinking abilities that may appear remarkably sophisticated when applied in familiar contexts, startlingly illogical in less familiar domains.

Piaget's account of thinking during early childhood is the starting point for several explanations of preschoolers' development, and the phenomena he observed, including egocentrism, precausal reasoning, and appearance/reality confusions, continue to be of interest to contemporary developmental psychologists. Today, neo-Piagetians are developing ways to adapt Piaget's theory to better explain the unevenness of preschoolers' thought, while information-processing theorists use computer models to understand these phenomena. Biologically oriented theorists search for the roots of development in the maturation of brain structures, while psychologists using the cultural-context approach look for sources of unevenness in the ways adults arrange the occurrence of basic contexts in which cognitive development takes place. While none of the theoretical approaches provides a complete explanation for development during early childhood, each contributes something to our understanding.

Chapter Outline

Psychologists' attempts to explain the unevenness of preschoolers' reasoning reflect their approaches to the basic questions of continuity versus discontinuity and the roles of nature and nurture in development.

I. Piaget's Account of the Preschool Mind

According to Piaget, preschool children's thinking is **preoperational**, that is, they are not yet able to engage in true mental operations. For example, they have difficulty keeping more than one aspect of a problem in mind at a time. During early childhood, children gradually overcome obstacles to logical thought; when, at the end of the pre-operational stage, they are able to combine, separate, and transform information mentally, they will be engaging in mental **operations**.

A. Piaget believed that 3-, 4-, and 5-year-old children interpret the world from the point of view of the self, or ego, and that this **egocentrism** is the cause of some of their difficulties in problem solving. For example, in the "three mountains problem," when asked to select the view that would be seen by a doll placed at the opposite side of the table, preschoolers tend to choose a picture showing the scene from their own view-point. In speech, egocentrism may result in children failing to include information their listeners need to know.

B. Their tendency to focus attention on the perceptual attributes of a stimulus may make it difficult for preschoolers to separate appearance from reality. Rheta De Vries showed children a cat wearing a dog mask. Most of the 3-year-olds believed that the cat had become a dog, while the 6-year-olds were more confident that such a trans-formation was impossible.

C. When engaging in **precausal thinking**, preschoolers confuse cause and effect. For example, one child believed that graveyards caused people to die and that, by avoiding graveyards, one could avoid death.

II. The Study of Preschool Thinking After Piaget

Piaget's view of preschool thinking is attractive because it is a comprehensive expla-nation; however, investigators have found grossly uneven levels of performance by preschoolers; they are capable of reasoning that Piaget considered characteristic of middle childhood.

A. Variations in children's performance from one problem to another—what Piaget called **horizontal decalage**—is a challenge to all theories of early childhood thought.
•When Helen Borke modified the "three mountains problem" to a more familiar scene, even 3-year-olds demonstrated that they could imagine perspectives other than their own.
•Experiments by John Flavell and his colleagues showed that, under some conditions, even 3-year-olds were able to distinguish between reality and a misleading appear-ance.
•Merry Bullock and Rochele Gelman demonstrated that 3-year-olds grasped the working of an apparatus which caused a Snoopy doll to pop up when a marble was dropped into one of two slots, although 5-year-olds had more adequate verbal explanations of the task.

Because Piaget's tasks are highly dependent on verbal explanations, they may underestimate preschoolers' competence. Seeking alternative explanations of preschoolers' thinking, psychologists have adopted neo-Piagetian, information-processing, biological, or cultural-context approaches.

B. **Neo-Piagetian** theorists, refining Piaget's theory to account for new evidence, tend to take one of two approaches. One view is that children acquire knowledge within narrow domains, so that there may be little correspondence between their levels of performance on unrelated though seemingly similar problems. The other view is that, if the logical structure of problems from different domains can be equated, performance levels on the two should be the same or similar.

C. **Information-processing** theorists view people's thought processes as analogous to the workings of a computer. In one kind of information-processing model, information is seen as first entering a **sensory register**, then **short-term memory**, where it is combined with information about past experiences from **long-term memory**. According to this perspective, as children develop they reduce—gradually, or in stagelike jumps—limitations on their ability to process information. These limitations include distractibility, lack of systematicity, inability to hold several items in mind at once, difficulties in focusing on relevant features, and lack of strategies for dealing with the information they take in. When tasks are arranged to reduce the load on children's information-processing systems, their cognitive performance is enhanced.

D. Biological theories view the limitations of preschoolers' thinking as a reflection of physical immaturity, to be overcome by the processes of growth.
•There is some evidence that developmental changes in preschoolers' brains correspond to changes in their behavior. Rapid growth in the auditory area may be related to language development; additional connections between the temporal, occipital, and parietal areas are associated with faster processing of temporal, visual, and spatial information. Myelination within the hippocampus is associated with improvement in short-term memory, and myelination of fibers connecting the cerebellum with the cortex allows better coordination of fine motor movements.
•Noam Chomsky's theory of language development has inspired some psychologists to propose a **mental module** explanation of cognitive development which hypothesizes highly specific mental faculties, tuned to particular kinds of environmental input. Modules are thought to be domain-specific, to have innately specified organizing principles, and to be only loosely connected to one another. The concepts of number, music perception, and other abilities have been suggested as examples of mental modules. The mental module approach is useful in explaining the accomplishments of child prodigies and of children with **autism**—a disorder that interferes with language and social interaction—who have particular areas of extremely high ability.
  While mental modules almost certainly play some role in causing unevenness of cognitive development in preschoolers, modularity explanations do not provide a full explanation of preschool mental development.

E. The cultural-context view emphasizes the way that adults promote development by arranging the environment to support children's efforts to master new forms of behavior.

•This approach views children's schemas—their organized patterns of knowledge about how to behave—as being closely connected to the **contexts** to which they are exposed by other people. As children grow, schemas and contexts develop together. For example, children, over the years, take on progressively more responsibility for taking baths, yet the activity "taking a bath" occurs at all ages.

•Children construct generalized representations—or **scripts**—for routine events such as birthday parties or going to restaurants. These scripts are guides to action that tell children what to expect. Scripted knowledge frees them to attend to more than the superficial details of an activity; it also helps them coordinate their activities with others who share the same scripts. In addition, scripts help children acquire abstract concepts—for example, playing house—by providing a framework into which specific examples can be fitted.

•Preschoolers typically engage in socio-dramatic play, in which they enact, with other children, scripts they have encountered in stories, on television, or in real life. Piaget viewed this kind of play as a manifestation of egocentric thought that should give way to rule-bound play in middle childhood. Pretend play does peak during the preschool period; however, fantasy does not disappear, even in adulthood. Lev Vygotsky viewed pretend play as a mental support system—a zone of proximal development—that allows children to perform more advanced behaviors than they are ordinarily capable of. An example is Maniulenko's study of self-control in which 4-year-olds were able to stand still longer when asked to pretend that they were honor guards at Lenin's tomb.

•Culture influences unevenness of development by arranging the occurrence of contexts, by arranging the frequency of contexts, by shaping the relationships among contexts, and by regulating the level of difficulty of children's roles within contexts.

•While the cultural-context approach is effective in explaining why preschoolers' cognitive development should appear uneven, it has difficulty explaining particular combinations of children's general and domain-specific abilities. To fully account for these would require exhaustive study of specific behaviors.

III. Applying the Theoretical Perspectives

Drawing is an activity in which the various approaches to preschoolers' cognitive development can be compared.

A. In all cultures in which children are given opportunities to draw, their drawing passes through similar stages, much as Piaget would predict. Children progress from scribbling to, at about age 3, representational drawing; between the ages of 7 and 11, their drawings become more and more realistic.

B. As predicted by the information-processing approach, children gradually learn to represent three dimensions in their drawings as they master drawing rules and become better able to hold several pieces of information in mind at a time.

C. Lorna Selfe has observed a number of children who had exceptional drawing skills despite low language and general mental abilities. These cases can be interpreted within a mental module view of the development of drawing.

D. The cultural-context approach emphasizes the fact that the process by which children's drawings become meaningful representations is culturally organized. For example, preschoolers are often asked, "What are you drawing?" This gives them the idea that drawings represent things. Children then begin to talk about their drawings as representations of things ("I made a mountain") even if they do not name their pictures until after they are completed. Instruction in drawing is organized so that children and adults come to share an idea of what "drawing a picture" means.

IV. Reconciling Alternative Perspectives

None of the theoretical approaches—Piagetian, neo-Piagetian, information-processing, biological, or cultural-context—provides a complete explanation of preschoolers' cognitive development. However, the theories can be viewed as complementary; in any case, the phenomena best explained by each would all need to be included in any comprehensive theory of preschool development.

Key Terms

Following are important terms introduced in Chapter 10. Write the definition for each after the term. Then match the term with the letter of the example that best illustrates it.

_____ Autism _____

_____ Context _____

_____ Egocentrism _____

_____ Horizontal decalage _____

_____ Information-processing approach _____

_____ Long-term memory _____

_____ Mental modules _____

_____ Neo-Piagetian approach _____

_____ Operations _____

_____ Precausal thinking _____

_____ Preoperational stage _____

_____ Scripts _____

_____ Sensory register _____

_____ Short-term memory _____

a. According to some theorists, language acquisition and the extraordinary artistic abilities of some autistic children represent examples of these.

b. Generalized event representations that specify the people, objects, and behaviors involved in, for example, birthday parties or visits to the dentist.

c. This is a general setting that gives meaning to the behaviors which occur within it.

d. A 3-year-old's speech is egocentric when he is answering a difficult question; when the question is changed somewhat, however, he is able to take account of his listener's knowledge.

e. A preschooler points to a picture in a book and asks, "What's this?" not understanding that her mother can only see the outside cover of the book and not the picture she is indicating.

f. These involve combining, separating, and transforming information within a logical system.
g. Information from the environment is detected in this earliest stage of information processing.
h. The behavior of children with this disorder is ritualized and compulsive, with retarded language development and a lack of normal social interactions.
i. Psychologists using this approach view children's thinking processes as analogous to the workings of a computer.
j. Children make use of this when they recall experiences from the past.
k. John tells his nursery school teacher, "when the trees outside move, it makes the wind."
l. We make use of this when we hold a phone number in mind long enough to write it down.
m. According to Piaget, this is a period during which children's thought is representational but not yet logical.
n. Psychologists using this approach seek to adapt Piaget's theory to account for new evidence about children's cognitive development.

Fill-in Review

Cover the list of answers next to the statements below. Then uncover each answer after you complete each statement.

1. Piaget used the term _____ stage to describe children's thinking during the preschool period. *preoperational*

2. Preschool children, according to Piaget, are _____—that is, they have difficulty adopting others' points of view. *egocentric*

3. The collective _____ is an example of egocentric speech. *monologue*

4. In Rheta De Vries's study, 3-year-olds were likely to believe that a cat could actually become a dog; this illustrates a confusion between _____ and reality. *appearance*

5. Some researchers have found that, at least under some circumstances, children display logical reasoning _____ than Piaget reported observing it. *earlier*

6. _____ are psychologists who are trying to adapt Piaget's approach to take into account current findings about children's thinking abilities. *Neo-Piagetians*

7. Robbie Case and his colleagues found that children performed equally well on two different tasks when the tasks were _____ equivalent. *logically*

8. Information-processing theorists understand children's thought by analogy with the workings of _____. *computers*

9. According to one information-processing approach, stimulation is first read into the system's _____ register; it is then stored in _____ memory. *sensory; short-term*

systematic

10. One limitation on preschoolers' ability to process information is a tendency to explore stimuli in a haphazard rather than a _____ way.

strategies

11. Generally, older children and adults have developed more effective _____ for dealing with problems than have preschoolers.

brain

12. Biological accounts of preschoolers' cognitive development emphasize developmental changes in the _____.

modules

13. A theoretical approach inspired by Noam Chomsky's theory of language development views the mind as a collection of mental _____.

autistic

14. The remarkable, highly specific abilities of certain _____ children lend support to the modularity approach.

adults

15. The cultural-context approach looks at the way _____ support children's development through the contexts they create.

scripts

16. According to Katharine Nelson, contexts are represented mentally as generalized event schemas or _____.

contexts

17. Culture contributes to the unevenness observed in children's development by regulating exposure to particular _____.

play

18. Lev Vygotsky believed that ____ serves as a mental support system to help children control their behavior.

scribbling

19. Children's earliest drawing takes the form of _____.

represent

20. At about 3 years of age children recognize that their drawings can _____ things.

rules

21. In the information-processing view, the developmental sequence children go through in learning to draw follows from their acquisition of drawing _____.

module

22. The mental _____ approach is best able to explain the extraordinary artistic ability of some otherwise developmentally disabled children.

cultural-context

23. The _____ approach has examined the ways that adults talk to children about their drawings, helping them discover the representational nature of art.

complementary

24. The various approaches to understanding preschoolers' development are best viewed as _____.

Practice Questions

1. In Piaget's framework, the preschool period is associated with the _____ stage of development.
   a. sensorimotor
   b. preoperational

  c. concrete operational
  d. postsymbolic

2. Which of the following characterize(s) preschool thought, according to Piaget?
  a. Egocentrism
  b. Autism
  c. Logical thinking
  d. All of the above

3. In studies designed to evaluate their thinking, preschoolers are often led astray by
  a. inability to verbalize what they think.
  b. difficulties making the required motor responses.
  c. having to keep their minds on one thing at a time.
  d. changes in surface appearance that contradict underlying reality.

4. _____ are psychologists who are working to apply Piaget's basic assumptions to new evidence about children's thinking abilities.
  a. Neo-Piagetians
  b. Neuropsychologists
  c. Information-processing theorists
  d. Modularity theorists

5. Preschoolers are fairly reliable as witnesses in court when
  a. they are asked for specific examples of events that occurred many times.
  b. they are allowed to reenact events with props.
  c. they are allowed to give their accounts and then are probed for more information.
  d. None of the above—preschoolers cannot remember most events for more than a few days.

6. Which occurs in short-term memory?
  a. Information is stored for several seconds.
  b. Information is combined with information from long-term memory.
  c. Both a and b.
  d. Information is stored for several weeks; if not retrieved by then, it is forgotten.

7. Which of the following occurs in children's brain development during the course of the preschool period?
  a. The brain attains 50 percent of its adult weight.
  b. Specific mental modules develop their physical structures.
  c. Excess myelin is dissolved from the hippocampus and cerebellum, allowing these areas to function more efficiently.
  d. New connections among different cortical centers allow better syntheses of information about different aspects of a problem.

8. Children's mental representations of routine events such as eating in a restaurant have been called _____ by psychologist Katherine Nelson.
  a. long-term memory
  b. scripts
  c. cultural contexts
  d. modules

9. According to Lev Vygotsky, in play children perform activities
   a. at lower developmental levels than their usual behavior.
   b. at the same developmental level as their usual behavior.
   c. at higher developmental levels than their usual behavior.
   d. that are more highly rule-bound than their usual behavior.

10. At about _____ of age, children begin to recognize that the lines they draw can represent things.
    a. 1 year
    b. 3 years
    c. 5 years
    d. 7 years

11. The unusual artistic ability of Nadia, an autistic child studied by Lorna Selfe, supports the _____ explanation of the development of drawing.
    a. mental module
    b. cultural-context
    c. information-processing
    d. All of the above equally.

12. The _____ view of the development of drawing emphasizes the way adults talk to children about the things they draw.
    a. mental module
    b. environmental-learning
    c. information-processing
    d. cultural-context

Short-Answer Questions

1. In what ways can preschoolers' thinking be characterized as uneven? Why is this a problem for some theories of development?

2. What are the strengths and weaknesses of biologically-oriented explanations of cognitive development during early childhood?

3. Develop a script, from a preschooler's point of view, for "eating in a restaurant." Develop the same script for a college student. How do these scenarios differ? Note particularly how the supportive roles played by other people differ between the two.

4. What are the characteristics of play during early childhood? How does play serve to promote development?

5. Show how the different theoretical perspectives discussed in the chapter can each contribute to our understanding of the development of drawing.

Sources of More Information

Caplan, Theresa, and **Frank Caplan.** *The Early Childhood Years: The 2 to 6 Year old.* New York: Bantam, 1983.
This book gives an overview of development during the preschool years, covering motor and cognitive development, social development, early literacy experiences, sexuality, and family situations.

Flavell, John H. Really and truly. *Psychology Today,* January, 1986, 38-39, 42-44.
The author discusses the problems of understanding appearance/reality distinctions among preschoolers of several cultures.

Goodnow, Jacqueline. *Children Drawing.* Cambridge: Harvard University Press, 1977.
An exploration of the development of children's drawings, from scribbles through representation.

Paley, Vivian. *Wally's Stories.* Cambridge: Harvard University Press, 1981.
Paley, Vivian. *Mollie Is Three.* Chicago: University of Chicago Press, 1986.
The subtle changes in children's behavior that occur between the end of infancy and the onset of middle childhood are poorly documented in standard research on early childhood. In these case studies of preschool children, the author vividly describes the unevenness of their thinking and the enormous amount of work that small children put forth daily in their efforts to understand the world around them.

Selfe, Lorna. *Normal and Anomalous Representational Drawing Ability in Children.* New York: Academic Press, 1983.
In this monograph, the psychologist who studied Nadia provides a wealth of examples of extraordinary drawing ability by children, illustrating the kind of phenomena emphasized by modularity theories of development.

Answer Key

Answers to Key Terms: h, c, e, d, i, j, a, n, f, k, m, b, g, l.

Answers to Practice Questions: 1. b, 2. a, 3. d, 4. a, 5. b, 6. c, 7. d, 8. b, 9. c, 10. b, 11. a, 12. d.

11

SOCIAL DEVELOPMENT IN EARLY CHILDHOOD

Socialization begins at birth with infants' first interactions with their parents, and throughout infancy the values, standards, and knowledge of their society help to organize children's experiences. But it is not until the preschool period that children are able to actually construct an understanding of the workings of their families and their communities. At first, children follow the rules of their societies under adult constraint; eventually, though, they internalize standards and follow them on their own. Psychologists believe that a process called identification, in which children mold themselves after important people in their lives, is helpful in socialization, but they differ in their ideas of how identification comes about.

Preschool children face many important developmental tasks in addition to making sense of the rules that govern their environment. They are expected to learn to control their own behavior, including their impulses to hurt others, and to be helpful and cooperative when it is appropriate. They may need to cope with the addition of younger siblings to their families, and they must come to terms with their identities as males or females and master the sex-typed behaviors appropriate to their society.

The task of socialization is by no means completed at the end of the preschool period, but by then children understand their society's rules and expectations well enough to be ready for the increased responsibilities that accompany middle childhood.

Chapter Outline

Social development is a two-sided process. **Socialization** is the process by which children acquire the standards, knowledge, and values of the society in which they live. **Personality formation** refers to their development of **personality**, a distinctive sense of self and characteristic ways of thinking and feeling. These two processes are closely intertwined but there is also tension between them, as children experience conflict between their desires and the rules of their society.

I. Acquiring a Social Identity

According to psychologists, socialization requires **identification**, a process that provides individuals with an idea of who they are and who they want to be. According to Freud, **primary identification** occurs during infancy, when babies recognize that some things in the external world are like them; **secondary identification**, which develops during the third year, involves molding oneself in some way after a particular other person. Psychologists do not agree about how identification is achieved.

A. Much of the research on identification focuses on how children acquire **sex roles**. Acquiring a sex-role identity involves identifying with the parent of the same sex.

B. Freud's theory of development emphasizes the changing forms of sexual gratification during different periods. Children pass through the **oral, anal,** and **phallic** stages before sexual desires are suppressed during the **latency stage**. at about age 6. Puberty marks the beginning of adult sexuality—the **genital stage**.

According to Freud, boys come to identify with their father though a process of *differentiation* from their mother, the parent with whom they had the closest relationship in infancy. During the phallic stage, Freud believed, a boy wants to take his father's place with his mother; he then defends himself against perceived threats from his angry father by using two **defense mechanisms,** *identifying* with the father and *repressing* his feelings toward his mother. Freud viewed the personality as being made up of three mental structures: the **id**, source of basic desires and mental energy; the **ego**, intermediary between the id and the social world; and the **superego**, representing the authority of the social group. The superego begins to form during the preschool period and takes on an important role during middle childhood.

C. Psychologists have viewed girls' identification with their mothers as a process of *affiliation*, in contrast to the differentiation that characterizes the formation of boys' sex-role identities. Freud viewed this process as a response to girls' guilt feelings over rejecting their mothers and competing for their fathers' affection. Girls, Freud thought, blamed their mothers for their lack of a penis. Psychologist Nancy Chodorow, in contrast, points out that parents themselves play significant roles in their children's sex-role identification.

D. Social-learning theorists such as Albert Bandura and Walter Mischel believe that all behavior, including sex-role behavior, is shaped by the environment. According to their view, children observe and imitate sex differences in behavior; they are also rewarded by adults for sex-appropriate behavior. Researchers have found that adults do, in fact, differentially reward children for sex-appropriate behavior; however, children's ideas about appropriate rewards are themselves sex-typed, and social learning theory does not explain where these preferences come from in the first place.

E. Cognitive theorist Lawrence Kohlberg viewed sex-role identification as a result of children's structuring of their own experience; a crucial factor is children's categorizing of themselves as boys or girls. In Sandra Bem's view of sex-role identification, children acquire a **gender schema** that guides their behavior and struc-

tures their perceptions. Children should then find sex-typed behavior rewarding because it is consistent with the identities—male or female—they have adopted.
•Researchers have found that, between the ages of 2 1/2 and 6, children gradually develop a well-articulated concept of what it means to be a boy or girl in their culture. Even before age 2 1/2, boys and girls behave differently in some ways; the source of these differences is still being debated. Children's ideas about sex-appropriate behavior will, however, continue to develop gradually over the course of early childhood.
•One aspect of children's sex-role identity formation is understanding the permanence of being male or female. Kohlberg found that, just as many 4-year-olds believed that a dog could become a cat, they believed that sex could be changed. By 6 years of age, most children understood that sex is a permanent feature of a person's identity.

F. The theories of identification discussed in this chapter are in agreement about children's abilities to notice the characteristics that they share with others and to form ideas about sex-appropriate behavior on the basis of categorization, observation, and imitation. They do not agree as to the role of culture in the process. While Freudian and cognitive theories deemphasize the role of the environment, social-learning theory highlights the role of culture.

II. Developing the Ability to Regulate Oneself

As children acquire a sense of identity, they also learn what behavior their parents expect of them. At first, children's ideas of bad and good are strongly influenced by adults' reactions to their behavior. Piaget called this **heteronomous morality**, or "the morality of constraint." In heteronomous morality, Piaget believed, intentions play little role and the objective consequences of an act—the amount of damage done, for example—are the basis for judging the seriousness of an offense. During middle childhood, according to Piaget, children develop an **autonomous morality** in which rules are seen as agreements among people, not as decrees handed down by adults.

A. When children can anticipate adult reactions to their behavior and want to behave in ways that will bring adult approval, they are said to have **internalized** adult standards. Children then feel guilt when they fail to live up to these standards. According to Erik Erikson's theory of psychosocial development, the main conflict faced by children during the preschool period is that between the need to take initiative in their behavior and their negative feelings when the results of that initiative work out badly.

B. Children need to develop self-control in order to balance their desires with the social standards they have internalized. Self-control involves inhibiting behavior that would otherwise automatically occur; for example, a child who has been hit would refrain from hitting back.

III. Aggression and Prosocial Behavior

The rudiments of both **aggression** and **prosocial behavior** are thought to be present during the newborn period.

A. **Aggression** is generally defined as an action intended to hurt another. The first signs of aggression are newborns' angry reactions when their sucking is interrupted. As children develop, they begin to exhibit first **instrumental aggression,** in which aggressive behavior is aimed at getting something they want, and later person-oriented or **hostile aggression,** performed for revenge or to gain dominance. Wanda Bronson, studying children's play in the laboratory, found that, while younger children might struggle over a toy, it was not until about 2 years of age that children began to worry about "ownership rights" and engage in more deliberately antagonistic disputes. Between 3 and 6 years of age, children have fewer physical tussles, but they now exchange more verbal threats and insults, and hostile aggression makes an appearance. In general, boys are more aggressive than girls, both physically and verbally.

B. Discovering the causes of aggression is one of the most important questions about human social relations.
•Charles Darwin pointed out that members of a species are essentially in conflict with one another to survive and that they pass on their inborn characteristics to the next generation. According to this view, aggression is natural and necessary, and automatically accompanies biological maturation.
•According to the social-learning view, aggressive behavior is learned. Gerald Patterson and his colleagues found that aggressive behavior increased when it was followed by rewarding consequences but was less likely to be repeated if negative consequences followed.
•Sometimes parents model aggressive behavior for their children in the very act of disciplining them. Bandura and his colleagues found that children who observed adult aggression in a laboratory situation imitated the aggressive acts they had seen.

C. Theories explaining the causes of human aggression also suggest ways of controlling it.
•Evolutionary theories suggest that once a **dominance hierarchy** is formed within a group the frequency of hostile interactions should diminish. There is some evidence that dominance hierarchies take shape among nursery school children.
•It is widely believed that **catharsis**—the opportunity to vent aggressive tendencies in harmless behavior—will reduce the incidence of actual aggression; however, research demonstrates that this is not the case. Shahbaz Mallick and Boyd McCandless found that helping boys to sympathetically reinterpret a peer's obtrusive behavior was more effective in diffusing hostility than letting the boys "blow off steam" by shooting at targets.
•Coercive child-rearing behaviors may develop when children inadvertently train their parents to use physical punishment; this may make the children themselves more aggressive as a result. If punishment is to be used to suppress aggressive behavior,

it should be administered consistently and by a person with whom the child strongly identifies.

•Teachers often find that the level of aggression in their classrooms declines significantly when they ignore aggressive behavior and only attend to and reward children's cooperative behavior. Allen, Turner, and Everett found similar benefits when teachers gave attention and advice to the victim of aggression but ignored the aggressor.

•Reasoning with children about aggression—cognitive training—is sometimes effective even with preschoolers. Shoshana Zahavi and Steven Asher found that children were better able to control their aggression when their nursery school teachers made them aware of the feelings of the children they aggressed against.

D. **Prosocial behaviors** such as altruism, cooperation, helping, and empathy develop during infancy and early childhood. Why do they occur?

•Evolutionary explanations emphasize that prosocial behavior, like aggression, is also characteristic of other organisms. However, human altruism, unlike that of animals, often extends beyond the kin group to total strangers. While humans obviously have a biological potential for prosocial behavior, it is also influenced by social circumstances and cultural traditions.

•**Empathy**, sharing another's emotional response, is an important stimulus for prosocial behavior. Martin Hoffman has traced the development of empathy through four stages. During the first year, babies cry at the sound of another infant's cry; this empathy is reflexlike, occurring even before infants have any real awareness of other people. During the second year, babies actively attempt to comfort a person in distress. Preschoolers can empathize with a wider range of feelings and, through the media, with people they have never met or with story characters. Finally, between 6 and 9 years of age, children begin to empathize with the social conditions of groups of people.

•Carolyn Zahn-Waxler and Marion Radke-Yarrow found that, based on mothers' observations, between 10 months and 2 1/2 years of age, children's responses to another person's distress develop from diffuse emotional reactions such as crying to active caregiving and comforting behaviors such as offering Band-Aids and blankets. Harriet Rheingold found that all the 2-year-olds she studied spontaneously helped their mother with household chores in a laboratory situation and that most of them even helped an unfamiliar woman.

•Although parents are the most significant figures in children's socialization, siblings also play an important role. Older siblings join in parents' interactions with the baby, and siblings play together and compete for their parents' attention. Judy Dunn and Carol Kendrick found that when mothers drew their older child into the care of the baby, the interaction between the siblings was significantly more friendly.

•Adults can increase children's prosocial behavior by giving them explicit rewards; however, there is a chance that they will then behave prosocially only when rewarded. Two less direct but effective methods are **explicit modeling**, in which adults behave in ways they want the child to imitate, and **induction**, in which explanations are used. Marion Yarrow and her colleagues found that when explicit modeling was carried out in a nurturing, loving way, the effects on preschoolers' behavior lasted for some time. Induction has more generally been used with older children.

IV. Taking One's Place in the Social Group

By the end of early childhood, children have accepted that conformity to social rules is inevitable. While they are by no means completely socialized, they have a great deal of knowledge about the social world that they can apply in a variety of contexts.

Key Terms I

Following are important terms introduced in Chapter 11. Write the definition for each after the term. Then match the term with the letter of the example that best illustrates it.

_____ Aggression _____

_____ Autonomous morality _____

_____ Dominance hierarchy _____

_____ Empathy _____

_____ Explicit modeling _____

_____ Heteronomous morality _____

_____ Hostile aggression _____

_____ Identification _____

_____ Induction _____

_____ Instrumental aggression _____

_____ Personality _____

_____ Prosocial behavior _____

_____ Sex role _____

_____ Social development _____

_____ Socialization _____

a. The process by which children acquire their society's values, knowledge, and standards.
b. A mother appeals to her children's pride and their desire to be grown-up in explaining how they should behave toward others.
c. A person's characteristic style of dealing with others, and the idiosyncrasies that make him or her distinctive.
d. A teacher demonstrates prosocial behavior for her pupils, hoping that they will imitate this behavior in their interactions with one another.
e. This occurs when someone hurts another person intentionally.
f. An attribute, usually based on a person's biological sex, that shapes many of his or her social roles.
g. When this develops in a nursery school, it determines who will typically be dominant and who will be submissive in an argument between two children.
h. Janet hits another preschool child in order to gain possession of the doll she is playing with.
i. Children have achieved this when they understand that rules are based on the agreement of those they govern and can be changed if everyone agrees.
j. This is a process with two aspects: in one, children become differentiated as individuals; in the other, they become integrated into the society of which they are members.
k. John calls a fellow kindergartner "stupid" just to hurt his feelings.
l. A baby cries when she hears another child crying.
m. Altruism, cooperation, and sharing are examples of this.
n. This is characterized by attention to the letter, rather than the spirit, of the law.
o. A child's desire to look, act, and feel like another person.

Key Terms II

Following are important terms introduced in Chapter 11. Write the definition for each after the term. Then match the term with the letter of the example that best illustrates it.

_____ Anal stage _____

_____ Catharsis _____

_____ Defense mechanisms _____

_____ Ego _____

_____ Gender schema _____

_____ Genital stage _____

_____ Id _____

_____ Internalization _____

_____ Latency stage _____

_____ Oral stage _____

_____ Personality formation _____

_____ Phallic stage _____

_____ Primary identification _____

_____ Secondary identification _____

_____ Superego _____

a. In Freud's theory, the mental structure that accomplishes its goals through perception, logical thought, and problem-solving.
b. The Freudian stage during which children develop sexual jealousy toward the parent of the same sex.
c. A father encourages his children to hit a punching bag to "blow off steam," hoping it will prevent them from punching one another.
d. This part of the personality, Freud thought, begins to develop during the preschool period and does not become a major force until middle childhood.
e. Children can guide their actions with this idea of their culture's conceptions of sex roles.
f. The first of Freud's stages of psychosexual development.
g. This happens during infancy when babies notice that there are other things in the world like them.
h. This Freudian stage begins at puberty and encompasses mature sexuality.
i. This part of the personality is our main source of mental energy.
j. We make use of these in seeking to protect ourselves from unpleasant thoughts.
k. The Freudian stage that occurs during the second year of life.
l. Freud's term for modeling oneself after another person.
m. This has occurred when children have accepted social rules and make an effort to follow them on their own.
n. The way children come to have a distinctive sense of themselves as well as distinctive ways of thinking, feeling, and behaving.
o. During this Freudian stage, sexual energy is channeled into acquiring technical skills.

Fill-in Review

Cover the list of answers next to the statements below. Then uncover each answer after you complete each statement.

socialization   1. One aspect of social development is _____, the process by which children acquire the standards, values, and knowledge of their society.

personality   2. A second aspect of social development is _____ formation, the way in which children come to have a sense of themselves and distinctive ways of thinking and feeling.

identification   3. Part of socialization involves _____, a process that provides children with a sense of who they are and who they want to be.

primary   4. In Freud's view, there are two kinds of identification: _____ identification, which occurs during infancy when babies realize their similarity to other people;

secondary   and _____ identification, which takes place during early childhood when children want to be like a specific other person.

phallic   5. Freud believed that around the age of 3, children enter the _____ stage of development, during which they develop sexual feelings toward the opposite-sex parent and jealousy or resentment toward the same-sex parent.

  6. According to Freud's theory, the personality has three parts: the id, which contains a person's basic _____; the ___, which is an intermediary between the

desires; ego

superego   id and the social world; and the _____, which represents the authority of the social group.

differentiation   7. Freud believed that in boys, identification occurs through _____

girls   while in _____ it occurs through affiliation.

social-learning   8. According to _____ theory, identification occurs through observation and imitation.

  9. In Lawrence Kohlberg's view, the most important factor in sex-role identifica-

categorize   tion is children's ability to _____ themselves as boys or girls.

different   10. By 2 1/2 years of age, most boys and girls like to play with _____ kinds of toys.

permanent   11. Children may not understand that a person's sex is _____ until late in the preschool period.

  12. Piaget labeled preschoolers' reasoning about moral issues heteronomous morali-

constraint   ty or a "morality of _____."

autonomous   13. During middle childhood, Piaget thought, children develop a more _____ morality, based on an understanding that rules are agreements between people and can be changed by common consent.

internalized   14. By the end of the preschool period, children have _____ many adult standards for behavior.

15. Children can only resolve the tension they feel between internalized standards and personal desires by developing _____.   *self-control*

16. _____ is behavior that is intended to hurt another person.   *Aggression*

17. Whereas _____ aggression is performed in order to obtain something desirable, _____ aggression is person-oriented.   *instrumental* *hostile*

18. According to some students of animal behavior, aggression is an important mechanism of _____   *evolution*

19. Learning theorists point out that aggression increases when it is _____.   *rewarded*

20. Children may also learn aggression from adults who inadvertently _____ aggressive behavior.   *model*

21. Formation of a _____ hierarchy reduces aggression by reducing the number of others an individual will fight with.   *dominance*

22. The idea that _____, or "blowing off steam," will reduce people's hostile impulses has not been supported by research.   *catharsis*

23. Because children are sometimes aggressive in order to gain attention, one way of reducing aggression is to reward only _____ behavior.   *nonaggressive*

24. Altruism, cooperation, helping, and empathy are _____ behaviors.   *prosocial*

25. Two effective methods of promoting prosocial behavior are explicit _____ and induction.   *modeling*

Practice Questions

Circle the letter of the word or phrase that correctly completes each statement.

1. _____ is the process by which children learn the standards, values, and knowledge of their society.
   a. Personality formation
   b. Prosocial behavior
   c. Affiliation
   d. Socialization

2. According to Freud, identification in males
   a. requires that they differentiate themselves from their mothers.
   b. requires that they differentiate themselves from their fathers.
   c. results in their remaining affiliated with their mothers.
   d. occurs because they are rewarded for imitating appropriate behavior.

3. In thinking about moral issues, preschool children
   a. have no sense of right or wrong.
   b. believe in obeying the spirit of the law rather than the letter of the law.

    c. judge the rightness or wrongness of actions by outcome, not intention.

    d. are inclined to question the judgment of people in authority.

4. Which part of the personality serves as a person's conscience?
   a. The id
   b. The ego
   c. The superego
   d. The unconscious

5. When children are able to pass up an immediate small reward to wait for a larger reward in the future, they are exhibiting
   a. repression.
   b. self-control.
   c. internalization.
   d. prosocial behavior.

6. The major developmental crisis of the preschool period, according to Erik Erikson, involves conflict between
   a. trust and mistrust.
   b. industry and inferiority.
   c. autonomy and shame and doubt.
   d. initiative and guilt.

7. When a child hurts a playmate for revenge or to assert dominance, he or she is engaging in
   a. hostile aggression.
   b. explicit modeling.
   c. instrumental aggression.
   d. a defense mechanism.

8. Children worry about "ownership rights" to toys and become serious about taking them from others
   a. from early infancy.
   b. only when they begin preschool.
   c. beginning at about the time they can walk.
   d. beginning at about 2 years of age.

9. Aggression among children is caused by
   a. frustration.
   b. adults who inadvertently reward aggressive behavior.
   c. inborn tendencies to compete with others.
   d. All of the above are causes.

10. Physically punishing children for aggressive behavior
    a. may make children even more aggressive.
    b. is the most successful way to inhibit aggressive behavior.
    c. has no effect on children's level of aggression.
    d. provides catharsis for parents and helps them cope better with their children's behavior.

11. When newborns cry in response to another baby's crying, they are displaying the first signs of
    a. self-control.
    b. frustration.
    c. empathy.
    d. learning.

12. Developmental psychologists tend not to recommend directly rewarding children for prosocial behavior because
    a. direct reward is not an effective way to increase prosocial behavior.
    b. children may act prosocially only when they are being rewarded.
    c. it is too difficult to find appropriate rewards.
    d. children usually engage in so much prosocial behavior that there is no reason to try to increase it.

Short-Answer Questions

1. Briefly describe the Freudian, social-learning, and cognitive approaches to explaining children's sex-role identification. What are the strengths and weaknesses of each?

2. Discuss what happens during each of Freud's stages of psychosexual development. How do Freud's stages differ from Erikson's stages of psychosocial development?

3. What factors are thought to be responsible for human aggression? What might help reduce aggression among children?

4. What is prosocial behavior and what is its course of development in children? How can prosocial behavior be increased?

Putting It All Together

In this section, material from Chapter 11 can be put together with information presented in Chapters 9 and 10.

I. One of the major accomplishments of early childhood is the growth of children's ability to regulate their own behavior. Show how developments in language ability and the growth of scripted knowledge help children to exhibit self-control and to interact socially with others.

II. Among preschoolers, the ability to reason about social categories such as sex is thought to influence the process of identification. Use examples to demonstrate the relationship between cognitive development and social development during early childhood.

Sources of More Information

Ames, Louise Bates, and **Carol Chase Haber.** *He Hit Me First: When Brothers and Sisters Fight.* New York: Dembner, 1982.
This book discusses sibling rivalry from the biological-maturational perspective of the Gesell Institute.

Freud, Anna. *Psycho-analysis for Teachers and Parents* (Trans. by Barbara Low). New York: Norton, 1979.

This book contains four lectures in which Sigmund Freud's daughter, a noted children's analyst, discusses the early stages of psychosexual development.

Galinsky, Ellen, and **Judy David.** *The Preschool Years.* New York: Times Books, 1988.

The authors present practical solutions to the problems faced by parents of preschool children.

Hall, C. S. *A Primer of Freudian Psychology.* New York: World, 1954.

This brief paperback account of Freud's thinking is one of the most accessible and comprehensive available.

Honig, Alice Sterling. Compliance, Control, and Discipline, Part I. *Young Children*, January 1985, 50-58.

Honig, Alice Sterling. Compliance, Control, and Discipline, Part II. *Young Children*, March 1985, 47-52.

These two articles discuss children's development of self-regulation and suggest techniques that can be used by adults to increase cooperation and compliance.

Kohn, Alfie. Beyond Selfishness. *Psychology Today*, October 1988, 34-38.

This article explores the roots of prosocial behavior and includes suggestions for raising helping children.

Paley, Vivian. *Boys and Girls: Superheroes in the Classroom.* Chicago: University of Chicago Press, 1984.

The focus of Paley's attention is the distinctive patterns of play that boys and girls display both in their fantasy play and in other preschool classroom activities.

Answer Key

Answers to Key Terms I: e, i, g, l, d, n, k, o, b, h, c, m, f, j, a.

Answers to Key Terms II: k, c, j, a, e, h, i, m, o, f, n, b, g, l, d.

Answers to Practice Questions: 1. d, 2. a, 3. c, 4. c, 5. b, 6. d, 7. a, 8. d, 9. d, 10. a, 11. c, 12. b.

12

SOCIALIZATION: CONTEXTS AND MEDIA

Children's development is influenced by the many contexts of their lives; their families, for example, belong to communities that, in turn, are parts of larger societies. Child rearing varies from society to society: a family of nomadic herders in North Africa and a family living in a New York City high-rise apartment will not teach their children the same survival and social skills. There are also differences in child-rearing practices within societies and corresponding differences in children's behavior. Many factors influence a family's child rearing, including the personalities of parents and children, the parents' occupational status, and the life stresses that affect the family at any particular time.

Even within the family, children are influenced by the world outside. Media such as television, newspapers, and books help to shape the behavior and beliefs of family members in the United States. Research on the influence of television on children indicates that it can have both positive and negative effects, depending on how it is used. Print media, particularly books, provide children with an introduction to literacy.

During early childhood, many children are cared for by relatives besides their parents or by day-care providers, either in other families' homes or in day-care centers. While high-quality day care does not harm children intellectually, the social effects are mixed. Not all families are able to arrange the best possible care for their children, but the long-term effects of poor-quality day care have not been determined.

Children also have out-of-home experiences in nursery schools or preschools—sheltered environments oriented toward enhancing their development. Special preschool programs have been created for economically disadvantaged children in the hope of giving them an educational "head start," and there is some evidence that preschool experience has long-lasting positive effects on such children's later school achievement.

By the end of the preschool period, children, while not completely socialized, will have a great deal of information about how their culture works and will be able to behave competently in the wide variety of situations with which they are familiar.

Chapter Outline

Chapter 12 discusses the ways that different family patterns of child rearing are shaped by the community's economic and cultural characteristics, as well as the influence of books and television and the effects of day care and nursery school on children's development.

I. Cultural Variations in Family Socialization

When Beatrice and John Whiting organized observations of child rearing in six diverse locales around the world, they found differences, not only in the circumstances of children's lives, but in the overall patterns of their behavior. Each cultural group socializes children in ways that will help them to fit in as adult members of that particular society.

A. While child-rearing behaviors differ in many ways among U.S. families, psychologists conceive of parenting styles as varying along two dimensions: from control to autonomy and from affection to indifference. Diana Baumrind and her colleagues found that, when measured on these dimensions, 77 percent of the families they studied fall into one of the following categories: **authoritarian parents**, who try to control their children's behavior and stress obedience to authority; **authoritative parents**, who encourage individualism and independence, while setting high standards for behavior; and **permissive parents**, who provide less discipline and demand less achievement and maturity than do parents in the other categories. Baumrind found that the children of authoritarian parents tended to lack social competence and intellectual curiosity, that the children of authoritative parents were more self-reliant and self-controlled, and that the children of permissive parents were relatively immature and less responsible than those of the other groups.

There are limits to the generalizability of these findings. First, the studies were of white, middle-class, two-parent families; they do not take account of ethnic differences in parenting styles. Also, many children are raised in single-parent families, and reasearch has found that divorce exerts long-lasting effects both on child rearing and on children's behavior. Third, children's own characteristics probably influence the child-rearing strategies adopted by their parents. Still, these findings have generated a great deal of interest and have inspired other researchers.

B. Family interaction patterns are influenced, not only by the characteristics of parents and children, but by circumstances outside the family. Laboratory and observational studies have demonstrated that when mothers are under stress they are more likely to adopt an authoritarian parenting style. Stressful events occur more often in poor families; low-income parents are also more likely to use authoritarian or inconsistent styles of child rearing. Melvin Kohn and his colleagues found that parenting style is significantly related to parental occupation. Middle-class occupations tend to require independence and self-directed work, while working-class occupations often demand obedience and punctuality.

C. Socialization practices generally support whatever social situation currently exists; this means that families can, through their patterns of child rearing, inadvertently perpetuate socioeconomic inequalities that affect their children.

II. Media Linking Community and Home

Children's behavior is shaped, not only by the members of their families and their communities, but by books, television, newspapers, and radio. Chapter 12 examines the influence of television and books.

A. Young children's difficulties in distinguishing between appearance and reality can greatly affect their understanding of television. They may have difficulty separating the actors from the characters they portray or understanding that the events depicted are not really happening.
•Techniques of television production such as close-ups, flashbacks, and changes of camera angle have meaning for older viewers but are confusing to preschool children, who may be able to keep track of less than half of what they see. The fast-paced nature of television also allows little time for reflection. Gabriel Salomon found that children socialized to learn from television had lower expectations of how much mental work was needed to learn from written texts.
•The content of television programs differs systematically from everyday reality. For example, prime-time programming tends to stereotype women, ethnic groups, and members of certain occupations; these stereotypes may work their way into children's basic assumptions about the world. Television also contains many violent episodes, and psychologists have noted an association between viewing violent television programs and aggression in children's play.
•The family has some influence on how children are affected by television. Children whose playground behavior is less aggressive also tend to be those whose viewing is limited and restricted to educational and children's programs and whose parents also take them to parks, museums, and cultural events.

B. Like television viewing, being read to requires children to construct meanings from words and pictures that represent elements of the everyday world.
•Virtually all preschool children are involved with print media in some form every day, if only for a few minutes. Many are read to by their parents or other adults. Children who are often read to at home generally learn to read easily once they begin school. In their interactions with children over books, parents often construct a zone of proximal development, asking questions suited to their children's level of knowledge.
•Adults have much greater control over the content of the books they read to children than over the content of television programs children watch. Some adults worry that certain literary forms such as fairy tales or nonsense verse are harmful to children's development; still others defend them as beneficial. It is difficult to characterize the influences of media in general terms—their effects depend on the social setting for which a child is being prepared.

III. The Child in the Community

Children are often left in the care of people other than their parents for several hours a day. This changes both the nature of their experiences and the nature of their parents' control over those experiences.

A. In 1987, more then 50 percent of U.S. mothers with preschool children were working and using some form of day care.
•In *home care*, children are cared for in their homes by relatives or babysitters.
•In *family day care*, children are cared for in the day-care provider's home, along with children from outside their families. Family day-care providers may be licensed by state, county, or local government, but most are unlicensed.
•Licensed *day-care centers* generally place more emphasis on formal learning experiences. Those serving fewer than 60 children tend to be more flexible and more responsive to individual children than larger ones; within a center, children receive more individual attention when placed in a group of less than 15 to 18 children.

B. There is disagreement among psychologists about the effects of day-care experience on children's development.
•Since much early research on day care was conducted in high-quality, university-affiliated centers, the results may not be generalizable to other settings. The long-term effects of day care have not yet been studied. And families who use day care may vary in significant ways from those who do not, raising the possibility that some "effects of day care" could be only effects of family situations.
•The intellectual development of middle-class children in day care is at least as good as that of their stay-at-home peers; low-income children seem to actively benefit from day-care enrichment programs.
•Children who attend day-care centers in the U.S. are more self-sufficient and independent, more cooperative, and more comfortable in new situations, though also less polite, less compliant with adults, and more aggressive than children who do not attend day care. Children in day-care centers and nursery schools engage in a great deal of group play and must therefore learn social skills such as how to enter groups of children who are already playing together and how to handle themselves when other children reject their overtures.

C. *Nursery schools* or *preschools* serve a primarily educational purpose; the children, who may range in age from 2 1/2 to 6, typically spend 2 1/2 to 3 hours per day engaged in a variety of activities designed to enhance various aspects of their development. The emphasis is usually on exploration rather than on performing correctly on preassigned tasks.
•Project Head Start was begun in 1964 in an attempt to narrow the educational gap between low-income and middle-class children by providing preschool-aged children with learning experiences they might miss at home. By 1967, it was a year-round program serving 200,000 children. Although many children benefited, the program lost favor after a 1969 study reported that the beneficial effects disappeared during the first years of elementary school. Supporters of Head Start were encouraged, however, by results of a 1983 follow-up of participants; this study showed that

children who had attended a preschool program achieved more and had higher aspirations than children with no preschool experience.

IV. On the Threshold

By the end of the preschool period, children have accumulated a great deal of knowledge about a wide variety of contexts; their ability to think about the world, to interact with other children, and to control their own behavior have all increased as well. In these ways they indicate their readiness to take on the roles and responsibilities they will face in middle childhood.

Key Terms

Following are important terms introduced in Chapter 12. Write the definition for each after the term. Then match the term with the letter of the example that best illustrates it.

_____ Authoritarian parenting pattern _____

_____ Authoritative parenting pattern _____

_____ Permissive parenting pattern _____

a. Janet's parents expect a lot of her and are fairly strict, but they are willing to explain the reasons for their decisions and to listen to her point of view. Janet gets along well with other children and is generally happy with her home life.
b. John's behavior is relatively immature for his age, but his parents are not especially concerned. They believe that children should learn through their own experiences. When John is ready to accept more adult responsibilities, he will indicate it through more mature behavior, they feel.
c. Jack is a quiet and well-behaved child, though his behavior seems to lack spontaneity. His parents are insistent that he follow the rules they set, and Jack knows that if he questions these rules he will be punished. In general, Jack prefers playing alone to dealing with the problems that accompany social interactions among children.

Fill-in Review

Cover the list of answers next to the statements below. Then uncover each answer after you complete each statement.

1. Beatrice and John Whiting's study of child rearing in six different locales revealed how differences in _____ are associated with differences in children's behavior patterns.   *culture*

2. Diana Baumrind characterized the U.S. parents in her study as _____, authoritative, or _____ with respect to child rearing.   *authoritarian*
permissive

3. Children of _____ parents tend to achieve more and be better adjusted socially both as preschoolers and as adolescents.   *authoritative*

4. Studies of single-parent families indicate that children who are _____ at the time their parents divorce seem to suffer less long-term disruption.   *preschool-aged*

5. Because lower-income families are subject to more _____ than well-to-do families, their parenting styles can be expected to be more _____.   *stress*
authoritarian

6. While middle-class occupations stress self-direction, working-class occupations place greater emphasis on _____ and punctuality.   *obedience*

7. Three- and 4-year-old children may not understand some television programs because of their problem distinguishing between appearance and _____.   *reality*

8. Frequently, television programs depict ethnic groups, women, and certain occupations in _____ ways.   *stereotyped*

9. Jerome and Dorothy Singer found that preschoolers who watched television frequently were more _____ at preschool.   *aggressive*

10. Children learn more from watching television when their _____ watch with them.   *parents*

11. Children acquire the beginnings of _____ at home, by being read to, looking at the writing on cereal boxes, or watching their parents read the newspaper.   *literacy*

12. The way parents interact with their children over picture books prepares them for the way they will be asked questions in _____.   *school*

13. A major difference between preschoolers' experiences with books and television is the greater _____ adults have over the content to which they are exposed.   *control*

14. The most popular day-care arrangement for preschool children is _____ day care, in which children are cared for in the home of a nonrelative.   *family*

15. In day-care centers, children receive more individual attention when cared for in groups of less than _____.   *15 to 18*

16. Attendance at well-staffed day-care centers has no negative effects on children's _____ development.   *intellectual*

17. The most clear-cut effects of day care are on children's _____ development.   *social*

Nursery   18. _____ schools came into being to "promote experiences of mastery within a child-sized world."

achievement   19. Preschool experience has been shown to increase school _achievement_ among low-income children.

       20. Preschoolers display surprising competence and maturity of reasoning when op-
contexts   erating in familiar _contexts_ for which they know the appropriate scripts and the roles they are to play.

Multiple-Choice Practice Questions

Circle the letter of the word or phrase that correctly completes each statement.

1. Diana Baumrind and her colleagues found that the parenting styles of middle-class Americans vary along dimensions of
   a. aggression and love.
   b. control and affection.
   c. guilt and initiative.
   d. confidence and empathy.

2. Compared with working-class parents, middle-class parents are
   a. more concerned about their children's futures.
   b. less concerned about their children's futures.
   c. more likely to emphasize self-reliance.
   d. more likely to emphasize obedience.

3. All children are affected when their parents divorce, but _____ in particular suffer long-lasting effects.
   a. preschoolers
   b. girls
   c. infants
   d. boys

4. Which is a possible source of misunderstanding when preschoolers watch TV?
   a. They may not know how to interpret special techniques such as scene changes or flashbacks.
   b. They may not understand that the events on the screen are not really happening.
   c. They may not be able to distinguish the actors from the characters they play.
   d. All of the above.

5. Which is true about the effects of TV violence on children's behavior?
   a. Unrestricted viewing of violent programs is associated with more aggressive behavior.
   b. Children who watch nonviolent children's programs like *Mr. Rogers' Neighborhood* are just as aggressive as those who watch violent programs.

    c. Only children who are predisposed to be violent are affected by violent programs.

    d. Children who "blow off steam" by watching violent programs are less aggressive in their play than children who watch nonviolent programs.

6. Which of the following serves as a "literacy experience" for young children?
    a. Listening to their parents read a letter aloud.
    b. Looking at the message on cereal boxes.
    c. Bringing home a note from their preschool teacher.
    d. All of the above.

7. Kornei Chukovsky, a Soviet poet, argues that nonsense verse
    a. is harmful to children's cognitive development.
    b. helps strengthen children's sense of reality.
    c. is fun for children but doesn't teach them anything.
    d. is confusing to children because they think the nonsensical things really happen.

8. Differences in _____ have been found between children who attend day care and those cared for at home.
    a. social development
    b. intellectual development
    c. attachment to their parents
    d. All of the above.

9. The most widely utilized form of day care is
    a. care in organized childcare centers.
    b. care in the child's own home.
    c. family day care.
    d. All are utilized equally.

10. Preschool-aged children have less trouble joining a group of children already playing together if
    a. they are girls.
    b. the group they are joining is composed of unpopular children.
    c. they ask the other children to explain what they are doing.
    d. they act as though they are already part of the group.

11. The main purpose of nursery schools is to
    a. take care of young children while their parents work.
    b. give children a head start in learning academic skills such as reading and writing.
    c. provide children with opportunities to practice developmental skills in a scaled-down environment.
    d. get children ready for school by teaching them to perform correctly on assigned tasks.

12. The most recent follow-up studies of Project Head Start showed that
    a. the program had no effect on children's development.
    b. the program had an initial positive effect on children, but the effect gradually disappeared once they began school.
    c. the program had long-lasting effects on school achievement and on occupational aspirations.
    d. the program left disadvantaged children even worse off than before.

Short-Answer Questions

1. What differences can be observed among children whose parents use authoritarian, authoritative, and permissive child-rearing strategies? Why is it hard to say whether the strategies actually cause the differences in children's behavior?

2. In what ways do parents' occupations and socioeconomic status influence the child-rearing strategies they use?

3. What problems may young children have in understanding what they see on TV? What similarities and differences are there between the way children learn from TV and the way they learn from books?

4. In what ways do day-care and preschool experiences affect children's intellectual and social development? What positive effects have been noted? Negative effects?

Sources of More Information

Fields, Marjorie V. *Literacy Begins at Birth.* Tucson, Ariz.: Fisher Books, 1989. The author discusses how children learn to read and write and how parents and teachers support the process.

Greenfield, Patricia Marks. *Mind and Media: The Effects of Television, Video Games, and Computers.* Cambridge: Harvard University Press, 1984.
The author shows how various media can be used to enhance children's learning and to promote social development.

Singer, Dorothy G., Jerome L. Singer and Diana M. Zuckerman. *Teaching Television: How to Use TV to Your Child's Advantage.* New York: Dial Press, 1981.
This book reviews the problems and possibilities of television watching, discusses how TV shows are put together, and covers stereotyping, violence, and other timely issues.

Trelease, Jim. *The Read-Aloud Handbook* (Rev. ed.). New York: Penguin, 1985.
This book discusses how being read to affects children's development and includes a bibliography of suggested stories and books for reading aloud to children of various ages.

Trotter, Robert J. Project Day-care. *Psychology Today*, December 1987, 32-38.
The author interviews Ed Zigler, a psychologist who helped start Project Head Start, about possible solutions to the childcare crisis facing U.S. parents.

Wallerstein, Judith S., and Joan Berlin Kelly. *Surviving the Breakup: How Children and Parents Cope with Divorce.* New York: Basic Books, 1980.
A summary of findings from the Children of Divorce Project, written for general readers.

Wallis, Claudia. The Child-care Dilemma. *Time*, June 22, 1987, 54-60.
This article describes the crisis developing as day-care facilities fail to keep up with the demand created as greater numbers of mothers join the workforce.

Answer Key

Answers to Key Terms: c, a, b.

Answers to Practice Questions: 1. b, 2. c, 3. d, 4. d, 5. a, 6. d, 7. b, 8. a, 9. c, 10. d, 11. c, 12. c.

13

COGNITIVE AND BEHAVIORAL ATTAINMENTS OF MIDDLE CHILDHOOD

Between 5 and 7 years of age, children change in a number of ways. Their bodies and facial features become more streamlined and their smiles show gaps and permanent teeth coming in. Less visible changes in their brains support more graceful movements and more efficient thinking. They are entering the developmental period called *middle childhood.*

During middle childhood, children's height, weight, and strength increase steadily. These changes are matched by new cognitive abilities and increasing competence in the many social contexts to which they have been exposed since the end of infancy. Already skilled speakers of their language, these older children can follow complex directions and, when assigned tasks, can perform them without constant adult supervision. They are better at remembering things and their thinking is more consistently logical than it was during their preschool years.

A reflection of children's new abilities is that adults now send them to be educated in schools or assign them economically important work to do. These new activities, in turn, stimulate further cognitive and social development. The behavioral changes of middle childhood can be understood more clearly when they are considered in terms of the many contexts in which development takes place.

Chapter Outline

It seems to be universal among cultures that when children are between 5 and 7 years old, adults begin to expect them to take on new responsibilities that involve working independently and planning ahead. Chapter 13 investigates the biological and psychological changes that underlie children's greater abilities and justify adults' expectations of children during middle childhood.

I.   Biological Developments

In many cultures the first loss of baby teeth marks the beginning of middle childhood, and the accompanying physical growth and brain development are the sources of children's new capacities.

A. Children increase in size and strength, putting on about 1 1/2 feet in height and 50 pounds in weight during middle childhood, although their actual rate of growth is slower than it was in previous years. Both genetic factors and nutritional status contribute to size differences between children.

B. Development of children's brains is at least partially responsible for increases in their agility, coordination, and problem-solving abilities. Some researchers attribute these behavioral changes to increases in **lateralization**, a process by which one hemisphere of the brain dominates the other, leading to smoother coordination of brain functions and allowing more complex thought. Some doubt has been cast, however, by more recent research showing that some lateralization of brain functions is present from the time of birth.

   Children's brains have a growth spurt between the ages of 5 and 7, and myelination of the cortex is almost completed during this time, leading to better connections between different areas of the brain. Now, children's brains have reached a nearly adult level of complexity, and electroencephalograms (EEGs) reveal a shift from a predominance of theta activity (characteristic of sleep in adults) to a predominance of alpha activity (characteristic of engaged attention) after age 7. Some researchers, notably Alexander Luria, have argued that development in the brain's frontal lobes underlies children's increasing ability to make plans and maintain goals. However, because the evidence is correlational, it is difficult to be certain whether changes in children's brains are the actual causes of the changes in their behavior.

II.   A New Quality of Mind?

Psychologists are interested in whether the changes in children's thinking during middle childhood represent a distinctive stage of cognitive development or whether they are simply a collection of gradual advances that have been occurring since the end of infancy.

A. During middle childhood, children can carry out a complex task when given instructions at the outset rather than needing to be guided at each step. Four factors seem to account for this increased memory performance:
•Children are able to hold more information in memory. Some researchers believe that their memory capacity actually increases; others believe that it remains constant but that older children are able to make more efficient use of their memory capacity.
•Children become better able to make use of **memory strategies,** patterned ways of learning. Studies by Keeney, Canizzo, and Flavell and by Jill Weissberg and Scott Paris have demonstrated that older children are more likely to use rehearsal in order to remember information. Children who do not spontaneously repeat material do

improve their performance when they are taught the technique. **Memory organization** also changes during middle childhood. For example, older children are more likely to link words to be remembered according to category (animal, color, etc.).
•Older children generally have a greater **knowledge base** and, therefore, better-elaborated concepts to draw on when they need to remember things relating to a particular topic. For example, Micheline Chi found that 10-year-old children who are expert chess players remember positions on a chess board better than college students do, though they are not as good at remembering random numbers.
•Seven- and 8-year-olds know more about their own memory processes (**metamemory**) than younger children and are therefore more likely to correctly estimate how much effort will be required to remember particular items.

These changes in different aspects of memory performance each appear quantitative and gradual. However, they add up to a sizeable difference in memory performance between preschoolers and 7- to 8-year-olds.

B. According to Piaget, the new behaviors that accompany middle childhood represent a new form of thought. **Concrete operations** are internalized mental actions that fit into a logical system and are based on the presence of physical objects rather than occurring on a purely abstract level. Children's thinking is now more flexible and, when solving problems, they can consider alternatives and retrace their steps. Conservation and logical classification are two activities requiring concrete operational thought.
•**Conservation** of properties such as quantity or number refers to children's understanding that these properties remain constant even when physical appearance changes; for example, the level of water rises when the water is poured into a taller, thinner glass. Most 3- and 4-year-olds are misled by changes in physical appearance because they focus their attention on only one aspect of a stimulus, such as the height of the water. When children conserve liquid quantity, they justify their insistence that "there is still the same amount of water" with one of the following arguments: **identity**, nothing was added and nothing was taken away; **compensation**, the new glass is taller but it is also thinner; and **reversibility** or **negation**, if the water were poured back into the original glass, it would reach the same level as before. Middle childhood sees an increase in children's ability to conserve. However, recent research has demonstrated more overlap in the conservation abilities of preschoolers and older children than was reported by Piaget.
•In logical classification, children show their ability to group objects according to more than one criterion. So, for example, a stamp collection might be organized by country, year, and denomination. Unlike preschoolers, 7- to 8-year-olds are able to answer questions requiring knowledge of the relationship between a category and its parts (for example, "Are there more roses or more flowers?").

C. Using concrete operations in solving problems means being able to think about two aspects of a thing at the same time.
•Preschoolers often center on only one aspect of a problem and fail to notice other features. For example, David Elkind found that while 8-year-olds generally perceived ambiguous figures in more than one way, 6-year-olds rarely pointed out alternatives and 4- to 5-year-olds often saw the figures in only one way even when

alternatives were pointed out. When presented with conservation problems, pre-schoolers looked at only one aspect—for example, height of the liquid—of a stimulus display set up by Kenneth O'Bryan and Frederic Boersma.

•During middle childhood, increasing ability to keep two things in mind leads to a better understanding of other perspectives and a decline in egocentrism.

•Children also become better at **social perspective-taking**—thinking about how their actions and ideas will be perceived by others. Both Robert Selman and Dorothy Flapan found that children become better able to understand the points of view of more than one character in stories and films and are better able to incorporate characters' psychological states into interpretations of their actions.

D. Are the cognitive changes accompanying middle childhood universal or are they products of schooling and other characteristics of industrialized societies? Two of the most frequently studied cognitive abilities connected with middle childhood are concrete operations and free-recall memory.

•Most research has found that children in nonindustrial societies achieve concrete operations a year or more later than children in Western industrialized societies. However, Patricia Greenfield found that many adults in certain cultures never showed an understanding of concepts like conservation. It has become evident that unfamiliarity with testing procedures is responsible for such extreme results and that, in fact, children in traditional societies may actually acquire some concepts—for example, conservation of quantity or understanding business transactions—earlier as a result of their greater experience with activities such as working with clay or helping their families market their products.

•Cross-cultural studies show that the development of memory skills during middle childhood takes a somewhat different course in nonindustrial societies. For example, Michael Cole and his colleagues found that, unless they had attended schools, tribal children in rural Liberia did not demonstrate the regular increase in free recall performance characteristic in industrialized societies. Educated Liberian children, like their U.S. counterparts, learned the stimulus list quickly and made use of its categorical structure in recalling the items. The non-schooled Liberians, however, learned the list easily when the items were presented, not randomly, but as part of a story. Barbara Rogoff and Kathryn Waddell found that Guatemalan children from a Mayan village also performed better on a memory task made meaningful in terms of their culture.

•On the basis of this evidence, it is difficult to say for certain whether middle childhood is a distinctive stage of development. Biological changes and changes in the way children are treated by adults appear to be universal but because the contexts in which children develop differ across societies, examination of psychological developments requires an understanding of the roles of such contexts as schools and peer groups.

Key Terms

Following are important terms introduced in Chapter 13. Write the definition for each after the term. Then match the term with the letter of the example that best illustrates it.

_____ Compensation _____

_____ Concrete operations _____

_____ Conservation _____

_____ Identity _____

_____ Knowledge base _____

_____ Lateralization _____

_____ Memory organization _____

_____ Memory strategies _____

_____ Metamemory _____

_____ Negation _____

_____ Rehearsal _____

_____ Reversibility _____

_____ Social perspective-taking _____

a. In answering a question about conservation, a child points out that two lumps of clay were the same weight to begin with and that nothing has been added or removed; therefore, they must still be equal although they now look different.

b. When asked if two lists of words are equally difficult to learn, a boy says that it will take longer for him to learn the longer list.

c. Understanding that objects' basic physical properties, such as weight, volume, and quantity, remain the same despite changes in appearance.

d. Procedures that help people remember things more effectively; for example, tying strings on their fingers or writing themselves notes.

e. A child realizes that the transformation performed in a conservation task can be undone; for example, by pouring the water back into the original container.

f. Ways of transforming information (combining, separating, etc.) that fit into a logical system.

g. A 10-year-old gets a phone number from "directory assistance" but has no pencil to write it down; she keeps it in memory by repeating it to herself over and over.

h. A boy notices that, when liquid is poured into another container, the greater height of the second glass is balanced by a decrease in width.

i. Children take advantage of internal structure in remembering a list of words, grouping the mammals together, the flowers together, and the fish together.

j. A mental operation in which a child thinks through an action and then reverses it.

k. This gets larger the more experience children have with particular topics or activities.

l. Being able to think about how other people will perceive one's actions and ideas.

m. This process is thought to be related to handedness.

Fill-in Review

Cover the list of answers next to the statements below. Then uncover each answer after you complete each statement.

teeth

1. In many cultures, children are considered ready for new responsibilities when they begin to lose their baby _____.

lateralization

2. Some biological theorists believe that many of children's accomplishments during middle childhood can be attributed to an increase in the degree of _____ of their brains.

3. Between 5 and 7 years of age, children's electroencephalograms begin to shift from a preponderance of theta activity to a preponderance of _____ activity.   *alpha*

4. Eight-year-olds, as opposed to younger children, are able to carry out tasks on the basis of preliminary _____.   *instructions*

5. It is not known whether older children have greater memory _____ or whether they simply use what they have more efficiently.   *capacity*

6. Two effective memory strategies are _____ and memory _____.   *rehearsal;organization*

7. We can say that a boy who has read many books about dinosaurs has a greater _____ base on this topic than one who has not.   *knowledge*

8. _____, knowledge about their own memory processes, is more developed in older children than in preschoolers.   *Metamemory*

9. When children mentally transform objects and information in a logical manner they are engaging in concrete _____.   *operations*

10. _____ is the Piagetian term for understanding that an object's underlying properties remain the same when its appearance is changed.   *Conservation*

11. Children explain their correct answers on conservation tasks in terms of negation or _____, identity, or _____.   *reversibility; compensation*

12. Middle childhood also sees an increase in children's abilities to logically _____ a collection of objects into groups and subgroups.   *classify*

13. Children perform better on tasks like the three-mountain problem and are better at communicating with other people as their _____ skills increase.   *perspective-taking*

14. According to John Flavell, because our own points of view are always the most accessible to us, even adults are "at risk" for _____ thinking.   *egocentric*

15. Many cross-cultural studies of cognitive development show that children from nonindustrial societies attain _____ _____ a year or more later than children from industrialized societies.   *concrete operations*

16. _____ them on conservation tasks is one way to determine whether children from traditional cultures understand conservation but fail to show their knowledge because of unfamiliarity with the task.   *Training*

17. Children with a great deal of practice in a particular activity attain concrete operations related to that activity _____ than children without comparable experience.   *earlier*

18. Some cultural differences on conservation tasks are due to experimenters' lack of fluency in the subjects' _____.   *language*

19. Children who have not attended school typically perform poorly on _____ _____ memory tasks, in which a large number of objects are presented to subjects in random order.   *free recall*

20. When items to be remembered are presented as part of a _____, unschooled villagers are quite skilled at recalling the items.   *story*

Multiple-Choice Practice Questions

Circle the letter of the word or phrase that correctly completes each statement.

1. When children are between the ages of 5 and 7, their brains
   a. double in size and weight.
   b. begin the process of lateralization.
   c. shift their electrical activity to a preponderance of theta waves.
   d. become nearly completely myelinated.

2. During middle childhood
   a. children grow at the same rate as they did during the preschool period.
   b. children increase in height by 1 1/2 feet and in weight by 50 pounds, on the average.
   c. children grow faster than at any time since early infancy.
   d. do not grow appreciably.

3. Increases in memory performance during middle childhood can be attributed to
   a. more efficient use of memory capacity.
   b. increased use of strategies such as rehearsal.
   c. an increasing knowledge base.
   d. All of the above.

4. Metamemory refers to a person's
   a. memory capacity.
   b. knowledge relating to the information being recalled.
   c. knowledge about the process of remembering.
   d. use of organization to help remember a list of items.

5. A child who, in correctly answering a question about conservation of liquid quantity, says, "They're still the same because, even though the level now looks higher, the second container is skinnier" is justifying her answer in terms of
   a. negation.
   b. reversibility.
   c. identity.
   d. compensation.

6. When shown a display of six daisies, three roses, and one daffodil, which child is likely to answer correctly when asked, "Are there more daisies or more flowers?"
   a. A 3-year-old
   b. A 5-year-old
   c. An 8-year-old
   d. All of the above.

7. One reason for preschoolers' problems on conservation tasks is that they focus their attention on
   a. only one aspect of the stimulus situation.
   b. two aspects of the stimulus at the same time.

c. other stimuli besides the ones presented.

d. their own actions with respect to the stimuli.

8. At about what age is egocentrism finally completely overcome?

a. 3 years

b. 5 years

c. 7 years

d. Never—even adults are sometimes egocentric.

9. People from traditional, nonindustrial societies perform better on conservation tasks when

a. the experimenters are fluent speakers of their language.

b. they are familiarized with the tasks through training sessions.

c. Both a and b.

d. None of the above—conservation performance is not greatly affected by task variables.

10. Schooled people have an advantage over unschooled people on which aspect of memory performance?

a. Rehearsal

b. Free recall tasks

c. Memory capacity

d. Remembering stories

Short-Answer Questions

1. Why is it difficult to determine the extent to which biological development during middle childhood *causes* the changes in behavior that characterize this period? Give examples.

2. Show how increases during middle childhood in children's ability to think about more than one thing at a time is reflected in their performance on perspective-taking tasks, measures of concrete operations, and in their increasing ability to communicate with others.

3. What important changes take place in children's memory performance during middle childhood? How are these changes affected by cultural context?

4. What cultural factors affect the age at which children attain concrete operational thought in a particular content area? What aspects of task presentation are important?

Putting It All Together

As children grow older, they learn more and more about the world. One thing they learn is that certain properties of people and objects remain the same despite changes in the way they look. Using examples, show how this knowledge develops in various ways during infancy, the preschool period, and middle childhood.

Sources of More Information

Cole, Michael, and **Silvia Scribner.** *Culture and Thought.* New York: Wiley, 1974.
This book describes studies of cognitive development carried out in Liberia.

Elkind, David. *Children and Adolescents: Interpretive Essays on Jean Piaget* (3rd ed.). New York: Oxford University Press, 1981.
This book of essays was inspired by Piaget's theory of cognitive development.

Inhelder, Barbel, and **Jean Piaget.** *The Early Growth of Logic in the Child.* New York: Norton, 1969.
The authors discuss the development of children's skills in logical classification.

Neisser, Ulric (Ed.). *Memory Observed: Remembering in Natural Contexts.* San Francisco: W. H. Freeman, 1982.
The selections in this book provide good examples of the effect of context on cognitive processes.

Serpell, Robert. Measures of Perception, Skills and Intelligence: The Growth of a New Perspective on Children in a Third World Country. In Willard Hartup (Ed.), *Review of Child Development Research.* Chicago: University of Chicago Press, 1982.
The author reviews research on cross-cultural variations in perceptual and cognitive tasks and discusses ways that imposing Western cultural interpretations on behavior can be avoided.

Tanner, J. M. *Fetus into Man.* Cambridge: Harvard University Press, 1978.
This is a comprehensive review of normal growth and development.

Answer Key

Answers to Key Terms: h, f, c, a, k, m, i, d, b, e, g, j, l.

Answers to Practice Questions: 1. d, 2. b, 3. d, 4. c, 5. d, 6. c, 7. a, 8. d, 9. c, 10. b.

CHAPTER

14

SCHOOLING AND DEVELOPMENT IN MIDDLE CHILDHOOD

Throughout the world, middle childhood is a time when children are expected to begin to learn the skills they will need in order to be productive adult members of their societies. In modern, industrialized countries, children of this age spend much of their time in school, learning literacy, mathematics, and other culturally valued knowledge.

When children begin school, they already know a great deal about language and may know the names of the letters of the alphabet, a system that represents each significant sound with a different symbol. They can usually count numbers and objects, using their fingers or other body parts to help keep track of quantity. They are also experienced at making inferences on the basis of partial signs; for example, they know that, if the car is not in the driveway, their friend next door may not be at home. In school, children will build on these skills, working within a specialized environment with its own rules and even its own ways of using language.

Most of the cognitive changes associated with middle childhood are not direct results of schooling; however, children who have been to school perform better on tasks that resemble school activities. Schooling has its greatest effect on opportunity: children who are not educated have little chance for later economic success.

Because of the importance of schooling for later success, there has been great interest in tests that will predict school performance, and intelligence tests are now routinely used for that purpose. In fact, psychologists do not agree on what intelligence is, but since tests of intelligence seem primarily to measure aptitude for schooling, they are moderately successful in predicting who will do well and who is likely to have problems. In addition to aptitude, students need environments conducive to learning in order to succeed academically. For many students, school atmosphere and teacher expectations can make a difference between success and failure.

Chapter Outline

Because of the importance of education in shaping children's later lives, the study of learning and development in school contexts is an active area of research for developmental psychologists.

I. The Contexts in Which Skills Are Taught

Although all children are raised to learn the basic knowledge, beliefs, and skills important in their culture, **education**—the deliberate teaching of specialized knowledge and skills—is not an important activity in all cultures. In hunter-gatherer societies, skills are taught as a part of everyday activity. Once societies become more complex, **apprenticeships**, which combine instruction with productive work, provide training for specialized occupations. In contrast to children taught in schools, apprentices learn through observation and practice, put their skills to work from the beginning, and are taught through oral rather than written language. The workshop is likely to contain people of all ages, and the master is a parental figure to the young apprentices.

II. The Nature of School Learning

Written notation systems serve as a form of memory, extending language in space and time. Historically, literacy and numeracy are fairly recent human achievements, having developed along with the rise of large civilizations.

A. Thousands of years ago, before writing systems were developed, small clay tokens served to represent objects used in trade. When the number of tokens increased to the point that the system became cumbersome, people began to substitute pictures of the tokens, then to represent the sounds of language. Since cuneiform writing was difficult to master, schools were established to train young people to be scribes.

B. It is only in more recent times, since the industrial revolution, that mandatory schooling and mass literacy have become widespread. At first, only children of the elite received a high level of education; today, many societies expect all children to attain such a level. This can, however, be a challenge to modern educational systems, which use teaching methods—based on drill and practice and oral imitation of the teacher—developed for large groups, and which are faced with an ever greater volume of information considered part of "the basics."

C. The modern alphabet was developed by the ancient Greeks and is a descendant of cuneiform writing. Each letter corresponds to a different basic sound or *phoneme*. In other kinds of writing systems, each symbol corresponds to a basic concept or to a unit of sound. For English and many other languages, a phonetic system is the most efficient, allowing all words to be represented using only 26 symbols.

D. Jean Chall has classified children's mastery of reading into six stages:

•Stage 0, *prereading* (birth-age 6). Children learn to interpret events on the basis of partial signs, can identify familiar logos, and have some knowledge of the properties of words.

•Stage 1, *decoding* (ages 6-7). Children learn the ways written symbols correspond to the sounds of spoken language.

•Stage 2, *confirmation, fluency, ungluing from print* (ages 7-8). Children now move to rapid and fluent decoding.

•Stage 3, *reading for learning something new* (ages 9-14). Children progress from "learning to read" to "reading to learn." Reading at Stage 3 involves both "bottom up" processing (sounding out letters to produce words, adding these together, etc.) and "top down" processing (integrating material with previous knowledge).

•Stage 4, *multiple viewpoints* (ages 15-18). Readers must reconcile different viewpoints in order to interpret the meaning of a text.

•Stage 5, *construction and reconstruction* (post-secondary level). Texts become aids in solving problems as readers use them to help construct their own knowledge.

E. Learning arithmetic in school builds on children's prior ability to do things with numbers. Children generally use body parts, such as fingers, to aid them in solving arithmetic problems; some societies have developed elaborate counting systems based on body parts or on conventional counters such as shells. When children first study arithmetic, they must learn the conventions of representing numbers in writing before they can actually learn to solve problems.

Throughout the years, there has been debate about the most effective ways to teach children reading and arithmetic. In the 1960s, the "look-say" approach to teaching reading, which had led to the use of greatly simplified texts, was replaced by more traditional phonics instruction, which had been popular during the nineteenth century. Today, instruction emphasizes both phonetic analysis and reading for meaning. In mathematics instruction, the debate has been between the "drill and practice" approach, which is very effective for learning rapid responses, and a "learning with understanding" approach, which is better at helping children generalize their knowledge to new problems. Recent research points to the importance of both types of instruction.

F. In school, children are exposed to **instructional discourse**, a pattern of language peculiar to that setting. Instructional discourse provides students with information about the curriculum and with feedback about the correctness of their answers while providing the teacher with information about their progress. A feature of instructional discourse is the **initiation-reply-evaluation sequence**; frequently, this takes the form of questions to which the teacher already knows the answer. In the specialized language of school, context does not always help children interpret the teacher's questions and they have to focus on language itself in order to master the information presented.

III. The Cognitive Consequences of Schooling

Since schooling provides children with instruction in remembering and in problem-solving and greatly expands their knowledge base, some of the cognitive changes associated with middle childhood might be attributed to schooling, not to general developmental processes. Psychologists have studied the effects of schooling on various aspects of cognitive development.

A. The evidence suggests that schooling does not affect children's attainment of concrete operations. However, school experience may increase children's familiarity with testing procedures, making their performance appear accelerated compared with that of unschooled children.

B. In the opinion of some psychologists, lexical organization of children's vocabularies is affected by schooling. For example, children who have attended school are more sensitive to the abstract, categorical meanings of words. They show this by responding with words from the same category when asked for associations to a particular word (a child might respond "salmon" to the word "trout").

C. Schooling appears to be the factor underlying cultural differences on standard memory tests. These differences are most pronounced in cases in which the materials to be remembered are not connected by an everyday script; they disappear when the materials are part of a meaningful setting. No evidence suggests that schooling increases actual memory capacity.

D. Schooling seems to influence the degree to which children can reflect on and talk about their own cognitive processes and explain how they reach solutions to problems. This ability is called **metacognition.**

E. Except for increasing children's ability to reflect on their own thought processes, schooling does not appear to change the basic cognitive processes associated with middle childhood, although schooled children have an advantage in performing cognitive tasks closely related to school activities. Probably the most important effect of schooling on children's lives is the opportunity it gives them to perform other activities later on, particularly those leading to economic power and increased social status.

IV. Aptitude for Schooling

For many years, the idea of intelligence" has influenced discussion of the question of why some children learn more easily in school than others. While people of all cultures have words in their languages referring to intelligence, the exact meanings of the terms differ across cultures. In the U. S., intelligence tests are used to predict children's aptitude for schooling; they also influence the kind of education children receive.

A. Once mass education became widespread, educators became interested in finding out why some children had difficulty learning in school. In 1904, Alfred Binet and Theordore Simon were commissioned by the French Minister of Public Instruction to develop a screening exam to identify children who needed special instruction. Binet and Simon based their test on the premise that a child who performed at the level of the average 7-year-old on their tasks had a **mental age (MA)** of 7, regardless of his chronological age. An intelligent child would have a mental age greater than his chronological age, while the MA of a dull child would be less than his chronological age. While Binet and Simon felt that performance on their test was determined by both "nature" and "nurture," they specified no way in which the effects of these factors could be separated.

B. Binet and Simon's test came into use in many countries. In the U. S., it was modified by Lewis Terman of Stanford University. An updated version of the Stanford-Binet is in use today, as are intelligence scales developed by David Wechsler for use with adults and children. The concept **IQ** (intelligence quotient), introduced by William Stern, refers to MA/CA X 100. So, for example, a 10-year-old with an MA of 11 would have an IQ of 110. Using IQ, the intelligence scores of children of different ages can be compared. The procedure underlying today's IQ tests, like those of the test developed by Binet and Simon, are as follows: create a set of test items on which the performance of children of the same age will vary; order the items in terms of difficulty; and make certain that performance on the test corresponds to school performance.

•The essential properties of intelligence continue to be a matter of debate for psychologists. Intelligence is usually thought of as a general characteristic of people's behavior, and indeed, performance on separate tasks within IQ tests is highly correlated. However, some scholars feel that IQ tests measure only those aptitudes which relate to success in school, and in fact school tasks do differ in systematic ways from those encountered in other settings. Some investigators have proposed the existence of many different kinds of intelligence. Naturally, not all of these would be measured by traditional IQ tests.

•Disagreements about the nature of intelligence are complicated by differences found between the average scores of members of different ethnic groups. According to the **innatist hypothesis of intelligence**, embraced by many psychologists during the 1920s, these differences are due to inborn variations and cannot be eliminated through training or other environmental manipulations. During the 1930s and 1940s, this view was balanced by the **environmentalist hypothesis of intelligence**, which viewed intelligence as greatly influenced by experience. The debate became more heated during the 1960s when it grew to encompass the question of whether federally funded projects such as Head Start were capable of improving children's school achievement.

•Currently, psychologists recognize that both genetic and environmental factors contribute to the intelligence test performance of individuals. It is difficult to specify the exact contribution of each for the same reasons—detailed in Chapter 2—that it is difficult to specify the genetic and environmental contributions to any human behavior. Because all intelligence tests draw on a background of learning that is culture-specific, comparisons of intelligence between cultural groups are extremely difficult to make. Studies indicate that within-group differences may have a substantial genetic component; however, because of noncomparability of environments, there is no evidence that average score differences between ethnic groups are due to genetic factors. In addition, because heritability is a population statistic—meaning that it applies to groups of people, rather than to individuals—measures of heritability do not tell the percentage of a person's IQ score that is attributable to heredity; instead, they estimate the percentage of variability within a group of people (raised under similar conditions) that is attributable to heredity. When environment is radically changed—for example, by a change in socioeconomic status—IQ will reflect this. For example, although U. S. blacks as a group score below the national average on standard IQ measures, Sandra Scarr and Richard Weinberg found that children of black working-class parents who were adopted by white middle-class families scored, as a group, almost precisely at the national average.

V. The School and the Community

Peer influence and school atmosphere, as well as inherited ability and home environment, affect the likelihood of children's success in school.

A. William Labov and Clarence Robbins examined ways that children's peer groups may negatively affect their school performance. Their study was carried out in central Harlem in New York City; the school performance of boys in grades 4 to 10 who participated in ganglike groups was compared with that of boys who did not. Labov and Robbins found that, while reading scores increased as nongroup members moved from grade to grade, group members made virtually no improvement over the course of the study.

B. Research by Michael Rutter and his colleagues indicates that schools are not helpless in the face of peer group influence, and that school atmosphere can make a difference in achievement. Studying secondary schools in central London, they found that the most successful schools were characterized by an emphasis on academics; teachers who were skillful at coordinating class activities; greater emphasis on praise than punishment; and the expectation that students should take on some of the responsibility for a clean and pleasant classroom atmosphere.

Other research has shown that children's performance is influenced by teachers' expectations. Robert Rosenthal and his colleagues found improvements in IQ scores among a group of children whose teachers had been led to believe that they were likely to "bloom" intellectually during the school year. Not all studies have found effects of teachers' expectations, but this may be due in part to differences in the ways teachers respond to such suggestions. Work by Carol Dweck and her colleagues has indicated that teachers have different expectations for boys and for girls, and that these are reflected in the kinds of feedback they give children and, in turn, in children's expectations about their own behavior.

C. Although schooling is an important part of middle childhood in many societies, it does not represent all of children's lives. Chapter 15 examines the characteristics of children's peer groups and the effects of peer interaction on development.

Key Terms

Following are important terms introduced in Chapter 14. Write the definition for each after the term. Then match the term with the letter of the example that best illustrates it.

_____ Apprenticeship _____

_____ Education _____

_____ Environmentalist hypothesis of IQ _____

_____ Initiation-reply-evaluation sequence _____

_____ Innatist hypothesis of IQ _____

_____ Instructional discourse _____

_____ IQ _____

_____ Mental age (MA) _____

_____ Metacognition _____

a. A kind of verbal exchange frequent in schools, in which a teacher asks a question, a student answers, and the teacher provides feedback.
b. This would be equal to 8 for a child who can answer questions on an intelligence test as well as the average 8-year-old.
c. In older children, this is more developed than it is in preschoolers, as reflected by their greater ability to explain their solutions to problems.

d. This form of deliberate teaching is not characteristic of hunter-gatherer societies.
e. A kind of language used in schools that varies in important ways from everyday language.
f. According to this idea, one would expect people's intelligence scores to be more highly similar the more closely related they are.
g. In this kind of job training, the participant often lives in the master's house.
h. A number used to compare the intelligence of different people.
i. This idea is supported by evidence that improving children's environments raises their scores on IQ tests.

Fill-in Review

Cover the list of answers next to the statements below. Then uncover each answer after you complete each statement.

1. _____ is a form of socialization involving deliberate teaching of specialized knowledge and skills; _____ is a form of education in which instruction and productive labor are combined. *Education* *apprenticeship*

2. The first precursors of literacy were small clay _____ that represented objects used in trade; when this system became too cumbersome, _____ writing on clay tablets was developed. *tokens* *cuneiform*

3. The first _____ were places where young men were trained to be scribes. *schools*

4. Before mass education became widespread, children of the upper classes were educated privately by _____. *tutors*

5. The rapid accumulation of _____ poses problems for modern systems of education. *knowledge*

6. The _____ is based on a system of representing each separate phoneme with a symbol; in some languages, symbols represent basic concepts or each possible _____. *alphabet* *syllable*

7. In the _____ stage, children learn to interpret events on the basis of partial signs, while in Stage 1, 6- to 7-year-olds learn to _____ the sets of letters that make up words. *prereading* *decode*

8. In Stage 2, the decoding of 7- to 8-year-olds becomes more rapid and _____. *fluent*

9. Stage 3 readers, 9- to 14-year-olds, read to _____ rather than simply learning to read. *learn*

10. During Stage 3, readers engage in _____ processing, in which the words and phrases they are reading are integrated with prior knowledge. *top-down*

11. Fifteen- to 18-year-old readers are expected to reconcile different _____ while reading; in the highest level of reading, Stage 5, post-secondary students need to use reading materials as aids to solving _____. *viewpoints* *problems*

counting   12. Many societies have developed elaborate _____ systems using shells, tokens, or parts of the body.

phonics   13. Educators have found that reading instruction which includes _____ is more effective than that based on the "look-say" method alone.

drill   14. Modern mathematics instruction includes both _____ in computation
generalizing   and practice in _____ computation skills to new problems.

discourse; evaluation   15. One kind of instructional _____ is the initiation-reply-_____ sequence.

Schooling   16. _____ does not have an appreciable effect on children's development of concrete operations.

17. When asked for their associations to a word, children who have been to school
category   are likely to respond with another word from the same _____.

remembering   18. Schooled children do better than unschooled children at _____ lists of unrelated materials; they are also better able to describe the logic underlying their
metacognition   solutions to problems, an ability called _____.

IQ; mental age   19. A child's _____ is arrived at by dividing his _____ by his chronological age and multiplying by 100.

innatist   20. According to the _____ hypothesis of intelligence, differences between people's intelligence scores are due mainly to inborn factors; the environmentalist hypothesis, on the other hand, view intelligence as being highly dependent
experience   on _____.

21. Modern intelligence tests are moderately good at predicting children's perfor-
school   mance in _____.

22. It has not yet proved possible to develop an intelligence test that is truly
culture-free   _____.

23. While about half the variability in IQ scores within ethnic groups may be due to
between   inherited factors, there is no evidence that differences _____ groups are genetically based.

24. Research by William Labov and Clarence Robbins demonstrated that participa-
peer   tion in some _____ groups may negatively affect children's school performance.

25. Michael Rutter and his colleagues found that the most successful schools were
academic; praise   those which had a strong _____ emphasis, which relied on _____ rather than punishment, which stressed student responsibility, and whose
teachers   _____ were skilled in coordinating the class.

Multiple-Choice Practice Questions

Circle the letter of the word or phrase that correctly completes each statement.

1. Schooling
   a. trains children to remember lists of unrelated items.
   b. expands children's knowledge base.
   c. trains children to explain their reasoning in solving problems.
   d. All of the above.

2. The symbols in the alphabet represent
   a. phonemes.
   b. morphemes.
   c. basic concepts.
   d. syllables.

3. When children can recognize the logo of their favorite fast-food restaurant
   a. it means that they know how to read.
   b. they are taking a first step in learning to read.
   c. they are using "bottom up" processing.
   d. it means that they have reached the stage of concrete operations.

4. Today, a typical reading curriculum emphasizes
   a. the look-say method.
   b. learning letter-sound correspondences.
   c. reading for meaning.
   d. both b and c.

5. Using the body as a counting device
   a. is a practice of certain Pacific Island cultures.
   b. is a universal strategy for keeping track of quantity.
   c. is a hindrance in learning to count.
   d. only works for numbers up to 10.

6. Which is an example of instructional discourse?
   a. On the first day of school, the teacher asks a child, "What is your name?"
   b. The teacher asks the class, "Has anyone seen my red pencil?"
   c. After writing a word on the blackboard, the teacher asks, "What does this say?"
   d. All of the above are examples.

7. Schooling affects children's performance on which of the following?
   a. Memory for items connected by an everyday script.
   b. Concrete operations in everyday contexts.
   c. Ability to describe their mental activities.
   d. All of the above.

8. A 9-year-old child with a mental age of 10 has an IQ of
   a. 90.

   b. 100.
   c. 119.
   d. 111.

9. Intelligence tests are composed of questions that
   a. can be answered equally well by children of the same age.
   b. are culture-free.
   c. are ordered from least to most difficult.
   d. are selected to be unrelated to school performance.

10. Studies of heritability of intelligence have shown that
    a. differences in IQ scores within cultural groups is attributable, to some extent, to genetic factors.
    b. differences in IQ scores between cultural groups are largely attributable to genetic factors.
    c. about 50 percent of each person's IQ score is caused by genetic factors.
    d. All of the above.

11. While studying secondary schools in central London, Michael Rutter and his colleagues found that the most successful schools were those that
    a. served students with higher IQs.
    b. punished students whenever they misbehaved.
    c. had more modern buildings and better paid teachers.
    d. expected a great deal of students and emphasized academic achievement.

12. Carol Dweck and her colleagues, studying teachers' expectations of boys and girls in the classroom, found that
    a. boys are better behaved than girls during elementary school.
    b. overall, teachers criticize girls more than boys.
    c. girls are likely to be praised for cooperation rather than intellectual accomplishments.
    d. boys are less likely than girls to blame others for their own poor performance.

Short-Answer Questions

1. Discuss the differences between apprenticeship education and school learning.

2. Trace the development of children's literacy skills from the preschool period to the post-secondary level.

3. What differences have been found between the performance of schooled and unschooled children on cognitive tasks?

4. Describe the basic elements of standardized intelligence testing.

5. What evidence is there for the importance of genetic factors in determining children's IQs? What evidence is there for the importance of environmental factors?

Putting It All Together

Look back at the information on gene-environment interactions in Chapter 2. On the basis of what you have learned from Chapter 2 and from Chapter 14, discuss why it is difficult to assess the role of genetic factors in intelligence. In what ways does feedback in gene-environment interactions complicate the picture?

Sources of More Information

Baumeister, Alfred A. Mental Retardation: Some Conceptions And Dilemmas. *American Psychologist*, 1987, *42* (8), 796-800.
This discussion of mental retardation touches on some of the issues involved in the use of standardized tests to measure intelligence.

Bissex, Glenda L. *Guys at Work: A Child Learns to Write and Read.* Cambridge, Mass.: Harvard University Press, 1980.
This case study follows one child from age 5 to age 11 as he learns to read and write.

Copeland, Richard. *How Children Learn Mathematics*, 4th ed. New York: Macmillan, 1984.
This is a Piagetian approach to the learning of mathematics in the elementary classroom. There are good descriptions of the many numerical concepts children acquire as they learn to manipulate numbers.

Eisenstein, Elizabeth L. On the Printing Press as an Agent of Change. In David Olson, Nancy Torrance, and Angela Hildyard (Eds.), *Literacy, Language and Learning: The Nature and Consequences of Reading and Writing.* Cambridge: Cambridge University Press, 1985.
This is a discussion of social change as related to the invention of literacy.

Gardner, Howard. *Frames of Mind: The Theory of Multiple Intelligences.* New York: Basic Books, 1983.
This book presents Gardner's theory that every person has a unique set of competencies that together comprise his or her intelligence. Gardner describes seven intelligences, some of which are not included in commonly used IQ tests.

Nichols, Robert C. Schools and the Disadvantaged (A Summary of the Coleman Report). In Urie Bronfenbrenner and Maureen Mahony (Eds.), *Influences on Human Development*, 2nd ed. Hinsdale, Ill.: Dryden, 1975.
A discussion of how the environment of education affects children's academic achievement.

Rubenstein, Joseph, and **Brent Slife** (Eds). *Taking sides: Clashing Views on Controversial Psychological Issues*, 5th ed. Issue #12: "Can Intelligence Be Measured With a Single Score?" Guilford, Conn.: Dushkin, 1988.
The two sides of this controversy are represented by the views of Arthur Jensen, who believes that intelligence is a single, unitary trait, and Howard Gardner, who believes in the existence of multiple intelligences.

Trotter, Robert J. Three Heads Are Better Than One. *Psychology Today*, August 1986, 56-62.
This article presents Robert Sternberg's triarchic theory, which hypothesizes componential, experiential, and contextual aspects of intelligence.

Answer Key

Answers to Key Terms: g, d, i, a, f, e, h, b, c.

Answers to Practice Questions: 1. d, 2. a, 3. b, 4. d, 5. b, 6. c, 7. c, 8. d, 9. c, 10. a, 11. d, 12. c.

15

THE SOCIAL RELATIONS OF MIDDLE CHILDHOOD

Although the changes that usher in the period called middle childhood are biological, behavioral, and social, it is in the social domain that the greatest discontinuities in development arise as children move from the shelter of parental supervision to new contexts and challenges. Six- to 12-year-olds are more often left to the company of their peers than they were during the preschool period. They are expected to take responsibility for their activities during this time, get along with other children, and follow the social rules of their society even when no one is watching. They are also expected to take on personal responsibilities, such as completing homework, practicing musical instruments, feeding pets, and regulating their own behavior in numerous other ways. Their play begins to include more complex and competitive games, and the role-playing of early childhood gives way to Scrabble and Monopoly.

These changes in social behavior depend to some extent on the cognitive abilities that children are developing. At the same time, new opportunities for interaction with other children serve in turn as stimuli for further cognitive development. Parents and teachers recognize children's greater competencies and adjust their expectations accordingly. And cultural variations in behavior become more pronounced as the adults in children's environments push them toward the kinds of skills and social interactions that are valued and useful in their particular societies.

Chapter Outline

During middle childhood, children spend more time than before with **peers**, children of their own age and status, and less time with parents. This leads to the development of new cognitive and social skills that complement those learned in school. Children's sense of themselves changes as they come to inhabit new contexts, and parental socialization techniques shift from physically removing them from danger to explanation and discussion. Because children spend more time away from adult supervision, it is also more difficult for psychologists to study their behavior in contexts outside of school.

I. Games and Group Regulation

Piaget suggested that game-playing was an important aspect of children's developing ability to regulate their own social interactions.

A. In middle childhood, children continue the fantasy play, based on *roles*, begun in the preschool period; now, however, games based upon *rules* move into a position of prominence. **Rule-based games** require children to pursue goals while keeping a set of overall instructions in mind, to engage in social perspective-taking, and to coordinate their own actions with those that other players may be planning. Rule-based games often involve large groups of children and typically last longer than preschoolers' interactions do.

B. According to Piaget, rule-based games are a manifestation of concrete operations in children's social spheres, and they contribute to development by providing structured circumstances in which children can practice balancing the rules of society against their own desires. Piaget studied children's ideas about rules by observing them playing the game of marbles. He concluded that preschoolers had no particular idea of the rules or any sense of competition. During middle childhood, children began to play to win. At first, children would not agree to any alterations in the rules, believing that they had been handed down by authority figures and could not be changed; between the ages of 9 and 11, they began to treat the rules as social conventions that could be changed if the other players agreed. Piaget found that boys engaged in more competitive play based on rules than girls did during middle childhood, a finding that has been confirmed by Janet Lever's observations. Boys also tend to play in larger groups. However, rule-based games increase in importance during middle childhood for children of both sexes.

II. Reasoning and Action in Different Rule Domains

During middle childhood, children must learn to understand social rules in several different domains. From most general to most specific, these are **moral rules**, such as prohibitions against killing and stealing that are found in some form in all societies; **social conventions** regulating such things as sex-typed behavior, which are specific to particular societies; **group norms**, which apply to small groups such as peer groups; and **personal rules**, which are created by individuals to regulate their own behavior. By the time children are 5 years of age, they can recognize the differences between moral principles and social conventions. Larry Nucci found that, when asked to compare violations of rules, children ranked moral violations as most serious, then violations of social conventions; they ranked violations of personal rules as least serious.

A. Piaget found that during late middle childhood, children began to judge behavior on the basis of autonomous moral reasoning. This, he thought, was a result of their increasing cognitive abilities and new forms of interaction with their peers. Lawrence Kohlberg elaborated on these ideas in an extensive research program studying the development of children's moral reasoning. Based on subjects' responses to a series of story-dilemmas, Kohlberg classified moral reasoning into six stages—two stages at each of three levels—representing people's thinking from 3 years of age through adulthood. At the *preconventional* level, corresponding to the preoperational stage of thought, moral judgments are based on the physical consequences of actions; at the *conventional* level, corresponding to concrete operational thought, moral judgments depend on conformity to others' expectations; at the *postconventional* level, corresponding to formal operational thought, judgments are based on abstract, universal principles.

B. Instead of studying moral reasoning, William Damon studied 4- to 12-year-olds' ideas about **positive justice**, how resources should be divided or rewards distributed. The responses he obtained indicated that, as with moral reasoning, ideas of fairness develop through a sequence of levels: under 4 years of age, children simply state their desires, giving no reasons for their choice; 4- to 5-year-olds state their desires but justify their choices on the basis of external characteristics ("The girls should get more," for example); 5- to 7-year-olds tend to believe that strict equality is the only fair treatment when dividing resources. From about age 8 on, notions of deserving-ness and merit enter their reasoning; 8- to 10-year-olds' responses reflect moral relativity; and children older than 10 are able to coordinate the claims of different people and the demands of the particular situation. Damon also compared children's reasoning levels with their actual behavior when they were asked to divide candy bars given as "payment" for making bracelets. He found that in about 50 percent of the cases, children's behavior matched their reasoning level; in 10 percent of the cases, their behavior was at a higher level; and in 40 percent, it was lower.

C. Elliot Turiel and his colleagues used an interviewing technique to study the development of children's reasoning about social conventions, such as the one that certain occupations are more appropriate for men or for women. He found that children passed through three levels of reasoning about conventions: at the first level, they treated conventions similarly to moral rules; at the second, they rejected the need for conventions; and at the third level, they recognized that, although they are arbitrary, social conventions do serve some purpose in regulating social life. While some cross-cultural studies have found similar results in other societies, there are cultures in which breaches of social conventions are treated more like moral violations than they are in our society. Children do not necessarily reason at the same level about all kinds of social rules. Most likely, children's evaluations of transgressions depend upon context, cultural norms, and other factors as well.

III. Relations With Other Children

During middle childhood, children need more than ever to be able to make places for themselves within the social group.

A. Children's ideas about friendship undergo development during middle childhood. Preschoolers' friends are the children who live near them and with whom they play frequently. By age 9 or 10, children consider friends to be people they know well, with whom they share interests and abilities, and who have compatible personalities. Friendship in middle childhood also has connotations of loyalty and commitment.

•Robert Selman predicted that those children who were skilled at taking another's perspective would also have more sophisticated ideas about friendship; when he measured children's performance on various tasks, he found this to be true. These results support the idea that perspective-taking is a key factor in developmental changes in concepts of friendship during middle childhood.

•Observations have shown that children can have true friendships even if they are not able to talk about them in conceptual terms; however, higher levels of reasoning about friendship give children **social repair mechanisms** that allow them to remain friends when differences arise, thus permitting greater freedom from adult supervision.

•During middle childhood, children tend to segregate themselves by sex, although boys and girls do participate in joint activities on many occasions. Boys tend to have larger groups of friends and to play more boisterous, competitive games; girls have fewer, more intimate friends with whom they share feelings and exchange confidences.

B. The relative popularity of children in a group can be studied using a **sociogram** of friendship choices. The children named as friends by the most people are assumed to be the most popular. Many studies have found that popularity is related to physical attractiveness; however, popular children tend to be friendlier, more outgoing and helpful, brighter, and more socially skilled than other children. Martha Putallaz found that the social skills boys revealed while playing with two unfamiliar children in the laboratory predicted their popularity in first grade, four months later. Researchers studying the emergence of group structure in play groups of previously unacquainted boys found that those who became popular were helpful, reminded others of the rules, and were not aggressive; the boys who were rejected were more physically and verbally aggressive than others and were also more talkative and active. Boys neglected by group members were those who rarely interacted with the others.

C. Even when adults are not present, they influence peer interactions through social norms that shape patterns of cooperation, competition, and conflict.

•Studies by Millard Madsen and his colleagues have explored the way that groups choose cooperation or competition to solve problems. He found that Israeli kibbutz children, socialized to cooperate, performed significantly better on a task requiring cooperation than did urban Israeli children. Research in other countries supports the finding that children from cultures that emphasize group cohesion over individualism are more willing to cooperate for the benefit of the group.

•Just as children must learn to get along within a group, groups must learn to get along with one another. Muzafer and Carolyn Sherif, in a summer camp experiment, found that intergroup competition can lead to conflict and hostility. Simply getting the members of two feuding groups together under pleasant circumstances did nothing to reduce hostility, the Sherifs found. Mutual respect replaced dislike only when members of both groups had to cooperate to solve problems affecting everyone's welfare.

D. Does experience with peer interactions help children to develop social perspective-taking ability? Marida Hollos found that while Norwegian and Hungarian children growing up on isolated farms scored just as well as village and town children on tasks measuring logical operations, they were less skilled at social perspective-taking tasks. It appears that peer interaction plays an important role in social-cognitive development during middle childhood; however, relations with parents also remain crucial.

IV. Changing Relations With Parents

By the time children are 8 or 9 years old, their parents are less willing to shelter them than they were previously; by the end of middle childhood, parents expect nearly adult behavior from them. Now, more of children's activities are carried out away from adult supervision. This is especially true for children of working mothers. Research on the effect of maternal employment suggests that it depends on such factors as socioeconomic status, race, family structure, parental attitudes, and where the family lives. Girls seem to be positively affected by having mothers who work, while sons of working mothers are somewhat less well-adjusted than boys whose mothers are not employed outside the home.

Parental child-rearing strategies shift during middle childhood; children are not punished as frequently, and when they do break the rules, the consequences are more likely to involve removal of privileges than spankings. **Coregulation**, in which responsibility for controlling children's behavior is shared by parents and children, becomes more frequent as children grow. Freud felt that during middle childhood, the superego becomes dominant, performing many of the same functions as the parents in regulating behavior.

V. A New Sense of Self

During middle childhood, children come to have a new, more complex understanding of themselves.

A. At the start of middle childhood, children think of themselves as defined by their bodies and the activities they engage in—a *physicalistic* view. They next develop a sense of separate physical and mental "selves," but believe that these must be consistent. But by about 8 years of age, children realize that outward appearance and inner experience may differ and that people have private selves which cannot always be read from their behavior.

B. Children now begin to define themselves in comparison with other children, a process called **social comparison**. Diane Ruble and her colleagues studied the development of social comparison in middle childhood by manipulating the feedback they gave children about their performance on a basketball task. Nine-year-olds who were told the hypothetical scores of previous participants rated their own performance as good or bad relative to these scores; however, 5- and 7-year-olds were equally pleased with their performance regardless of the supposed scores of other children.

C. The new expectations faced by children during middle childhood are challenges to their self-esteem. Susan Harter found that by the time they are 8 years old, children could evaluate themselves, not only in terms of total self-worth, but in terms of cognitive, social, and physical competence. Children's ratings of themselves in these areas, she found, were significantly correlated with their teachers' ratings of their competencies. Stanley Coopersmith discovered that 10- to 12-year-old boys with high self-esteem had parents whose style of child-rearing included acceptance, clearly defined limits, and respect for individuality—characteristics similar to those of Diana Baumrind's "authoritative" parents.

VI. Middle Childhood Reconsidered

When the biological, behavioral, and social components of middle childhood are considered separately, development appears relatively continuous with that of the preschool period. However, the consequence of changes in these domains is a distinctive combination of factors resulting in a bio-social-behavioral shift to a new period of development.

Key Terms

Following are important terms introduced in Chapter 15. Write the definition for each after the term. Then match the term with the letter of the example that best illustrates it.

_____ Coregulation _____

_____ Group norms _____

_____ Moral rules _____

_____ Peers _____

_____ Personal rules _____

_____ Positive justice _____

_____ Rule-based games _____

_____ Social comparison _____

_____ Social conventions _____

_____ Social repair mechanisms _____

_____ Sociogram _____

a. "Start on homework right after school" is an example.
b. Baseball is one of these.
c. For young children, these are provided by caretakers; for older children, their ability to reason about interpersonal relationships is a source of these.
d. For a child in the third grade, these would be other third-graders.
e. This is arrived at by asking each child in a group which children he likes to play with.
f. "It is wrong to kill other people" is an example.
g. A child describes herself as "the best reader in the class."
h. The Girl Scout Laws are examples.
i. Children learn, for example, how to divide a dozen cookies among five children.
j. Wearing a bathing suit to school would violate one of these.
k. This involves sharing responsibility for children's behavior between children and parents.

Fill-in Review

Cover the list of answers next to the statements below. Then uncover each answer after you complete each statement.

adult

1. It can be difficult to study children's social development during middle childhood because much of their behavior takes place outside _____ supervision.

2. While the play of preschoolers is based largely on roles, that of older children is characterized by games based on _____. *rules*

3. Piaget felt that rule-based games are a manifestation of _____ in the social sphere. *concrete operations*

4. During middle childhood, children learn to understand social rules at three different levels: _____ rules, such as prohibitions against killing; _____ conventions, such as what clothes people should wear in public; and _____ rules, such as completing homework before watching T.V. *moral* *social* *personal*

5. Boys are more likely than girls to engage in games based on explicit _____; girls tend to play less complex games in _____ groups. *rules* *smaller*

6. Lawrence Kohlberg classified children's moral reasoning into stages on three levels: the preconventional level, corresponding to the stage of _____ thought; the _____ level, corresponding to the stage of concrete operational thought; and the _____ level, corresponding to the stage of formal operational thought. *preoperational* *conventional* *postconventional*

7. Children need to achieve the moral reasoning of Stage _____, characterized by "instrumental morality," before they can get along with one another without adult supervision. *2*

8. William Damon studied children's ideas about _____, the process of deciding how resources or rewards should be distributed. *positive justice*

9. Damon found that about half of the time the level of children's reasoning matched their _____ in a real situation. *behavior*

10. While Lawrence Kohlberg's view was that moral reasoning grows out of reasoning about social conventions, Elliot Turiel and his colleagues demonstrated that the two kinds of reasoning are _____. *independent*

11. To _____, friends are children of the same age and sex, who live near one another and play together. *preschoolers*

12. During middle childhood, children's ideas about _____ come to include mutual responsibility and support. *friendship*

13. According to Robert Selman, developmental changes in conceptions of friendship are a result of changes in children's ability to take another person's _____. *perspective*

14. While preschoolers and people who are developmentally delayed are capable of true friendship, higher reasoning levels provide older children with social _____ mechanisms that make relationships work more smoothly. *repair*

15. During middle childhood, boys tend to have _____ groups of friends than girls, while girls' friendships tend to be more _____ than boys'. *larger* *intimate*

16. Children's _____ within a group is related to physical attractiveness and social skills. *popularity*

cooperation

17. Children from cultures that value group cohesion over individualism perform better on problem-solving tasks requiring _____.

18. Muzafer and Carolyn Sherif found that by setting up situations requiring two groups of boys to cooperate with one another, they could reverse hostility caused by _____ between the groups.

competition

peer interaction

19. Marida Hollos found that children who had many opportunities for _____ performed better on a perspective-taking task than those growing up in isolation from peers.

20. According to psychiatrist Harry Stack Sullivan, if children fail to form _____ during middle childhood, their later interpersonal relationships will suffer.

friendships

21. During middle childhood, parental control over children's behavior is gradually replaced by _____.

coregulation

22. Preschoolers have a physicalistic view of the self, equating it with particular _____ parts; older children realize that a person's outward appearance may differ from his or her _____ experience.

body
psychological

comparison

23. Social _____ becomes more important in children's self-definitions during middle childhood.

24. Parents who are accepting of their children, set clearly defined limits, and respect their children's individuality, have children with high _____.

self-esteem

25. Although the changes associated with middle childhood do not appear stagelike when viewed separately, taken together they form a _____ shift.

bio-social-behavioral

Multiple-Choice Practice Questions

Circle the letter of the word or phrase that correctly completes each statement.

1. Compared with parents of younger children, parents of children in middle childhood are more likely to
   a. restrict the time children spend with peers.
   b. use physical force to control their children.
   c. rely on coregulation in controlling their children's behavior.
   d. supervise their children closely.

2. During middle childhood, _____ become(s) more important in children's play.
   a. rule-based games
   b. role-playing
   c. props such as blocks and dolls
   d. fantasy

    c. have respect for their individuality.
    d. All of the above.

Short-Answer Questions

1. Why did Piaget feel that rule-based games were an important part of development during middle childhood?

2. Give examples of the kinds of moral reasoning typical of children in Lawrence Kohlberg's Stages 1, 2, and 3.

3. What changes occur in children's ideas about friendship between the preschool period and the end of middle childhood? What relationship exists between these changes and the development of children's perspective-taking abilities?

4. In what ways do children's peer interactions during middle childhood affect their development? Give examples.

5. What major changes occur in children's sense of themselves during the years of middle childhood?

Putting It All Together

Look back at the material on play in Chapters 7 and 10 for help in completing this assignment.

I. Match each of the following examples of play to the developmental period of which it is most characteristic.

_____ 1. Stirring a cup of sand "coffee" with a twig.
_____ 2. Playing police and robbers.
_____ 3. Playing kickball.
_____ 4. Banging a hammer on the table.
_____ 5. Jumping rope.
_____ 6. Cooking a meal on a play stove.
_____ 7. Dressing up in extremely sex-stereotyped clothes.

a. Early infancy (less than 18 months)
b. Late infancy (18-30 months)
c. The preschool period
d. Middle childhood

II. Using an example from each period, show how children's play during infancy, the preschool period, and middle childhood reflects their increasing cognitive skills and how play, in turn, promotes further cognitive development.

CHAPTER

16

BIOLOGICAL AND SOCIAL FOUNDATIONS OF ADOLESCENCE

The end of middle childhood is announced by radical biological changes. During puberty, young people's bodies become adult, both in size and in their capacity for biological reproduction. In industrialized nations, the age at which puberty occurs has gradually fallen over the last 200 years; at the same time, technological developments have increased the amount of education young people need in order to become independent members of society. The result has been a shortening of middle childhood and a lengthening of adolescence—the transitional stage between biological maturity and the full independence of adulthood.

According to many theorists, adolescence is a time of emotional upheaval caused both by hormonal changes and by new social arrangements that characterize this stage. After a long period of relative segregation, boys and girls develop an interest in one another, and peer groups support them in establishing attachments with members of the opposite sex. Relations with parents are also in transition, as adolescents move from positions of dependence to more egalitarian relationships. Many adolescents hold paying jobs, contributing to their feeling of independence. Still, according to our society, adolescents are not ready for adult privileges and need to be protected from adult responsibilities. The resulting separation between biological, behavioral, and social aspects of development gives adolescence its unique character.

Chapter Outline

The bio-social-behavioral shift that marks the end of childhood includes major changes: the greatest biological transition since birth results in reproductive capability; boys and girls begin to interact in new social configurations; and children's relationships with their parents change as they become more independent.

I. Traditional Conceptions of Adolescence

Modern conceptions of adolescence still reflect the opinions of eighteenth- and nineteenth-century scholars who wrote of it as a distinct period of life. According to Jean-Jacques Rousseau, adolescents are characterized by heightened emotional instability as they **recapitulate** earlier stages of development; their cognitive processes undergo a change to self-conscious thought and logical reasoning ability. At the end of the nineteenth century, Rousseau's ideas were adopted by G. Stanley Hall and other psychologists, who attempted to construct a theory of individual development based on Darwin's ideas of evolution. In particular, Hall felt that "ontogeny recapitulates phylogeny"—that is, the evolutionary history of the species is repeated in the development of the individual child. This idea, now discredited, influenced many theorists.

II. Modern Theories of Adolescence

Although no one theory of adolescence is widely accepted at this time, there are theories based on the four theoretical approaches to understanding development.

A. Two influential theorists have brought biological-maturation perspectives to the study of adolescence.
• Arnold Gesell agreed with Hall and others that children's development recapitulates human evolutionary history; therefore, he thought, "higher" human traits such as abstract thought, imagination, and self-control appear late in development, during adolescence. Gesell believed that biological factors determine the basic pattern of adolescent psychological functioning.
• In Sigmund Freud's theory, adolescence corresponds to the genital stage of development. Reawakening primitive instincts upset the adolescent's psychological balance, producing conflict and erratic behavior, and young people must rework old conflicts associated with earlier stages.

B. Environmental-learning theorists such as Albert Bandura and Richard Walters have argued that biological-maturation approaches overestimate the degree of discontinuity between childhood and adolescence and overestimate the importance of biological factors in shaping behavior. According to the environmental-learning approach, the same principles that explain behavior in all other age groups can be applied to understanding the behavior of adolescents.

C. The interactional perspective is represented by the theories of Jean Piaget and Erik Erikson. Piaget and his colleague Barbel Inhelder emphasized the transition during adolescence from concrete to formal operational thought. This new mode of thinking, they felt, affected many aspects of adolescents' lives. According to Erikson, the main developmental task facing adolescents is to incorporate into a healthy personality their new sexual drives and the new social demands made upon them—to form an **identity**. Erikson views adolescence as an important time during which individual and social identity must be made compatible.

D. Psychologists who view adolescence from the cultural-context perspective note that while in some societies adolescence appears to be a distinct stage of life, this is not universally true. For example, in some nonindustrial societies children reach biological maturity later than they do in industrialized nations; by the time young people in these societies are biologically mature, they are also competent to support themselves and raise a new generation. Children from industrialized nations, on the other hand, may not be ready for independence until 7 to 9 years after they reach biological maturity.

III. Puberty

Puberty is a series of biological events that transform individuals from physical immaturity to physical and reproductive maturity. In the brain, the hypothalamus begins the process by signalling the pituitary gland to produce greater amounts of growth hormones and to produce gonadotrophic hormones that will stimulate the testes to produce androgens or the ovaries to produce estrogen and progesterone; these, in turn, trigger the physical changes that accompany puberty.

A. One of the first signs of puberty is a growth spurt during which boys and girls grow faster than at any time since infancy and reach 98 percent of their adult height. The cephalocaudal and proximodistal patterns of growth no longer hold; leg length typically reaches a peak first, followed by trunk length, and shoulder and chest width. The brain grows little, although the head increases in size as the skull bones thicken. Girls' hips widen and their breasts develop, while boys develop broader shoulders and thicker necks. Puberty also leads to differences in strength. Boys develop greater strength and greater capacity for exercise; girls, however, will on average live longer and be better able to tolerate long-term stress.

B. The **primary sexual organs**, those involved in reproduction, become mature during puberty. In males, this means the production of sperm cells and semen; in females, it means that mature ova are released and menstruation occurs. During this time, **secondary sexual characteristics**—outward signs that distinguish males from females—appear.

Girls experience **menarche**, the first menstrual period, about 18 months after the growth spurt reaches its peak. Ovulation typically begins 12 to 18 months after menarche.

C. There is wide variation between children in the age at which puberty begins. Both genetics and environment play a part in this. Identical twin girls reach menarche much closer in time than do fraternal twins, illustrating the role of genetics. The role of the environment can be seen in the effect of socioeconomic factors; on the average, girls from more affluent families go through menarche 11 months earlier than girls from poor families. In addition, a look at historical trends shows that, at least in industrialized countries, the age of menarche has been gradually declining during the last 150 years. Boys also seem to pass through puberty earlier than they did before.

D. Does the fact that an individual matures sexually earlier or later than his or her peers influence social adjustment, personality, or peer relations? In an early study, Mary Cover Jones and Nancy Bayley found early-maturing boys to be more psychologically and socially mature and better socially accepted than late maturers, who often compensated by attention-seeking behavior or withdrawal from social interaction. Later studies, however, have uncovered disadvantages of early maturation; for example, early-maturing boys are more likely to smoke, drink, use drugs, and get in trouble with the law. Studies of girls have also shown a mixed picture, but early maturation has fewer benefits for girls than for boys and is associated with increased social pressures. Little is known about how being an early or late maturer affects later life; by the time they are approaching 40, differences between the groups studied have largely disappeared.

IV. The Reorganization of Social Life

The biological changes that mark the end of childhood affect young people's social development in various ways.

A. Peer relationships change during adolescence. Instead of gathering in same-sex groups, young people get together in increasingly heterosexual groups. Friendships become more complex and intense. And peers take over much of the confidant role previously played by parents.

•Friendship during adolescence implies intimacy, mutual understanding, and loyalty. Adolescents appreciate their friends' different personalities and are appreciated in turn. Friends are expected to be accepting and to keep to themselves knowledge of intimate feelings that has been confided to them. Researchers have noticed some differences in the development of friendship in boys and girls. At about 11 or 12 years of age, girls focus on doing things together with female friends; around age 14, the emphasis changes to intimacy and loyalty as friends become confidants with whom they can check the acceptability of their behavior and thoughts concerning boys. This leads to a certain amount of possessiveness, which eases later in adolescence when girls need their best friends less and are therefore more tolerant of their friends' differences and their relationships with others. Fourteen- to 16-year-old boys form somewhat less close friendships than do girls. Because they are more concerned with their relationship to authority than girls are, boys need the loyalty and support of male friends to help them remain independent from parents and other adults. Friends help adolescents of both sexes to confront and deal with anxiety-provoking situations. As more situations are negotiated successfully, dependence on friends lessens.

•Popularity is a bigger issue for adolescents than it is for younger children. James S. Coleman found that both boys and girls felt that "having a good personality" was the most important characteristic for being in a "leading crowd" at school. Boys also ranked a good reputation, participation in athletics, good looks, nice clothes, and good grades as important; for girls, the other important things were good looks, nice clothes, and a good reputation. One out of five boys and girls said they would like to change themselves so as to be accepted by the leading crowd. August Hollingshead, examining the effect of socioeconomic class on friendship, found that adoles-

than boys have their first experience with someone they know well and keep the same partner for a longer time. Boys are more likely to report that their first intercourse was a positive experience.

•Never-married adolescent girls engage in sexual intercourse in greater numbers than they did several decades ago; boys are likely to have a greater number of sex partners than they did in the past. There is, however, little evidence that this is the result of a "sexual revolution"; instead, it appears to be part of a trend that began early in the century. An increase in the availability of contraception may have played some role in this trend, but most sexually active adolescents are inconsistent users of contraception. Recent worries about AIDS may slow the trend toward earlier sexual activity and multiple partners.

•Although surveys show U.S. teenagers to be no more sexually active than those in other countries, they are more likely to become pregnant. About 40 percent of the pregnancies of 15- to 19-year-old girls and more than 50 percent of the pregnancies of girls under 15 end in abortion. Girls who give birth are more likely to keep their babies, even if they are unmarried, than to give them up for adoption. Race, social class, educational aspirations, and religious beliefs all affect the likelihood of a particular decision. Teenage motherhood is likely to interfere with a girl's educational plans and lead to economic hardship. In addition, babies of adolescents have higher rates of mortality and illness than do those born to older women.

C. During adolescence, young people's changing relations with their peers are accompanied by changes in their relationships with their parents.

•Although teenagers' appearance, dress, and behavior often suggest membership in a separate "youth culture," research shows that adolescents and their parents are in agreement about most important issues. A majority of the high school students surveyed by Denise Kandel and Gerald Lesser considered themselves "extremely" or "quite" close to their parents and wanted to be like their parents in many ways. Adolescents are more likely to discuss personal matters with their mothers, seeking out fathers primarily when special advice is needed. Adolescents spend about equal amounts of time with parents and peers. However, time with parents is largely devoted to everyday activities such as shopping and eating, while relaxation and play are activities most often shared with peers.

•Peer pressure to conform is strongest during early adolescence but depends on the type of activity involved. While increased pressure increases the probability of misconduct, teenagers are, on the whole, more likely to give in when the suggested behavior is prosocial. Some behaviors considered antisocial in adolescence—smoking and drinking, for example—are considered acceptable for adults, demonstrating the possibility that adolescents may simply be modeling adult behavior when they engage in these activities.

•What are the subjects of adolescent-parent conflict? Mihaly Csikszentmihalyi and Reed Larson found that many of the conflicts center around matters of taste. These, however, may actually be expressions of conflict over independence and responsibility. Both parents and peer groups are important in the process of individuation, which results in adolescents taking on a more equal role and more equal responsibilities within their families.

D. Children's first work experience comes from doing household tasks, perhaps followed by neighborhood jobs such as babysitting and newspaper delivery. By age 15, many adolescents have regular part-time jobs. And recent studies indicate that as many as 40 percent of tenth graders and more than 50 percent of high school seniors are employed at some time during the school year. Part-time employment has both positive and negative aspects. While it increases adolescents' self-confidence and provides practical knowledge of the business world, it does not typically provide on-the-job training that will be useful in adulthood, nor does it keep teenagers out of trouble. Employed teenagers also are less involved with school and their grades may decline, especially if they work many hours per week. Each job that adolescents hold tends to be more responsible and substantial. By their mid-twenties, young people are generally working in adult careers.

E. The basic bio-social dilemma of adolescence is that, in societies where adult rights and responsibilities are delayed relative to puberty, adolescents are biologically mature but socially immature and dependent. The gap between puberty and adulthood has widened over the years and the organization of work and schooling tends to segregate adolescents from adults and increase the influence of peers. The next chapter will examine the ways changes in the quality of mind that accompany adolescence contribute to psychologists' understanding of this unique period of development.

Key Terms

Following are important terms introduced in Chapter 16. Write the definition for each after the term. Then match the term with the letter of the example that best illustrates it.

_____ Identity _____

_____ Menarche _____

_____ Puberty _____

_____ Primary sexual organs _____

_____ Recapitulate _____

_____ Secondary sexual characteristics _____

a. These are directly involved in reproduction.
b. The age at which girls reach this developmental milestone has declined by more than a year since the turn of the century.
c. According to Erik Erikson, this is achieved when adolescents incorporate their new sexual drives and the new social demands to which they are subject into a healthy and fully integrated personality.
d. These outward signs of being male or female develop as a result of hormonal changes during adolescence.
e. This series of biological changes constitutes the most radical change in physical development since birth.
f. Some theorists believe that adolescence is a time when young people do this with respect to the crises of earlier stages of development.

Fill-in Review

Cover the list of answers next to the statements below. Then uncover each answer after you complete each statement.

social

1. During adolescence, biological changes are accompanied by changes in _____ life.

emotional

2. Jean-Jacques Rousseau felt that adolescence was a time of _____ conflict and instability and that biological and social changes during this stage were accompanied by changes in _____ process.

cognitive

recapitulate

3. Rousseau also believed that adolescents _____ earlier stages of life, an idea that influenced later theorists such as G. Stanley Hall and Sigmund Freud.

4. Some modern-day theories, such as those of Arnold Gesell and Freud view adolescence as primarily the result of biological _____.

maturation

social

5. Environmental-learning theorists point out that _____ environment plays an important role in shaping adolescent behavior.

6. Piaget believed that during adolescence, young people progress from concrete to _____ operational thinking.

formal

7. According to Erik Erikson, adolescents' most important developmental task is to establish _____.

identity

8. Psychologists who take the cultural-context perspective point out that in some cultures adolescence appears as a distinct _____ of development and in others it does not.   *stage*

9. _____ is a series of biological developments that transforms individuals from being biologically immature to being capable of sexual reproduction.   *Puberty*

10. A _____ spurt is one of the first signs of puberty; generally, the ____ are the first area of the body to reach their peak.   *growth; legs*

11. By the end of puberty, _____ are the stronger and more athletic sex, while females, on the average, live _____ and are healthier.   *males*
longer

12. During puberty, the primary sexual organs, those involved in _____, enlarge and mature. At the same time, _____ sexual characteristics, such as breast development and voice changes, appear.   *reproduction*
secondary

13. _____, girls' first menstrual period, occurs about 18 months after the growth spurt reaches peak velocity.   *Menarche*

14. In the U.S., both boys and girls reach _____ earlier than they did in 1905.   *puberty*

15. There is some evidence that _____ -maturing boys are also more psychologically and socially mature; however, the picture for _____ is not so positive.   *early*
girls

16. Adolescent girls tend to want friends in whom they can _____, while boys want friends who will support them in troubles with _____.   *confide*
authority

17. Both boys and girls agree that having a good _____ is important for getting into the "leading crowd" in high school.   *personality*

18. Adolescents tend to date and form friendships with others from similar _____ backgrounds.   *socioeconomic*

19. In early adolescence, young people gather primarily in same-sex _____ but increasingly spend time in heterosexual crowds.   *cliques*

20. Peer group _____ generally are the ones who model the transitions to heterosexual relationships for the rest of the crowd.   *leaders*

21. Psychologists such as John Gagnon and William Simon point out that the actions making up sexual activity—hand holding and kissing, for example—can be thought of as a kind of _____.   *script*

22. Individuals whose sexual preference is bisexual are more likely to have been influenced by social-learning factors than those whose preference is exclusively _____.   *homosexual*

23. Biological and social factors result in adolescent girls being more committed to romantic love and adolescent boys being more committed to _____.   *sexuality*

24. Surveys have revealed that males and females report different responses to their first intercourse; in general, _____ have more positive feelings about this experience.   *males*

25. Although U.S. teenagers are no more sexually active than their European counterparts, they become _____ in much greater numbers.   *pregnant*

conform
prosocial

26. Adolescents are somewhat more subject than younger children to peer pressure to _____; they are more likely to follow their peers' lead, however, in _____ than in antisocial behavior.

Conflict

27. _____ between adolescents and their parents often centers on matters of taste.

work

28. Teenagers who ____ in addition to attending school benefit in many ways but their schoolwork may suffer.

Multiple-Choice Practice Questions

Circle the letter of the word or phrase that correctly completes each statement.

1. Jean-Jacques Rousseau believed that adolescents
   a. are, in a way, being born for the second time.
   b. recapitulate earlier stages of development.
   c. are subject to emotional ups and downs.
   d. All of the above.

2. In Freud's theory of development, the period of adolescence corresponds to the _____ stage.
   a. latency
   b. oedipal
   c. phallic
   d. genital

3. Adolescents must establish _____, a pattern of beliefs that reconciles the ways in which they are like others with the ways in which they are different.
   a. identity
   b. formal operational thought
   c. autonomy
   d. self-esteem

4. The _____ produce(s) the hormone that is responsible for the adolescent growth spurt.
   a. hypothalamus
   b. adrenal cortex
   c. pituitary gland
   d. ovaries and testes

5. Which is correct about the physiological differences between males and females in adolescence and adulthood?
   a. Males are stronger, healthier, and better able to tolerate long-term stress.
   b. Males have greater capacity for physical exercise but females are healthier and longer-lived.
   c. Females have larger hearts and lower resting heart rates and can exercise for longer periods.

d. There are no appreciable differences between males' and females' capacities for exercise and athletic performance.

6. The timing of the events of puberty
   a. is the same, on the average, in all cultures.
   b. is earlier in children from poor families than children from affluent families.
   c. is earlier in many societies than it was 100 years ago.
   d. is equally similar for identical and fraternal twins.

7. Adolescents tend to choose friends
   a. who live close by.
   b. from the same socioeconomic background.
   c. who are several years younger.
   d. from a different socioeconomic background.

8. Which describes an adolescent clique?
   a. A group of 15 to 30 boys and girls
   b. A loosely associated group of couples
   c. A group of 6 or 7 friends, usually of the same sex
   d. Any of the above

9. Cross-cultural studies of sexual behavior indicate that
   a. adolescents in many cultures are bisexual.
   b. traditional societies are generally less restrictive about premarital intercourse than industrialized societies.
   c. the standards for adolescent sexual behavior is the same in all cultures.
   d. different cultures may have very different scripts for learning sexual behavior.

10. Under what circumstance are pregnant teenagers likely to choose abortion?
    a. If they are over 15 years of age
    b. If their mothers are well educated
    c. If they are doing poorly in school
    d. If their families are on welfare

11. Adolescents generally report that
    a. they spend little time with their parents and a great deal of time with their peers.
    b. they are closer to their fathers than to their mothers.
    c. they disagree with their parents on most important issues.
    d. despite disagreements, they feel close to their parents.

12. Most of the time, adolescents' jobs
    a. pay the minimum wage.
    b. prepare them for future careers.
    c. result in contact with many adults.
    d. offer good opportunities for advancement.

Short-Answer Questions

1. Discuss the interpretations different theorists have given Rousseau's idea that earlier stages of development are recapitulated during adolescence.

2. What evidence is there that early maturation may be socially and psychologically beneficial to adolescents? What exceptions to this picture have been noted?

3. What factors contribute to teenage pregnancy? What factors influence whether a girl will terminate her pregnancy or keep her baby?

4. Discuss the advantages and disadvantages of adolescents holding jobs outside school hours.

Sources of More Information

Berndt, Thomas J. The Features and Effects of Friendship in Early Adolescence. *Child Development*, 1982, *53* (6), 1447-1460.
The author examines the literature on childhood and adolescent friendship and discusses the major findings in this area of study.

Cole, Sheila. *Working Kids on Working.* New York: Lothrop, Lee, and Shepard, 1980.
The author has interviewed more than two dozen working children about why they work. The book also deals with questions about working and the law.

Hass, A. *Teenage Sexuality: A Survey of Teenage Behavior.* New York: Macmillan, 1979.
This is an account of adolescent sexual behavior, based on the survey responses of American teenagers.

Malinowski, Bronislaw. The Social and Sexual Life of Trobriand Children. In Wayne Dennis (Ed.), *Historical Readings in Developmental Psychology.* New York: Appleton-Century-Crofts, 1972.
This observation, first published in 1929, describes the coming of age of children in a society very different from our own.

Money, J., and **A. Erhardt.** *Man and Woman, Boy and Girl: The Differentiation and Dimorphism of Gender Identity from Conception to Maturity.* Baltimore: Johns Hopkins University Press, 1972.
This is a discussion of the complex factors involved in becoming male or female, biologically and psychologically.

Rubin, Zick. *Liking and Loving: An Invitation to Social Psychology.* New York: Holt, Rinehart and Winston, 1973.
This book provides an entertainingly written account of how psychologists study friendship and love.

Ruble, Diane N., and **Jeanne Brooks-Gunn.** The Experience of Menarche. *Child Development,* 1982, *53* (6), 1557-1566.
This article reports the attitudes and emotional reactions of adolescents and preadolescents to menarche.

Answer Key

Answers to Key Terms: c, b, e, a, f, d.

Answers to Practice Questions: 1. d, 2. d, 3. a, 4. c, 5. b, 6. c, 7. b, 8. c, 9. d, 10. b, 11. d, 12. a.

CHAPTER

17

THE PSYCHOLOGICAL ACHIEVEMENTS OF ADOLESCENCE

Psychologists from various theoretical orientations agree that adolescents' thought processes are more sophisticated than those of younger children. Piaget felt that adolescence was characterized by the emergence of formal operations, a type of systematic, logical thinking, while other investigators feel that the characteristics of adolescent cognition can be accounted for by the development of more advanced problem-solving rules and strategies. Cross-cultural differences complicate the matter, but thinking skills very much like formal operations appear in people of all cultures, applied in specific contexts in which they are appropriate.

Adolescents' improved thinking skills are applied to social, political, and moral as well as academic problems. Capable of seeing the faults in existing systems, they may feel frustrated by the seeming impossibility of social change. Young people face important personal tasks during adolescence. They must loosen their attachments to their parents and look outside their families for someone to love. At the same time, they must establish identities, developing and committing themselves to their own points of view in many domains, including sex role, occupational choice, and friendship as well as political and religious orientation.

Adolescence exists because of delays in some components of the bio-social-behavioral shift that mark the end of childhood. It is not surprising, therefore, that adolescence as a separate, unified stage of development is not universal across societies; in this sense it is more like a long transition period between middle childhood and adulthood than a separate stage of development.

Chapter Outline

Many theorists agree with Jean-Jacques Rousseau that the transition from middle childhood to adolescence requires the development of a new quality of mind.

I. Research on Adolescent Thought

Daniel Keating has suggested that adolescent thinking is characterized by the following: thinking about possibilities not present to the senses; thinking ahead, rather than considering only the present; thinking through hypotheses, considering "what if"; thinking about thought, including **second-order thinking**, which involves rules about rules; and thinking beyond conventional limits about such topics as politics, morality, and religion. While there is a great deal of evidence for these characteristics of adolescent thought, psychologists disagree about their cause and about whether they are universal among adolescents.

A. Piaget felt that changes in the way adolescents think about themselves, their social relationships, and their society have their source in the development of **formal operations**, a new level of logical thought. In contrast to concrete operations, formal operations involve, he believed, the ability to think systematically about all logical relations within a problem. Analyzing the performance of children and adolescents on tasks such as the "combination of chemicals" problem, Piaget found that adolescents' reasoning could be described as a **structured whole**—a system of relationships—while younger children's reasoning was characterized by partial, unconnected links.

While Inhelder and Piaget's work suggests that formal operations universally affect adolescent thought, other studies have found formal operational thinking among only a minority of subjects. Robert Siegler and Robert Liebert found that 10- and 13-year-olds who were tutored in using a systematic approach on similar problems were able to solve a railroad-track switching problem analogous to Inhelder and Piaget's chemicals task; without tutoring, none of the 10-year-olds and only 10 percent of the 13-year-olds were successful. Failure to use a formal operational approach is not limited to young adolescents. Noel Capon and Deanna Kuhn found that only 20 percent of adult shoppers used formal operational thought when asked to judge which of two sizes of garlic powder was a better buy.

When Anita Meehan surveyed 150 studies involving formal operational tasks, she found that, while in many studies there were no sex differences in performance, when sex differences did occur they generally favored males. To some extent, this may be caused by the content of formal operational tasks, which are often science-oriented and of greater interest to males. There is some speculation that differences in performance are linked to sex differences in spatial ability; however, there is as yet no conclusive evidence that spatial abilities are strongly related to performance on formal operational problems.

Are there cultural differences in the incidence of formal operational thought? Cross-cultural work indicates that people from small societies that are not technologically advanced rarely demonstrate formal operations when tested with Piagetian methods. Piaget considered two possible explanations. Perhaps a certain amount of environmental stimulation is necessary for formal operational thought to develop; life in small, traditional societies may not provide stimulation of the right kind. Alternatively, all normal people may attain formal operations, but may manifest this mode of thought "in different areas according to their aptitudes and their professional specializations." In the end Piaget found the second explanation a more likely one.

B. Several alternative accounts of adolescent thought have been suggested by theorists who question Piaget's interpretation.

•Information-processing theorists disagree with Piaget's idea of a qualitatively different mode of thought emerging during adolescence. Instead, they argue, increasing information-processing capacity and more efficient problem-solving and memory strategies can account for the differences in performance between adolescents and younger children. When Robert Siegler applied the information-processing approach to Inhelder and Piaget's balance beam problem using 5- to 17-year-olds as subjects, he found that, with increasing age, subjects acquired more powerful rules for solving the problem and applied them more reliably. However, even the oldest subjects failed to solve all forms of the problem, indicating the absence of the generality one would expect in formal operational thought.

•Theorists from a number of traditions view adolescent thought as strongly influenced by increasing ability to use abstract verbal concepts. Heinz Werner and Bernard Kaplan found that 11- and 12-year-olds were better able than younger children to integrate information over many examples when inferring the meaning of an unfamiliar word. And Philip Levinson and Robert Carpenter concluded that, while 9-year-olds found quasi-analogies ("A bird uses air, a fish uses _____") easier to solve than true analogies ("Bird is to air as fish is to _____"), 15-year-olds found both types equally easy, showing a greater ability to coordinate the meanings of separate words into a logical system.

•While Piaget sought to describe adult thought with a single logic, cultural-context theorists attempt to understand adult thought by analyzing the different settings adults frequent and their associated scripts. This approach expects variability in thinking from one context to another, and cross-cultural studies have found evidence of such variability. For example, Edwin Hutchins showed that techniques used by Micronesian navigators to sail from one island to another were examples of formal operational thought. Yet, while they were sophisticated problem solvers during navigation, the same Micronesian subjects did not perform at high levels on a traditional Piagetian test of formal operations. Although high school-educated Micronesians could not use the navigational system, some showed formal operations in the traditional Piagetian task, presumably because that task was more familiar from their school experiences.

People regularly demonstrate their ability to apply formal operations in everyday situations requiring organization and planning ahead; for example, arranging for a holiday meal. However, their reasoning in everyday contexts may vary (for example, by using short cuts) from their reasoning on formal tasks designed as logical puzzles. In fact, several studies of everyday reasoning have cast doubt on the hypothesis that once individuals become capable of formal reasoning, it becomes a general characteristic of their thinking. Judy Tschirgi found that even when the logic and materials of the problems are the same, subjects may respond differently depending on whether they view an outcome as positive (one they want to maintain) or negative (one they want to change). In Tschirgi's study, college students and second-graders were equally likely to follow this pattern.

It has also been observed that expert problem solvers such as chess players and scientists often take shortcuts in reasoning, not looking at all possible combinations of factors, but only those that have proved important in the past. Taken together, these findings suggest that formal operations are, indeed, acquired in a context-specific manner.

II. Adolescent Thinking About the Social Order

Do the characteristics of adolescent thought, as measured in formal problem-solving contexts, explain the ways adolescents actually reason about their likes and dislikes, relations with parents and peers, moral and political problems, and other areas of vital interest to them?

A. While children think seriously about social realities during middle childhood, their reasoning changes in predictable ways during the course of adolescence.
•Based on interviews with adolescents from Germany, England, and the U.S., Joseph Adelson and his colleagues concluded that, at about 14 years of age, adolescents began to speak in terms of abstract principles when asked to respond to questions about society. Older adolescents also viewed social control differently; while 12- to 13-year-olds tended to give authoritarian answers when asked about law-breaking and punishment, 15- to 16-year-olds thought in terms of reform and rehabilitation. This shift in reasoning corresponds to changes in mid-adolescence noted by Inhelder and Piaget in their studies of scientific problem solving.
•Adolescents are especially interested in political and religious ideologies because of their new ability to think logically and to find inconsistencies in long-held beliefs. They may, however, find it difficult to work out alternatives to the existing social and political order.

B. There is some evidence that, like thinking about politics or scientific problems, reasoning about moral issues undergoes development during adolescence. Stage 4 reasoning in Lawrence Kohlberg's system appears during adolescence, though stage 3, based on relations between individuals, remains the most commonly seen mode of reasoning. Stage 4 reasoning is based on fulfilling duties to which one has agreed and focuses on relations between the individual and the group. Moral behavior is, therefore, behavior that maintains the existing social order. Stage 3 and stage 4 reasoning depend on partially attaining formal operations. Stage 5 reasoning in Kohlberg's system generally does not appear until early in adulthood and is rarely seen even then. Rather than focusing on maintaining the existing social order, stage 5 thinkers seek possibilities for improving it. Stage 6 reasoning is even rarer and involves placing certain self-accepted moral principles above the rules of society. Stages 5 and 6 require fully consolidated formal operational thought.

Several controversies surround Kohlberg's theory of moral development. First, while most studies show subjects progressing through the stages in order, others have found regressions and skipping of stages. Similar problems have arisen with respect to the correspondence between moral and cognitive stages. Finally, there is uncertainty about the relation between moral reasoning and actual moral behavior. People who can reason morally may not always behave morally. However, some evidence of correspondence is provided by a study of University of California students during the protests of the Free Speech Movement. Those who risked arrest by participating in sit-ins also scored at higher levels than other students in their reasoning about moral dilemmas.

•If, as Piaget thought, moral reasoning has its origins in the games of middle childhood, are girls less developed in moral reasoning, given that their childhood games are less complex? Carol Gilligan has hypothesized that male-female differences may occur due to differences in "moral orientation," with males more oriented toward individual rights and females more oriented toward responsibility for others. In fact, however, most studies show no significant differences between males and females on tests of moral reasoning.

•Cross-cultural studies reveal that people from small, technologically unsophisticated societies rarely reason beyond Kohlberg's stage 3, and often reason at stage 1 or 2. Kohlberg explained this as the result of differences in attainment of formal operational thought. Other investigators, such as anthropologist Richard Shweder, have pointed out that Kohlberg's stage sequence itself contains value judgments specific to Western traditions of liberal democracy. In any case, data from many societies indicates that, by the time they reach adolescence, young people can reason at stage 3—on a level corresponding to the Golden Rule.

III. Integration of the Self

In order to form the basis of a stable adult personality, the adolescent needs to come to terms with the problems that accompany sexual maturation and with the social relations that accompany work and taking on adult roles in the community.

A. In Freud's theory, adolescence is a time when young people must rework, in new forms, the conflicts of earlier stages. For example, reworking the oedipus conflict results in seeking love outside the family, "one of the most painful psychical achievements of the pubertal period," according to Freud. He believed that the stresses of the new demands of adolescence made young people especially vulnerable to personality disorders.

B. Erik Erikson also believes that adolescent development involves reworking previous **developmental crises** involving trust, autonomy, initiative, and industry. In addition, the major task of adolescence, **identity formation**, requires that the resolutions to all four of these crises be integrated into a healthy personality. Adolescents must resolve their identities in both the individual and the social spheres and establish "the identity of these two identities," according to Erikson. Identity formation can be difficult, and adolescents in a state of identity confusion may vent their feelings in antisocial or even criminal acts. Adolescents are also at greater risk of dying as a result of accidents or suicide than are younger children.

•It is not easy to objectively evaluate Erikson's ideas about identity. Erikson himself has carried out biographical case studies of famous men, but this method is not practical for use with large numbers of ordinary teenagers. Instead, James Marcia and his colleagues have used interviews to elicit information about the degree to which young people have adopted and committed themselves to well-thought-out views on politics, religion, occupation, friendship, dating, and sex roles. On the basis of the answers they obtained, the researchers identified four categories: *identity achievers*, who had experienced a decision-making period and decided on their own views; *fore-closers*, who had not gone through an identity crisis but had simply adopted their parents' identity patterns; *moratoriums*, who were experiencing an identity crisis at the time of the interview; and *identity diffusions*, who had tried on several identities but had not settled on one. Many studies have indicated that, as they grow older, more and more adolescents can be classified as identity achievers and fewer as identity diffusions, a trend that continues into adulthood. Harold Grotevant and Catherine Cooper examined the relation between identity achievement scores and family interaction; they found that family systems which offer support and security while allowing adolescents to create distinct identities are the most effective in promoting identity achievement.

•Like Freud, Erikson believes that girls and boys tend to follow different paths to identity achievement, but the evidence for sex differences is weak. Cultural differences seem more probable; U.S. teenagers face many occupational, political, and social choices compared with adolescents in more traditional societies.

IV. The Transition to Adulthood

The period between middle childhood and adulthood does not entirely fit the pattern of earlier stages. In some societies, puberty begins later than it does in industrialized countries and coincides closely with marriage and taking on adult responsibilities. And in societies such as our own with a long delay between puberty and adult status, biological, social, and behavioral changes are not coordinated in the same way as in earlier stages.

A. Is adolescence really a distinctive stage of development, rather than a slow transition between childhood and adulthood? Historical and cross-cultural evidence suggests that while the transition from middle childhood to adulthood is universal, a stage of adolescence as we conceive it exists only under particular cultural circumstances.

B. Adolescence in modern industrialized societies is closely associated with the existence of formal schooling or other specialized training. Schooling introduces a long delay in reaching economic self-sufficiency and prolongs the process of socialization. Therefore, while changes in certain social domains, for example, relations with the opposite sex, change in a logical manner in response to biological developments, in other social domains, work and starting a family, for example—full adult power and responsibility are delayed. This unevenness in the social sphere is most likely the reason for much of the unevenness in adolescents' thinking and behavior.

C. Current trends requiring higher levels of educational knowledge may, by delaying young people's working lives and prolonging their economic dependence, have the effect of prolonging adolescence or may even result in a new stage of development between adolescence and adulthood.

Key Terms

Following are important terms introduced in Chapter 17. Write the definition for each after the term. Then match the term with the letter of the example that best illustrates it.

_____ Developmental crisis _____

_____ Formal operations _____

_____ Identity formation _____

_____ Second-order thinking _____

_____ Structured whole _____

a. Adolescents are doing this when, for example, they make mental comparisons between two possible systems of rules for electing class officers.
b. In Erik Erikson's system, one of a set of developmental tests that an individual must face before moving on to the next life task.
c. A kind of systematic logical thinking on which adolescent thought is structured, according to Piaget.
d. Piaget considered this system of relationships an important characteristic of adolescent thought.
e. According to Erikson, this requires the integration of the solutions to all the developmental crises of childhood.

Fill-in Review

Cover the list of answers next to the statements below. Then uncover each answer after you complete each statement.

1. Daniel Keating has suggested that adolescent thinking is characterized by thinking about possibilities; thinking _____; thinking through hypotheses; thinking about thought, or _____ thinking; and thinking beyond conventional limits.

   ahead
   second-order

2. Piaget believed that the new forms of thought which characterize adolescence are based on a logical structure called _____ operations.

   formal

3. Adolescents' performance on problems such as the combination of chemicals task demonstrates, in contrast to that of younger children, the presence of a _____ whole.

   structured

4. While many studies show no differences in performance between males and females, those differences that are found generally favor _____; females with little interest in _____ perform better on tasks with "female-oriented" content.

   males
   science

5. While _____ operational abilities appear to be universal, it is possible that _____ operations develop in different areas of thought, according to an individual's aptitudes and interests.

   concrete
   formal

6. On the balance beam problem, adolescents' problem-solving skills can be described as a gradual acquisition of more powerful _____, according to Robert Siegler.

   rules

7. Increasing ability to solve analogies is one sign of the changing relation of thought to _____ during adolescence.

   language

8. The cultural-context perspective assumes that, while people in all cultures acquire the ability to think systematically, the settings in which this ability is used will ____.

   vary

9. Diverse activities such as Micronesian-style navigation and planning a holiday meal require the use of _____ thought.

   formal operational

10. In contrast to formal problem solving, when people reason about _____ situations, they may take shortcuts based on intuition.

    everyday

11. Judy Tschirgi found that when confronted with an everyday problem, people's expectations about the _____, not their cognitive competencies, may control their reasoning.

    outcome

12. Most studies indicate that formal operations are a context-specific rather than a _____ feature of adolescent thought.

    general

13. Joseph Adelson and his colleagues found that a major change occurs in adolescents' reasoning about politics at about _____ years of age.

    14

14. While 12- to 13-year-olds suggest that severe _____ is the best way to deal with law-breaking, older adolescents think more in terms of reform and rehabilitation.

    punishment

ideal   15. When separating themselves from the value systems of their parents, adolescents may seek out an _____ person or system to follow.

16. While adolescents' reasoning abilities make them skillful at identifying the faults of existing political and social systems, they find it difficult to work out
alternatives   _____.

moral   17. Stage 4 _____ reasoning appears during adolescence; however, most adoles-
3   cents reason at stage ___.

18. Stage 5 moral reasoning focuses on democratic processes, while stage 6, rarely
ethical   encountered, is based on universal _____ principles.

19. Carol Gilligan believes that male moral reasoning is focused on individual
rights; responsibility   _____, while female moral reasoning is based on a sense of _____ for other people.

reworking   20. According to Freud, a major task of adolescence is _____ the conflicts of earlier periods of development.

identity   21. Erik Erikson believes that _____ formation is the most important developmental challenge of adolescence.

22. James Marcia and his colleagues found that adolescents' responses to questions
achievers   about identity formation identified them as identity _____, foreclosers,
identity   moratoriums, or _____ diffusions.

family   23. A _____ that offers support and security can be helpful in promoting identity achievement in adolescence.

cultural   24. While there is little evidence for sex differences in identity formation, _____ differences are likely to exist.

25. Only in societies in which there is a relatively long separation between biological maturation and the assumption of adult roles does adolescence seem to exist as
stage   a unified _____ of human development.

Multiple-Choice Practice Questions

Circle the letter of the word or phrase that correctly completes each statement.

1. Which of the following are characteristics of adolescent thinking?
    a. Planning ahead
    b. Formulating hypotheses
    c. Thinking about one's own thought processes
    d. All of the above

2. According to Piaget, which of the following first makes its appearance in formal operational thought?
    a. The ability to construct others' points of view
    b. A system of relationships that can be logically described and thought about

    c. Conservation of liquid quantity

    d. The ability to generate a classification system

3. To which types of problems are adolescents and adults most likely to apply formal operations?

    a. Problems whose content is unfamiliar

    b. Problems that cannot be solved using concrete operations

    c. Problems of familiar and interesting content

    d. All of the above equally

4. According to the cross-cultural perspective, formal operational thought

    a. is applied in the same contexts in all societies.

    b. occurs only among people whose culture stimulates them to develop it.

    c. does not occur in most normal people.

    d. is applied in different contexts in different cultures.

5. People from which age group tend to be authoritarian in their views on social control and to conceive of the law as a way to prevent antisocial behavior?

    a. 12- to 13-year-olds

    b. 15- to 16-year-olds

    c. College-age young people

    d. Adults

6. When adolescents reason about political processes

    a. they generally see no problems with current systems.

    b. they are able to suggest workable solutions to current political and legal problems.

    c. they can see problems in current systems, but find it difficult to work out alternatives.

    d. their approaches are not significantly different from those of younger children.

7. The most common mode of moral reasoning during adolescence is Kohlberg's

    a. stage 2.

    b. stage 3.

    c. stage 4.

    d. stage 5.

8. Which of Kohlberg's stages of moral reasoning is based on maintaining the existing social order?

    a. Stage 2

    b. Stage 3

    c. Stage 4

    d. Stage 5

9. Which is an objection to Kohlberg's theory of moral development?

    a. Some studies have found no correspondence between moral reasoning and cognitive development.

    b. The method of scoring answers can be difficult to use.

    c. The relationship between moral reasoning and moral behavior is unreliable.

    d. All of the above

10. Freud believed that adolescents need to _____ earlier conflicts; for example, the oedipus conflict.
    a. rework
    b. repress
    c. succumb to
    d. recognize

11. According to Erik Erikson, establishing _____ is the fundamental task of adolescence.
    a. intimacy
    b. identity
    c. autonomy
    d. foreclosure

12. Adolescence is a separate stage of development
    a. in all societies.
    b. only when there is a long gap between biological maturation and the granting of adult social status.
    c. in males but not in females.
    d. for the last 100 years.

Short-Answer Questions

1. Discuss the differences between adolescents' thinking and the thinking of younger children. How are these differences explained by Piaget? By information-processing theorists?

2. How does culture affect performance on measures of formal operational reasoning? How does it affect performance on moral reasoning tasks?

3. Discuss the important developmental tasks of adolescence according to Freud and Erikson.

4. What evidence is there that adolescence is a distinct stage of human development? What evidence is there that this is not the case?

Putting It All Together

Match each example with the stage of which it is most characteristic:
   a. infancy
   b. the preschool period
   c. middle childhood
   d. adolescence

_b_ 1. Lisa is developing scripts that help her get through activities such as birthday parties, visits to the dentist, and meals in restaurants.

_d_ 2. Anne views laws as beneficial, not just a means of preventing bad behavior.

_d_ 3. When asked to figure out what combination of paints produces a particular color, Frank uses pencil and paper to keep track of the combinations he has tried.

_c_ 4. Children of Janet's age are learning that other people have feelings that may not always show in their behavior.

_a_ 5. Luke's major tasks in personality formation involve establishing first trust, then autonomy.

_c_ 6. Games with rules are now important in Jonathan's play with his friends.

_d_ 7. Michael no longer automatically accepts his parents' view of the world and is formulating his own opinions about politics, religion, and occupational choices.

_b_ 8. To Susan, friends are playmates—other children in the neighborhood whom she sees frequently.

_b_ 9. Richard's reasoning can be primitive or fairly logical, depending on his familiarity with the task and on whether he has scripted knowledge about the situation.

_d_ 10. Sara needs a best friend to supply feedback about her behavior and her feelings about boys.

Sources of More Information

Colt, George Howe. Suicide. *Harvard Magazine*, September/October 1983, pp. 46-53, 63-66.
Suicide is a greater risk among adolescents than among children in younger age groups. This article discusses the search for causes and evaluates prevention programs.

Erikson, Erik. *Identity: Youth and Crisis.* New York: Norton, 1968.
The author discusses adolescent identity formation and some of the difficulties involved in this process.

Keating, Daniel P. Thinking Processes in Adolescence. In J. Adelson (Ed.), *Handbook of Adolescent Psychology.* New York: Wiley, 1980.
In this chapter, the author describes the characteristics of adolescent thought and takes up problems of stage versus continuity and competence versus performance.

Linn, Marcia, Cathy Clement, and **Steven Pulos.** Is It Formal If It's Not Physics? (The Influence of Content on Formal Reasoning). *Journal of Research in Science Teaching*, 1983, *20* (8), 755-770.
This article examines the effects of content and subjects' expectations on performance on tests of formal operational reasoning.

Marcia, James E. Identity in Adolescence. In J. Adelson (Ed.), *Handbook of Adolescent Psychology.* New York: Wiley, 1980.
In this chapter, the author discusses his findings on adolescents' identity statuses.

Piaget, Jean, and **Barbel Inhelder.** *The Origin of The Idea of Chance in Children.* New York: Norton, 1975.
Reasoning about chance and probability are examples of logical thought. Piaget and Inhelder report on their studies of the development of these concepts in children with reasoning levels from preoperational through formal operational.

Overton, Willis F., and **Anita M. Meehan.** Individual Differences in Formal Operational Thought: Sex Role and Learned Helplessness. *Child Development*, 1982, *53* (6), 1536-1543.
The authors explore factors that can lead to sex differences in performance on tests of formal operations.

Siegler, Robert S. Three Aspects of Cognitive Development. *Cognitive Psychology*, 1976, 8, 481-520.
This article describes the author's information-processing approach to Inhelder and Piaget's balance beam problem.

Answer Key

Answers to Key Terms: b, c, e, a, d.

Answers to Practice Questions 1. d, 2. b, 3. c, 4. d, 5. a, 6. c, 7. b, 8. c, 9. d, 10. a, 11. b, 12. b.

Answers to Putting It All Together: b, d, d, c, a, c, d, b, b, d.

CHAPTER

18

DEVELOPMENT AND LATER LIFE

In many ways, adulthood is different from the periods of life discussed in earlier chapters. Change is no longer clearly in an upward direction—toward becoming taller, having a larger vocabulary, being faster at solving arithmetic problems. Instead, many aspects of adult life—biological functioning, some cognitive skills, and certain forms of social and economic involvement—can be characterized as smooth curves, reaching peaks in early adulthood or middle age, followed by gradual declines or lessening of activity. Yet there are also similarities between adulthood and earlier periods. Discontinuities occur in adulthood just as they do in childhood. Beginning a career, marriage, parenthood, retirement, and other culturally organized milestones all initiate stagelike changes in the roles adults play and the range of situations they encounter.

Theorists have differed in their approach to change during adulthood. Freud and Piaget viewed adulthood as a long plateau during which psychological functions remain at the level they reached during adolescence, while Erik Erikson's theory divides adulthood into several stages, each characterized by a particular developmental task. Of course, no one view of adulthood describes the experience of all people; the actual course of adulthood varies somewhat according to an individual's sex, social class, culture, and the historical era in which he or she lives. Adulthood has been the last major life period to attract the attention of students of development, but it challenges theorists of all orientations to reexamine their definitions of developmental change.

Chapter Outline

People are recognized as "grown up" when, at the end of adolescence, they become economically independent and take on adult career and family roles. Is development over once an individual reaches adulthood, or is it a process continuing throughout life?

I. The Discovery of Adulthood

People of different cultures have differed about the degree to which they conceive of adulthood as a period with its own psychological characteristics and about the ages at which they expect significant transitions to occur.

In Europe and the United States, **adulthood**, bounded on one side by adolescence and on the other by old age, has only recently been conceived of as a life stage. During the nineteenth century, the periods of adolescence and old age elicited social concern because of the perceived needs to integrate young people into society and to provide for people who could no longer care for themselves. Adolescence was institutionalized first through extended education and the passage of child labor laws. Increases in life expectancy during the twentieth century dramatically increased the number of people surviving 70 years or more; this, combined with the problems brought about by massive unemployment during the Great Depression of the 1930s, resulted in greater attention to old age as a distinct life period.

II. Theoretical Approaches to Adulthood and Old Age

When only biological processes are considered, change appears to be on a downward course once individuals develop the ability to reproduce. However, when the ability to engage in *cultural* reproduction is considered, change in adulthood can be viewed as developmental in nature, with adults of all ages contributing to their families and to their societies. Psychologists have been divided over this issue. For example, G. Stanley Hall divided the years from puberty until death into only two parts: a lengthy adolescence, lasting until the 30s or 40s, and a period of senescence that began when adolescence ended. Interactionists such as Freud and Piaget disagreed, seeing adulthood as a long plateau during which psychological processes remain fundamentally unchanged.

Psychologists who view culture as an important aspect of development tend, on the other hand, to consider development a process spanning the lifetime and including stagelike patterns of psychological processes brought about in accordance with sociohistorical circumstances. Psychologists working in the tradition of L.S. Vygotsky have described the years from 18 to 30 as a time of productive work, the period from 30 to 60 as a time of creativity, and the years beyond 60 as a time to reflect on and theorize about life. Erik Erikson has proposed three stages occurring during adulthood: **early adulthood**, from approximately 20 to 35, a time to make a commitment to a love relationship; **middle adulthood**, from approximately 35 to 65, a time to make a commitment to productive work; and **old age**, from 65 years onward, a time to make sense of life and to develop wisdom.

Scholarly attention focused on adulthood during the last two decades has led to the development of two approaches to its study. In the **life-span approach**, a psychological phenomenon—problem-solving ability, for example—is traced from infancy through old age to determine the changes effected by psychological and social change. The **life-course approach** examines the relationships between individual change and such major life events as beginning school or retiring from work.

III. The Biological, Social, and Behavioral Course of Later Life

Human beings change in certain fairly predictable ways as they age.

A. Biological changes during adulthood do not involve increases in functioning such as those that characterized earlier periods. In fact, the patterns of increase level off by about the age of 20 and biological capacities slowly begin to decrease, although it may be years before such decreases are noticeable. Sometime between the ages of 45 and 55, women experience **menopause**, the cessation of ovulation and menstruation, and are no longer able to bear children. Menopause is the only real discontinuity in adult biological functioning before 65-70 years of age. Sometime after age 65, the bodies of both men and women undergo a marked decline in biological functioning; the age at which this occurs depends upon both an individual's biological makeup and upon the healthiness of his or her environment.

B. The extent of cognitive change during adulthood can be difficult to assess because its course is different for different cognitive functions and the estimate of change is affected by the methods used to measure it.
•Performance on some kinds of cognitive tasks declines during adulthood, while for other tasks it remains the same or even improves. For example, the ability to memorize a list of unrelated words declines after age 30, while the ability to interpret spoken or written communications increases until age 60. According to John Horn and Gary Donaldson, performance on tasks depending on **fluid intelligence**—intelligence that requires the manipulation of new information to solve a problem—is biologically based and declines with age as other biological capacities decline. But performance on tasks requiring **crystallized intelligence**—intelligence built up through the experiences of a lifetime—continues to increase until a great deal of deterioration has taken place in its biological foundations. Paul Baltes and his colleagues have a similar view, suggesting that, during adulthood, increases in an individual's knowledge base can compensate for the brain's gradual loss of efficiency.
•Because many real-life problems require the use of both biologically based and culturally organized abilities, it can be difficult to test theories about adult cognitive change. Further complications arise when cross-sectional methods are used since historical factors, such as growing up during the Great Depression, can differentially influence the performance of subjects in certain age groups. This problem can be overcome using longitudinal studies; in fact, much of the decline on cognitive tasks as a function of age disappears when performance is examined longitudinally, suggesting that much of the observed decline is attributable to the use of cross-sectional studies. Elderly subjects also perform better on tasks relevant to life than they do on typical laboratory tasks presented out of context. In light of these and other similar findings, psychologists are reexamining the nature of cognitive change during adulthood.

IV. Social Factors and Later Psychological Change

Because the biological and cognitive changes that occur during adulthood do not, in general, represent stagelike discontinuities, it is important to look at the extent to which stagelike changes in adulthood and old age are products of events in the social domain. Age-related changes in family life, occupational status, and economic power have been examined by Robert Atchley. He found that in modern industrial societies there are three cycles involving important landmarks in an individual's changing social life. The work cycle involves several stages, beginning with preparation for an occupation (from infancy to mid-adolescence) and ending with retirement and removal from the workplace. The work cycle is paralleled by family and economic cycles. Added together, these cycles produce a "developmental contour," a social life cycle of heavy involvement in many areas during youth and middle age, with decreasing involvement thereafter.

While the buildup and decline of social involvements appear to parallel those of biological and cognitive capacities, there are important differences. Changes in the social sphere are marked by discontinuities arising from two sources: first, changes in social category often go along with changes in accompanying social roles—for example, becoming a parent results in marked changes in role and in the situations in which one finds oneself; second, changes in social category result in being treated differently by others—for example, once a woman is married she may be treated as fully adult by other family members. Discontinuities of this nature occur at many points during life, and each time one occurs, individuals are confronted with qualitatively new experiences to which they must actively adapt.

A. As Atchley himself points out, family, occupational, and economic timetables are not the same for all individuals. For example, these cycles do not adequately represent the experiences of middle-class adult women and working-class and poor people of both sexes. Even greater variations from the typical middle-class life trajectory are found in nonindustrialized societies—for example, there are no social institutions corresponding to retirement; instead, old people continue to play active roles until the end of their lives. The elderly in nonliterate societies may be especially respected because of the vital knowledge they have accumulated over their lifetimes. Historical events such as World War II or the Great Depression are further sources of variability in the patterns of people's lives. Though such events affect whole generations, their impact may differ according to a person's age at the time the event occurred. For example, individuals who were young children during the Great Depression were more negatively affected than those who were teenagers when the economic crisis began.

B. As first discussed in Chapter 5, experience shapes biology as well as the other way around. To what extent might socially mandated life changes—retirement, for example—influence changes in biological and cognitive functioning? Research indicates that disengagement from work and family responsibilities in old age contributes to biological and cognitive decline. For example, placing elderly people in institutions increases their chances of dying sooner, even when the institution provides an adequate physical environment. The loss of ability to adapt to new environments seems to be related to the phenomenon of learned helplessness in infancy. In an effort to determine whether social intervention could help overcome this problem, Ellen Langer and her colleagues assigned nursing home residents to one of two interview conditions: "reciprocal self-disclosure," in which interviewers talked frankly about their own lives while eliciting information from the elderly subjects about theirs; and a control condition in which researchers asked questions but did not volunteer personal information. Nurses later rated the reciprocal self-disclosure group as having higher levels of awareness, sociability, health, and well-being. This group also performed better on formal memory testing than did subjects interviewed in a less interactive way. These and similar results demonstrate that the changes which accompany aging are the result of complex interactions between social, behavioral, and biological processes that are shaped by, and help to shape, the cultural contexts in which they occur.

V. Decline or Continuing Development?

While the picture of growth followed by a plateau and gradual decline seems to apply to biological capacities and, at least under certain circumstances, to cognitive abilities and social participation as well, this pattern does not apply at the level of individual psychological experience. Instead, adults of all ages experience development as a process of encountering new and unexpected situations, adapting to new circumstances, and seizing opportunities to pursue goals and discover new insights.

Key Terms

Following are important terms introduced in Chapter 18. Write the definition for each after the term. Then match the term with the letter of the example that best illustrates it.

_____ Adulthood _____

_____ Crystallized intelligence _____

_____ Early adulthood _____

_____ Fluid intelligence _____

_____ Life-course approach _____

_____ Life-span approach _____

_____ Menopause _____

_____ Middle adulthood _____

_____ Old age _____

a. This is used when an individual manipulates new information to solve a problem.
b. Social problems caused by increases in both longevity and unemployment during the Great Depression resulted in this being perceived as a distinct period of life.
c. A psychologist using this approach studies memory by looking at how it works in age groups ranging from infants to retirees.
d. A period of life bounded by adolescence on one side and old age on the other.
e. According to Erik Erikson, people who do not commit themselves to a love relationship during this period may develop a sense of isolation.
f. This is the only clear biological discontinuity to occur in adulthood before age 65 or 70.
g. A way of studying development that focuses on events such as beginning and ending formal schooling, marriage, and retirement.
h. Performance on tasks that require mainly this capacity may increase during the course of adulthood.
i. In Erik Erikson's theory, this is a period when it is important for adults to engage in productive work.

Fill-in Review

Cover the list of answers next to the statements below. Then uncover each answer after you complete each statement.

1. The period of life between adolescence and old age is called _____.   *adulthood*

cultural 2. When _____ reproduction is included as one of its goals, human development can be seen as a lifelong process.

3. G. Stanley Hall viewed the period from puberty onward as having only two parts:
senescence adolescence and _____.

Interactionist 4. _____ theorists such as Freud and Piaget view adulthood as a plateau during which psychological functions do not change significantly.

5. According to Erik Erikson, during early adulthood people commit themselves to
love; work ____; during middle adulthood they commit themselves to productive *work*; and during old age they attempt to make sense of their lives and incorporate the choices they have made.

life-span 6. Psychologists using the _____ approach trace changes in phenomena such as memory or problem-solving from birth through old age, while psychologists
life-course using the _____ approach are concerned with the relationship between individual change and major life events such as marriage or retirement.

7. The only measurable biological discontinuity in adulthood before the age of 65
menopause or 70 is _____.

8. Although the timing varies from individual to individual, a sharp deterioration
65 in the body's functioning begins sometime after age ___.

fluid 9. Performance on cognitive tasks requiring _____ intelligence tends to decline
crystallized with age, while performance requiring _____ intelligence may improve over the course of adulthood.

cross-sectional 10. Studies using _____ designs are especially likely to overestimate cognitive changes due to advancing age.

11. When people's occupational, family, and economic life cycles are added together, they produce a developmental contour, with heavy involvement during
middle age youth and _____ and a decline in activity thereafter.

social 12. Unlike changes in the biological and cognitive spheres, changes in the _____ sphere during adulthood are marked by clear discontinuities.

13. Historical events affect people differently depending on their age: Glen Elder found that while the Great Depression was especially difficult for younger chil-
teenagers dren, _____ experienced the fewest difficulties.

dying 14. Radical changes in an elderly person's environment—being placed in an institution, for example—increase his or her chances of _____ sooner.

15. Ellen Langer and her colleagues found that nursing home residents interviewed
memory using reciprocal self-disclosure performed better on a formal _____ test than those who were asked questions by interviewers who did not reciprocate.

unexpected 16. At any age, adults, like children, encounter sudden, _____ events that bring new opportunities for psychological growth.

Practice Questions

Circle the letter of the word or phrase that correctly completes each statement.

1. When cultural reproduction is considered as one of its goals, development appears to
   a. continue until about 20 years of age.
   b. continue until about 35 years of age.
   c. continue until about 65 years of age.
   d. be a lifelong process.

2. According to _____, adolescence lasts into a person's 30s or 40s and is followed by a period of senescence.
   a. Freud
   b. Piaget
   c. G. Stanley Hall
   d. L.S. Vygotsky

3. Erik Erikson views _____ as the time when people should commit themselves to a love relationship.
   a. adolescence
   b. early adulthood
   c. middle adulthood
   d. old age

4. Menopause
   a. is the only clear biological discontinuity in adulthood to occur before the age of about 65 or 70.
   b. occurs in both men and women.
   c. is a matter of great concern to most people at the time they are experiencing it.
   d. All of the above

5. Crystallized intelligence
   a. declines as other biological capacities decline.
   b. is based on knowledge gained through experience.
   c. involves manipulating new information to solve problems.
   d. is rarely used in solving problems in everyday contexts.

6. _____ studies are likely to overestimate the amount of change in cognitive functioning due to increasing age.
   a. Observational
   b. Longitudinal
   c. Cross-sectional
   d. Naturalistic

7. Most of the stagelike changes in adulthood arise from the _____ domain.
   a. cognitive
   b. biological
   c. psychological

d. social

8. Robert Atchley's time line showing age-related changes in family life, occupational status, and economic power reflects mainly the experience of
   a. middle-class men.
   b. working-class men and women.
   c. people from nonindustrialized societies.
   d. white people from all socioeconomic groups.

9. In nonliterate societies, old people
   a. enjoy an early retirement.
   b. live longer than those in modern industrialized societies.
   c. are repositories of knowledge for the group.
   d. are valued less than they are in literate societies.

10. Which technique did Ellen Langer find to be effective in improving the memory test performance of elderly people?
    a. Asking them questions about their lives and confiding in them in turn
    b. Rewarding them with social approval
    c. Placing them in high-quality nursing homes
    d. Providing them with vitamin supplements

Short-Answer Questions

1. In what ways is change during adulthood different from that in earlier periods of life? In what ways is it similar?

2. Compare these theorists' views of adulthood: G. Stanley Hall, Jean Piaget, Erik Erikson.

3. How does cognitive functioning change during the course of adulthood? What factors can lead to overestimates of the degree of change that occurs?

4. Why is it often difficult to determine whether changes that accompany aging are the result of biological, behavioral, or social processes? Give examples.

Putting It All Together

As discussed in Chapter 5, experience shapes biology as well as the other way around. Compare learned helplessness in infancy with its occurrence in old age and discuss how it can be avoided. Then find another example, from another period of development, of how biological development or functioning is affected by environmental factors.

Sources of More Information

Erikson, Erik H. *The Life Cycle Completed: A Review.* New York: Norton, 1982. This compact discussion of Erikson's psychosocial theory provides a good review of the topic.

Horn, Jack C., and **Jeff Meer.** The Vintage Years. *Psychology Today*, May 1987: 76-77, 80-84, 88-90.
The authors discuss the likely results of the aging of the population and describe the behavior of older people as a group.

Newman, Barbara M., and **Phillip R. Newman.** *Understanding Adulthood.* New York: CBS College Publishing, 1983.

This textbook provides a general overview of adulthood, including aging, sexuality, and cognition.

Restak, Richard M. *The Mind.* New York: Bantam Books, 1988.
A synthesis of findings from psychology and the neurosciences, this book contains chapters on development, language, thinking, aging, and other topics.

Rosenfeld, Anne, and **Elizabeth Stark.** The Prime of Our Lives. *Psychology Today,* May 1987: 62-64, 66, 68-72.
This article summarizes research showing that differences due to the era in which an individual lives strongly affect the milestones of adult development.

Toal, Jeanne. The Fear of Forgetting. *American Health,* October 1986: 77-78, 80, 82-84, 86.
The author discusses the way memory changes with age and describes techniques that combat forgetfulness.

Answer Key

Answers to Key Terms: d, h, e, a, g, c, f, i, b.

Answers to Practice Questions: 1. d, 2. c, 3. b, 4. a, 5. b, 6. c, 7. d, 8. a, 9. c, 10. a.